Y0-BQI-001

The Grammar of Autobiography:
A Developmental Account

The Grammar of Autobiography: A Developmental Account

Jean Quigley

Trinity College
Dublin, Ireland

LAWRENCE ERLBAUM ASSOCIATES, PUBLISHERS

2000   Mahwah, New Jersey   London

LIBRARY
COLBY-SAWYER COLLEGE
NEW LONDON, NH 03257

PE
1315
.M6
Q54
2000
c.1

#43185961

The final camera copy for this work was prepared by the author, and therefore the publisher takes no responsibility for consistency or correctness of typographical style.

Copyright © 2000 by Lawrence Erlbaum Associates, Inc.

All rights reserved. No part of this book may be reproduced in any form, by photostat, microfilm, retrieval system, or any other means, without prior written permission of the publisher.

Lawrence Erlbaum Associates, Inc., Publishers
10 Industrial Avenue
Mahwah, NJ 07430

Cover design by Kathryn Houghtaling Lacey

Library of Congress Cataloging-in-Publication Data

Quigley, Jean.
    The grammar of autobiography : a developmental account /
Jean Quigley.
        p. cm.
Includes bibliographical references and index.
ISBN 0-8058-3483-4
    1. English language—Modality.   2. English
language—Grammar. 3. Children—Language. 4. Narration
(Rhetoric) 5. Autobiography. I. Title.

PC1315.M6 Q54 2000
425—dc21   99-087293
                                              CIP

Books published by Lawrence Erlbaum Associates are printed on acid-free paper, and their bindings are chosen for strength and durability.

Printed in the United States of America
10 9 8 7 6 5 4 3 2 1

For Rik

Contents

Preface

No argument is presumably necessary for the mutual relevance of psychology and linguistics but the self-evidence of the connection is commensurate only with the difficulty encountered in actually establishing it. Garcia (1990, p. 301)

Word is a two-sided act, always suspended in meaning between speaker and listener. Volosinov (1976, p. 86)

This discussion is situated at the interface of psychology and linguistics where discourse, language, and grammar form the point of contact between the two disciplines. In this psychology, the importance of language as a dynamic, social interactive phenomenon in the development and daily life of the individual is highlighted. Its linguistics counterpart describes a child who is actively learning to use language for interpersonal and social purposes. This psychological and social approach to discourse pays close attention to the use of linguistic forms, bringing grammar to bear on questions of self and identity.

The theoretical basis within psychology for this book lies in what has been called the "second cognitive revolution" (Harré, 1992a). The first cognitive revolution, in the 1960s, precipitated a shift away from behaviorism toward the study of cognition. Psychology was the study of mind as mental processes, as a central information-processing system behind what one says and does. Interestingly, Bruner, one of the main figures in the first movement, was also heavily involved in this later revolution. This time, things were proceeding against the psychology of the individual, the "myth of the mind": in philosophy, with Wittgenstein as the major influence, in sociology, in anthropology and the so-called "cultural psychology", in linguistics, but also with certain psychologists, including Bruner and Harré. This time around, the cognitive revolution is interested in the study of cognition "where it lives, in discourse, considered in a broad sense to include all sorts of symbolic manipulations according to rules" (Harré 1992a, p. 7).

This book explores the role played by grammar in the construction of the child's social practices and in the construction of the self. This assumes that language helps to create reality, that some of the objects and events one talks about are constituted by the ways in which one speaks about them. Using certain linguistic forms or constructions (e.g., tense or aspect markings, voice, indexicals) actually brings about certain types of discourse and contexts. It has been proposed that certain characteristics of the self are maintained through language and this is a study of how these characteristics are actually brought about in part via modal utterances in autobiography.

Discourse in this approach amounts to more than the sum of its utterances.

Meaning is conveyed via complex exchanges involving a host of factors, including the participants' beliefs and expectations and the shared knowledge between speaker and listener. Most research studies the speaker-proposition relationship, rather than the relationship between the speaker and the addressee with the proposition serving as a means of actualizing the latter relationship. I agree with Guo (1994) that this is the more important one.

Discourse provides information, not just about cultural meaning systems but also about a speaker's individual meaning system. Therefore, an ethnographic approach to grammar can be adopted (Gee, 1985) and grammatical constructions can be analyzed from the point of view of the speaker. This involves asking not just what a particular construction means, but how it works, what language does in various contexts rather than what it is (i.e., the social effects of language use *for the child*).

In this framework, the child is actively learning to use grammar for various purposes. Of course, the constructions are preformed and to that extent determine these purposes. The child is also constrained by the linguistic habits and practices in which she or he takes part. But by the same token, the child's participation in linguistic practices allows her or him to appropriate language forms for the construction of agency and perspective taking, of subjectivity and intersubjectivity (Bamberg, 1997, p.86). In a very real sense, grammar is distributed. The speaker always has a choice. Different forms are said to provide a kind of "typological slot" for the speaker (Gerhardt & Savasir, 1986) such that an intentional stance is implied by the use of a particular form. This means that different intentions and attitudes are structured into discourse as a result of speaking in one way as opposed to another.

This book describes how the child uses grammatical forms to imply different types of interpersonal motivation and the different social and discursive effects produced as a result. Development is described in terms of how different linguistic constructions are put to use for different discursive purposes at different ages and in various situations. The child actively assembles a grammar for discourse purposes and in so doing constructs self and other. "Language as a force pushes towards self-construction and moral order. The goal is the creation and situation of self and others in a moral order via the coordination of linguistic forms and functions" (Bamberg 1997, pp. viii-xi, 85-88).

The focus is on grammatical or linguistic forms in the context of autobiographical discourse, specifically, the development and use of the English modal auxiliaries, *can, could, will, would, may, must, might, shall, should, ought* in conjunction with other co-occurring grammatical constructions. The aim is to describe and to account for the role of these constructions within autobiographical narratives that, it is claimed, the modal auxiliaries actually help to bring about. The domain being investigated is grammar for autobiographical discourse or narratives. Language forms or construction types, especially the modal auxiliaries, are building blocks and the construction of autobiographical narratives is the activity in which these blocks are assembled (Bamberg, 1997, p. 85). One of the most powerful discourse forms is the narrative. According to

Bruner (1990), it is a push to construct narrative that determines the order of acquisition of grammatical forms by the young child. The extreme sensitivity to narrative and the tendency to narrativize experience links one's sense of self and one's sense of others in the social world. In the view of some authors, not only does narrative provide a privileged focus for examining the culture of language but there may also be a special affinity between narrative and self, such that narrative can be said to play a special role in the process of self-construction (e.g., Miller, Mintz, Hoogstra, Fung & Potts, 1991).

Detailed analysis of stories of personal experience reveals that a wide range of devices, from all levels of the linguistic system, are used to convey both the point of the narrative and, in turn, information about the narrator. One can analyze how different linguistic forms are used to take particular perspectives on events and to express different types of intention, how acts of commitment are tied to speakers and how responsibility is distributed (Harré & Mühlhäusler, 1990, p. 57); how reality is rendered subjunctive by language via a shift from expository to perspectival narrative language (Bruner, 1987); and the importance of modal (as opposed to chronometrical) time in the telling of one's story (Bowie, 1993) and so on.

In order to make use of "modal colorings" use must also be made of psychological theories of what and who one is. Individuals must be aware constantly of the relationships holding between them and those with whom, and about whom, they converse. This research studies grammatical distinctions based on the different perceptions and perspectives of the young child and traces the psychological validity of changes in these linguistic forms over time. Of course, one expects changes in a system as it accommodates to adult usage but, at first, it is interesting to look at the particular linguistic forms used that seem to serve an important definitional function for the child. The underlying assumption is that children are motivated to form their own connections between language form and language function. It is precisely these links that are of interest here; the functions of these linguistic devices as children begin to strategically employ them in their production of discourse.

Using a form of variation analysis (Schiffrin, 1994), within elicited autobiographical discourse the linguistic constructions of the modal auxiliaries were the starting point for a description of how linguistic forms are recruited for discourse functions related to the construction and presentation of self within the context of autobiographical narratives at different ages. The project was not conceived to test specific hypotheses but to try "to reveal the structure of discursive productions in which psychological phenomena are immanent" (Harré & Stearns, 1995, p. 1).

The analysis works its way up from the modal auxiliaries in used speech as linguistic forms that, because they have been chosen or recruited for use, make other forms and constructions be chosen. Throughout the discussion, the patterns of use of the modal auxiliaries, and their grammatical and discursive environs, can be seen to develop alongside, and to be consistent with, the development of the child's self-concept and with narrative and language development in general in the literature. What is known of the young child's developing sense of self and identity is matched with the child's linguistic formulations as he or she constructs his or her autobiography. That is, a relationship (although not necessarily a casual one) is established between the grammar of the modal auxiliaries and developmentally diverse concepts of self.

This requires some discussion of independent measures of the construct(s) under investigation. To address any circularity in the argument of the analysis, it makes sense to deal with an independent measure of the concept of self, apart from the linguistic forms. This involves models of the self that could be considered to fit in with, or at least not to conflict with, a discursive approach. Damon and Hart's (1988) psychological model of the development of self-as-subject and self-as-object is interesting in that they talk about components of the self and then look for indicators of those components as children talk about themselves, which can also be sought in the particular language constructions used.

Linde's (1993) literary model of social identity argues that some aspects or qualities of the self are actually maintained and supported by language (i.e., a sense of continuity, of distinctness and of reflexivity), which she discusses in terms of the narrative presupposition and the effort to establish an overall system of coherence in narrative. Including some measures of the self or some way of talking about the self that fits with the theoretical orientation of this study allows an exploration of the ideas of discursive psychology, and the idea that grammar and particular linguistic constructions can impact (at least) on the sense of self. Using these theories and models, a grammar of the child's developing autobiography based on the modal auxiliaries can be described.

There is a strong case for the modal auxiliaries as the linguistic forms most productively studied in this context. The use of modals is commonly seen as an indication of commitment, as constituting the subjectivity of an utterance. Lyons (1977) referred to subjective epistemic modality or the locutionary agent's qualification of his or her epistemic commitment. Individuals express an attitude or a stance toward the content of their utterances using modal expressions, that is, they use them as illocutionary markers. In this sense, the modal system, involving notions like possibility, necessity, obligation and permission is an especially fruitful aspect of language to study in terms of language-thought issues (Shatz & Wilcox, 1991). Modality is described as an area of language where speakers can either simply describe or actually mold by describing (Sweetser, 1990). In relation to children's developing autobiography, I show how they assign themselves roles, responsibility and agency, how they convey an attitude to or evaluate what they are saying and how they construct agency relationships as they account for, and report on, their own and others' actions in their personal narratives.

Modality is very important in relation to taking up a position in narrative and accordingly, there are several ways to express modality in English. Among the most important and the earliest acquired by children are the modal verb constructions, including modal auxiliaries and semiauxiliaries. A verb is said to be modal when it expresses the speaker's attitude to what is being said in the rest of the sentence. Modality (a modal auxiliary for the verb) subjectifies the action. The action of the verb is transformed from being a fait accompli to being psychologically in progress (Todorov, 1976). In English, the set of modal auxiliaries bear the burden of expressing modality. According to Stubbs (1996), "the expression of commitment and detachment or of modality in all its senses can be seen as a central organizing principle in language" (p. 4).

When analyzing the narratives, measures based on co-occurrence are used, which suggests that where words appear together, one word provides the context for the other, thus making the distributional aspect explicit. This interpretative strategy is based on the assumption that the co-occurrence between certain items within a clause indicates a "rapport" between those items (Whorf, 1956) such that they can be said to be included in the same semantic field (Gerhardt, 1991). In short, the aim is to organize this analysis of the children's discourse around a central set of concepts (and a set of speaker locations: spatial, temporal, moral, and social) that it is argued, make up the sense of self, including the concepts of agency, continuity, distinctness, and reflexivity. The point then becomes to explore the relation between the interpersonal discourse function of the targeted forms and their meanings from a functional perspective.

Overview

The first chapter situates the discussion in relation to psychological and linguistic approaches to discourse that recognize the constitutive use of particular linguistic forms in context. This is followed by a chapter that sets out the relation among the modal auxiliaries, subjectivity, and the self and the particular relevance of the modals for autobiographical discourse. Some theoretical issues in the linguistic conceptualization of modality, constraints on acquisition and some of the more interesting universal aspects of modal development are briefly discussed.

Part I is a detailed grammatical analysis of the patterns and occasions of use of the modal auxiliaries in the children's autobiographical narratives. Part II looks at the range of co-occurring grammatical features relevant to self-construction and presentation. The particular forms chosen for analysis reveal the ways in which different grammatical options and choices function for children to allow them to situate narrative events (and the self) in time, in space, and in relation to each other.

Part III explores the role of the modal auxiliaries with respect to the surrounding discourse. The discourse functions of the modal auxiliaries as used by the children in an autobiographical context are described, that is, the auxiliaries' particular contribution to narrative identity as it is grammatically constructed. Developmental trends in modal functions (i.e., a description of the changing discourse functions of the modal auxiliaries within the child's developing autobiography, including any parallels with the diachronic development of the modal forms) are described.

The book concludes by highlighting some of the more interesting temporal aspects associated with the differential deployment of the modal auxiliaries in the children's autobiographical stories. The self constructive implications of the use of the modal auxiliaries are discussed. Overall, this is an exploration of the idea of grammar as implicated in the construction of self and the special role played by the concept of modality and the modal auxiliaries in this process. The aim is to show how certain characteristics of the self it is proposed are maintained through language are actually brought about and supported via modal utterances in autobiography.

1

The Discursive Self

Don't look for anything behind the phenomena; they themselves are the theory. Goethe (1983, p. 74)

The task of psychology is to lay bare our system of norms of representation and to compare and contrast the enormous variety of systems: the rest is physiology. Harré (1989, p. 34)

What sort of psychology is being advocated, or more importantly perhaps, what is this psychology against? The short answer is all forms of positivism. As to what this means exactly, "it is only a slight exaggeration to say that all one can reasonably infer from unexplicated usage of the term 'positivism' is that the writer disapproves of whatever he or she is referring to" (Hammersley, 1995, p. 2). Somewhat more specifically, this approach opposes what Shanon (1993) has summarized very neatly as the Representational-Computational View of Mind (RCVM). Although this has dominated in psychology since the 1960s or so, that is not to say that it has gone unchallenged for all that time. The seminal critique in relation to the semantic representation of meaning was presented by Wittgenstein as early as 1953 but it is probably fair to say that even now the cognitive science model remains the most important general framework in use in psychology.

The tradition of the person as a central information-processing mechanism has dominated psychology. Initially, the cognitive revolution of the 1960s was greeted with welcome relief after the radical behaviorism that had been in place for so long with such disastrous effects for psychology's advancement. At last, meaning seemed to be reclaiming its place center stage. However it did not work out exactly like this, surplus baggage along the lines of a Platonic central mechanism that was abstract, fixed, and universal, came too. This occasioned the now familiar research heuristic in psychology that draws a strict line between internal psychological structures and processes and external environmental content, the latter having to be cleared away in order to get at what is "really real".

If the computational model concentrates on information processing, then discursive psychology is interested in meaning and meaning making (Bruner, 1990[1]); where the traditional model treats of the system of already-spoken words, the new paradigm's aim is to describe words in their speaking (Shotter 1993a).

---

[1] See Edwards (1997) on what he calls the thorough-going cognitivism of Bruner and also Chafe's narrative psychology.

Shanon's (1993) work is useful here as a backdrop against which to present a description of the basic premises of Discursive Psychology, although his critique of the RCVM model is primarily a cognitive rather than a philosophical one. However, it is not confined to this sphere. There is occasion to refer to his argument in relation to developmental, conceptual, methodological, and empirical considerations throughout this discussion.[2]

Specifically, Shanon said that semantic representations, defined as exhaustive and determinate, cannot fulfill their stated function. They can neither capture the knowledge that people clearly manifest nor can they account for the relation between cognition and the world. He proposed presentations rather than representations as the important structures.[3] The presentational view of the world is of "a matrix of meanings which cannot be separated from the beings who live in the world or from their interactions with it" (1993, p. 294), rather than a collection of things out there, an independent reality. If Shanon's emphasis still seems quite cognitivistic, it is important to remember that, in what is often referred to as the Second Cognitive Revolution, mental entities have not disappeared from the scene altogether. They have just been relocated in the discursive scheme. Relocation is a theme that is reiterated throughout this discussion. It is worth treating his work here because of his focus on the semantic representation of the meaning of linguistic expressions in particular and also because he is generally in favor of redefining the locus of psychology from the internal realm to the outside. In a similar vein, Harré (1995) moved the origin of the self from the inside of the person outwards, in that the language one learns, and the culture and system in which one learns that language, make possible a distinct type of self. In many ways, Shanon's arguments encapsulate a lot of the problems discursive psychology has with formalist models of language, for example, those of Fodor and Chomsky.

Shanon's (1993) argument runs that, rather than being the basis for cognitive activity, representations, if they exist at all, are instead the products of cognitive activity. Whatever it is that underlies cognitive or mental activity, it is not a repertory of well-defined, well-structured abstract symbols. Nor should we be tempted to neatly equate the workings of the mind with the computational manipulation of symbols of this sort. Instead he made some very interesting points about what this substrate should be. Namely, that it should not be fixed by any coding system that has been defined a priori; it should afford maximal

---

[2] Shanon has characterized development in terms of two principal lines of progression: one of decontextualization and autonomy, where development progresses from total immersion in the given context and dependence on it toward greater ability to divorce oneself from the context and gain relative freedom from it and the second line of differentiation and solidification, from that which is undifferentiated to that which is differentiated, leading to internal structuring, from that which is ill-defined to that which is articulated. It results in a fixation of meaning (1993, pp. 277-278).

[3] This point is discussed later, specifically in relation to grammaticalization and contextualization. (Cf. Fox, 1994, p. 33 on the nature of a distributed grammar and on Pribram's, 1991, holonomic brain theory. In this model sensory input is transformed into distributed, enfolded presentations that are not isomorphic with the organization of the sensory array and that bear little resemblance to what linguists think of as grammatical categories.)

sensitivity to unspecified dimensions and distinctions; it should be context sensitive; and it should be embedded in the framework of the organism's action in the world. There should be no distinction made between medium and message, both the body on the one hand and the ecological environment of the organism on the other must be taken into account.

What this is, is "an ever-active network which can resonate to and thus record whatever stimulation impinges on it" (Damasio, 1994, p. 17), which is both tied to the organism's being and action in the world and reflects the biological structuring of the brain. A fundamental property is that it can crystallise into "verbal and musical expressions, thought sequences and dreams as well as gestures and bodily expressions" (Shanon, 1993, p. 80). The emphasis on plasticity is interesting. Benson (1993a) said the idea of the brain as plastic in the face of experience is "a particularly helpful conceptual bridge between brain sciences and cultural sciences" (p. 4). There is evidence that the brain's neurobiological mechanisms can alter as a result of different social environments and discursive practices (Harré & Gillett, 1994).

Although Shanon's (1993) project is different to mine, there are important points of convergence that provide a good place to start. In his view, the domain of the conscious is not confined to the internal world but also takes in overt behavior in the external world. When discussing language, which he calls the hallmark of representationalist, internal science, he highlights its twofold character.[4] It is concrete and embodied on the one hand, but we must not forget that it could not exist without there being cognitive agents to produce it. So we think with words, just as we do with tools and instruments (reminiscent of Vygotsky's work)[5].

One final point of Shanon's is mentioned here and developed later: that conscious material is always experienced in terms of narratives.[6] In the same way, he said we should strive to understand cognitive tasks rather than to model them, that is, to "appreciate the factors involved in the execution of these tasks, the conditions which affect them, the dynamics of their execution and the course of their acquisition. In a nutshell to tell a story, a comprehensible narrative of these tasks" (1993, p. 363). This is what this book sets out to do, through an examination of a small part of language, to tell a story.

---

[4] The dual role of language in discursive psychology refers to its active use and to its use in second order commentaries.

[5] See Frawley's (1997) Vygotskyan cognitive science based on the notion that sociocultural theory of the mind and cognitive science's computational model are perfectly compatible and in fact complement each other.

[6] Tugendhat (1986) also said that the framework in which we formulate and justify decisions about how we shall live must assume a narrative form.

Discursive Psychology: An Alternative

According to Shotter (1993b) what is common to all versions of social constructionism[7] is the assumption that "it is the contingent flow of continuous communicative interaction between human beings which becomes the central focus of concern: a self-other dimension of interaction" (p. 12). This approach assumes that central to an understanding of anything psychological is an understanding of the role of language in human affairs. Cognitive psychology assumes a stable, well-formed and orderly reality independent of language. The newer approach works with the idea of a vague, only partially specified, unstable developing world open to further specification as a result of human communicative activity. The focus is on the dialogic use of words that structures our behavior, the "responsive or directive form of language use" (Shotter 1993b, pp. 162-165) and he quoted Wittgenstein (1969): "Language did not emerge from reasoning, the origin and primitive form of the language-game is a reaction: only from this can more complicated forms grow" (# 475). My interest is also in the situated use of words, in this reactive, responsive quality of language, the interpersonal functions of words in context.

What model of (self-)consciousness does this imply? Tugendhat's (1986) model of self-consciousness and self-determination based on an interpretation of Wittgenstein (1953), Heidegger (1973), and Mead (1934) has many points of contact with the model adopted here and could be useful to discuss. We already find many of the central themes of this work in Tugendhat's model. He wanted to break away from the traditional notions of consciousness and, like many others, was especially anxious that we finally drop the idea of "privileged access" to self-consciousness. We have no special access to ourselves, not through some sort of inner perception nor through any other channel. Consciousness is not a private, individual affair. Instead, one relates to oneself practically in relating to (i.e., deliberating about) the issue of how one is going to live.

This touches on some of the most important issues raised by the discursive turn in psychology, namely, the issues of personal responsibility, agency and the practical relation of oneself to oneself. Our relation to ourselves as agents is constituted by virtue of the choices we make in relation to "who" we are going to be, what we are going to do with our lives. We see just how important and formative the narrative drive is in the formation of the self.

But it is also important to consider in detail the ways in which our choices are constrained: essentially by the facts that we are embodied beings and that the rules of discourse are not arbitrary. This saves discursive psychology from the frequent criticism that it represents a descent into relativism. Nor is it some sort of freewheeling determinism along the lines of a more sophisticated dressed-up

---

[7]There are many points of contact between Shotter's Social Constructionism and Harré's discursive psychology, particularly in relation to ontological assumptions, but we must not forget to account for the differences between the approaches (e.g., Van der Merwe & Voestermans, 1995). According to Harré (1992b), the one shared thesis is that "all psychological phenomena *and the beings in which they are realised* are produced discursively" (p. 154).

behaviorism. Fox (1994, p. 11) reminds us that behaviorism, although not the only alternative to mentalism, is nonetheless often seen as its flip side and in that respect does not represent an alternative at all.

I want to argue that discursive psychology is, as she puts it, outside the mentalism-behaviorism paradigm altogether. Harré (1995) espoused a version of Wittgenstein's "moderate foundationalism"[8] rather then the radical relativism of which he is often accused. He said that "human forms of life must be fitted to the human condition and that includes the material basis for life" (1995, p. 371). So even though it is argued that our use of language in some ways structures our experiences of the world, this does not, and could not, happen in an arbitrary fashion but only in relation to the forms of life that characterize our experiences of the world.

According to Tugendhat (1986), the topic of self-consciousness is not a unitary one but has to do with both a first-person knowledge of one's own conscious states and a practical relation to oneself that each agent necessarily adopts in deciding how to live one's life. For instance, in a practical sense, he says we are required to define our identity which we do by deciding what we want to make constitutive of our "existence." The constructing and presenting of our autobiography, what we include or leave out and the ways in which we choose to structure our life story, is one important way in which we do this. Another way in which we as agents relate to ourselves is by adopting a self-questioning reflective stance in regard to those choices.

An idea of particular interest in this language-analytical philosophy, based on Wittgenstein (1953), is that concepts can be clarified only by studying the rules of use of the corresponding words and that the states of mind to which the phenomena of self-consciousness refer are propositional attitudes. That is, self-consciousness is not about reflecting on some inner sphere but is inextricably linked to the rules of intersubjective speech and also to the social community in which the agent is placed. All phenomena, for instance, wishing, believing, knowing, are initially given in a linguistic form. Their grammatical object is never an expression that designates an ordinary object but is always a nominalized sentence. So we are back to a sense of self that is constituted in, and by, language, rather than one arrived at through a special form of inner perception.

---

[8] See Cronen and Pearce (1992) who accuse Harré of a "creeping foundationalism."

A New Object for Psychology

The poet does not write with thoughts but with words.
Mallarmé (1974, p. 90)

Linking our psychology with our social worlds is hardly novel (Mead, for one, was already doing it in 1934). Proposing language as mediator between the two is new (as outlined, for instance, by Sapir in 1956, also heavily indebted to Vygotsky). Language now is not only representative but is also formative. It functions to construct situations as situations, not just to report on them. Our thoughts are not just the source of our talk but are also constituted or formulated in our talk. The focus of this psychology is on the social and linguistic construction of our reality insofar as it is true that it is language that has us and not the other way round.

But is the move toward social constructionism a genuine paradigm shift? Harré (1992b) would say they are at least enlarging it. What all these approaches have in common, and what unites them against the computational view of mind, is that they break down the individual-social, internal-external dichotomy to set the mind up as intrinsically social. And if psychology is the science of mind, then the object of psychology is not individuals but what goes on in the space between them. This concept is pivotal for theorists like Fox (1996) and Guo (1994) who assert that grammar is ultimately distributed. This means studying the relation between words and world, not between mind and world. It is not cognition but language that gives us the world and therefore it is not the individual thinker but primarily the world of relations that should concern us.

To answer my own question, this psychology operates in an unstable, developing world open to change as a result of our communicative activity, rather than in the independent knowable reality of cognitive psychology. Discourse is the characteristic feature of life and therefore the study of everyday language use or discourse, and of the psychological entities constructed therein, is one of its key tenets.[9] Language, as a tool and in its active use (to use Budwig's, 1995b, distinction), is one of the most important discursive activities we engage in to accomplish a number of different ends and will be the main focus of this book.

This constructivist psychology affords language a central and formative role in the child's developing sense of self, and it similarly affords the child the role of active participant in the process of acquiring a language and developing a sense of self. The development and experience of the sense of self is explored as the most important concept constituted by language and the aim is to outline a vocabulary of self, to extrapolate a set of rules or a grammar for the uses of words and linguistic forms that can be said to express local norms, "to formulate a concept of agency without the myth of the will" (Harré, 1989, p. 22).

---

[9] A second fundamental thesis concerns the active role of people makers (we see later with particular reference to Bruner's thesis based on Vygotskyan principles how older people teach mindedness to infants (Harré, 1995, p. 2); and also how children are not just passive acquirers of culture but also producers of culture (Much, 1992).

What Sort of Linguistics is Required for a Constructivist Account of Self?

There is not a private speaker behind the public speaker. There is just private and public speaking and listening, real and imaginary interlocutors. There is only one speaker per person and there is nothing behind that speaker but linguistic and other semiological powers and abilities and their neurological groundings. This is the foundation of the relation between grammar and self. Harré and Mühlhäusler (1990, p. 30)

The tone of a story or autobiography is largely achieved through the medium of grammar. Story structure is of course important, it also builds character but grammar is the poet's essential tool. Capps and Ochs (1995, p. 186)

The theoretical position just outlined vis-à-vis the self presumes that in the act of autobiographical discourse, people are actually constructing a version of self as they speak, on-line as it were. The self is a working concept, a tool, or an organizing principle. It is a set of experiences that are to count as equivalent. The question is how do people come to categorise a set or strip of experience (Denzin, 1995) as the self? How is this process manifested and worked out in the linguistic constructions people use, and how do they build a set of rules or a grammar of the self? We know there is considerable flexibility in how a person conceptualizes the self on different occasions; the suggestion is that this process can be seen at work through a description of situated language use.

If the self is a "continuous production" structured by discourse, rather than something inside a person, we need to understand the individual's "self-locations and the discursive contexts in which they are formed and expressed" (Corson, 1995, p. 426). The development of a sense of self can be traced in two directions: at first, mainly through the language to which we are exposed and later, through our own linguistic choices in various discourse contexts. Meaning is defined both by the individual and by the culture in which she or he participates (Bruner, 1990). If words are bearers of concepts, as discursive psychology would suggest, then an analytic study of the words and forms used in children's autobiographical narratives should afford a view of the child's working concept of the self.

An Alternative to Formalist Accounts of Language

What theory of language does this imply? The search for an alternative to formalism in linguistics, as with positivistic psychology, does not readily yield a well-defined coherent theory but "a complex of views that defines language more socially and cognitively and that characterizes the language acquisition process in more social-psychological terms, what we might call the social-pragmatic view of language acquisition" (Tomasello, 1992a, p. 68). This includes research that accords language and narrative a special role in the process of self-construction, especially the work of Bruner, and the insights of cultural psychology (e.g., Cole, Rogoff, Vygotsky).[10] Learning to use linguistic constructs for socially appropriate purposes is taken to be deeply embedded in cultural practices (e.g., Miller, Mintz, Hoogstra, Fung & Potts, 1991). Children come to know the world largely through how those around them represent the world through language.

> We all readily believe that children acquire language in some sense. We are less ready to believe that "language acquires children". We need a theory of what happens between speakers, and especially a theory of the interaction between how the child acquires language cognitively and how a society acquires a child functionally. (Dore, 1989, p. 256)

Ochs and Schieffelin's (1995) Language Socialization model of grammatical development explores the relationship between grammar and wider cultural aspects. They account for the child's grammatical development in terms of the indexical meanings of grammatical forms.[11] This is based on the idea that in every speech community, these forms are tied to, and hence index, culturally organised situations of use and that the indexical meanings of grammatical forms will therefore influence children's use and production of these forms.[12] Language is "a source for children to acquire the ways and world view of their culture" (p. 74). Language acquisition and grammatical development is something that takes place almost on a level beyond the person. It is played out between people who interact on a regular basis and who belong to a community with a shared history and a future: a culturally organized means-end model of grammatical development. Members of (speech) communities (including language-acquiring children) use grammatical forms to build speech acts and express stances that, in turn, are part of more complex social identities and activities (Ochs, 1993). Sociocultural meaning is acquired along with the formal features of language. A lengthy quote here emphasizes the distributed and dynamic processual nature of grammar, and speech, central to this approach.

> What we often refer to as a 'construction' is in fact a highly complex set of interacting patterns, observable at differing levels of abstractness, from specific lexical collocations to more abstract patterns of form-function relationships which begin to resemble a partial template. This 'coarse' system works because we as speakers are not left alone with just these to navigate with:

---

[10] One of the most important functions of language for Locke is not to function as a system for exchanging ideas with others, but to provide a kind of memory bank for storing ideas for oneself and *of* oneself (Mengham, 1995). See also Nelson (1993b, 1996) on language and the autobiographical memory system.

[11] Fox (1994) referred to the omni-indexical nature of language (based on Garfinkel), that is, that grammatical methods and practices are distributed across participants, context and environment (pp. 29 and 32). She said that indexicality is a pervasive design feature of talk (p. 1).

[12] According to Fox (1994) "human societies, human brains/minds and human language have co-evolved; it should thus not be a surprise that the design features of one exactly fit with the design features of the others" (p. 34, no. 10).

language exists only in use, and in that use we are assisted by other participants, the socially organised environment and the prior linguistic context. *These interacting forces in our larger talking ecology bring into existence for the moment an ordered bit of grammar* [italics added]. (Fox, 1994, p. 23)

The child's development of a sense of self in this framework is a process of appropriation rather than internalization. On the one hand, the grammatical means exist before being put to use in social practices, but on the other, children from the beginning are putting these tools to use for themselves. This sort of approach shows how "developmental considerations enable one to reconstruct a child's own efforts to acquire and use a language in increasing accord with cultural demands as to a telos of language development" (Bamberg & Marchman, 1990, p. 121).

Ethnographic Exploration

The claim is that language plays a role in creating the very social reality of which it speaks. We have seen that discourse carries information about both cultural and individual meaning systems. How exactly? To answer this, and to address the role language plays in the construction of self, we need to study language from the point of view of the speaker using it. This involves describing words in their speaking rather than a set of already spoken words, as "the reactance occasioned by the use of a word only shows up in the context of its use" (Shotter, 1993a, p. 10). There is often difficulty with the idea that language is essentially responsible for one's sense of self. The point is not that other factors do not play a role in self construction, just that language provides "distinct grammatical options for situating the subject" (Budwig, 1995a, p.3) that are interesting to look at in a developmental framework. It is not necessary to establish a causal relationship, only to indicate that grammar used to create a context can be shown to include knowledge of the social-psychological conventions of the culture. Each provides a set of epistemological resources for the speaking subject to insert self and other into discourse, so that subtle variations can be said to actually provide distinct positional fields[13] for the subject. The most important factor to keep in mind is that language is an instrument for making and conveying meaning (constructed jointly, in conversation, rather than located inside someone's head), that its structure reflects its function, and that therefore it can only ever be properly understood in terms of its function. Language is our most important "prosthetic device"[14]. To study language without recourse to meaning

---

[13] On the concept of positioning see Davies and Harré (1990); Smith (1994); Harré and Van Langenhove (1991, 1993). See also Frawley (1997) for cross-linguistic data on this point.

[14] Shotter (1993b, p. 33). Cassirer (1946, 1953) also made this point: "as soon as man employs a tool, he views it not as a mere artifact of which he is the recognised master, but as a Being in its own right, endowed with powers of its own" (p. 59).

"is like studying road signs from the point of view of their physical properties or like studying the structure of the eye without any reference to seeing" (Wierzbicka, 1996, p. 1). But this is how many linguists proceed: "that paradigmatically hard-nosed area of linguistics: syntax" (Reilly, 1995) still occupies a far more central place in academic enquiry than semantics, the study of meaning.

However I do not wish to put forward an argument for ignoring syntax to focus on so-called higher level systems. After all, I am focusing on the closed set of modal auxiliaries.[15] I just want to make the point that the language functions traditionally dealt with independently, referential-ideational and communicative-interpersonal, ought to be deconstructed. And to state that syntax in this approach, usually understood as static and described in terms of competence (exceptions include Chafe, 1980, 1994; Fox, 1987, 1994; Fox, Hayashi, & Jasperson, 1996; Fox & Hopper, 1994) is dynamic, locally managed and is constantly being reshaped by language use.

Elements of a typological approach are used here because it allows something specific to be said about the constitutive role of language. Although there is a lot of discussion in general terms of the importance of language and discourse in relation to development of the self and identity, there are still very few attempts at detailed explication of how exactly the self, or different presentations of the self, might be constructed via language. There is also comparatively little discussion of how exactly language might feature in children's self-development, which is another reason for choosing to carry out a tightly focused description of grammatical regularities in children's elicited autobiographical speech. Specific discourse needs are created, and therefore must be met, in each communicative context, and it is important to address how this process works.

Once more, it's hardly new to say that language has a role to play in development, but perceptions of what that role might be are certainly changing. There is a shift away from language as method (for the researcher) to language as mechanism (for the child). There is new interest in the way "language might provide the child with a wedge for actively constructing self" (Budwig, 1995b, p. 4). Language as method, language pressed into service by the researcher to "get at" other processes, is an idea that ought to be left behind.[16] There has been a perceptible shift within psychology concerning the relation between language and general functioning, but a lot of developmental work is still done from the point of view of language as a tool for understanding what is presumed to be going on elsewhere, as a means to uncover the child's underlying conceptual categories. This work focuses on language as a tool, not only for the researcher

---

[15] Johnstone (1996) warned that "formal syntax abstracts away from the self altogether. But linguists who work in depth with particular extended instances of language use sometimes come to connect them with their producers in ways that those who work with constructed data do not" (p. 183).

[16] Taking McGregor's (1997) point that we should neither refuse to acknowledge the significance of language in use and relegate instances of it to the ragbag of "mere performance data", nor, on the other hand, is it necessary to stop at speech and refuse to identify a system behind it (p. 18).

but also for the child, to gain access to culturally, and otherwise indexically appropriate, and useful, notions of self (Budwig, 1995a, 1995b).

Language and Grammar

This exploration combines a grammatical approach, which focuses on the modal auxiliaries, with a more psychological-social account of how speakers use language to situate self and other. In other words, a form of variation analysis[17] that allows exploration of several levels simultaneously. This involves not just looking at grammatical possibilities but what is actually said in real discourse situations.

Slobin's (1991) answer to the question of what it is one learns on learning the grammar of one's native language situates perfectly the sort of grammatical analysis being constructed. He said that in addition to a system of grammatical forms and semantic-communicative functions, "the child comes to adopt a particular *framework for schematizing experience*" (p. 7). His thesis was centered on the—for our purposes very useful—idea that "a special kind of thinking is called into play, on-line,[18] in the process of speaking in a particular language", "When I present a situation to you in any language I take a grammaticized point of view" (Slobin, 1991, p. 11). Grammar provides a set of options for schematizing experience for the purposes of verbal expression. Any utterance I make is multiply determined according to: what I have seen or experienced and therefore what needs to be conceptualized, my version of events; my purpose in telling about it; and the distinctions that are embodied in the grammar of my language, what can be readily and easily encoded and what is left to slow contextual inference. Every language trains the child to attend to a set of particular distinctions in the course of the acquisition of grammar, to attend to the "rhetorical slant" of their particular language. This implies that much of grammar is concerned, not with mental images or perceivable reality, but with marking distinctions that are relevant to discourse. In fact, some distinctions can never be articulated outside of a complex grammatical system. They can neither be pointed out to the child nor can they be directly experienced. They must be learned through the linguistic devices themselves that are "the only means for 'pointing' to the relevant event categories" (Slobin, 1985, p. 236).

This is exactly the process of acquisition and development of the modal auxiliaries in discourse as children start by using a particular grammatical form in a particular way that they must then learn to use differently. Slobin's (1991) position was interesting in that instead of trying to grapple with the language-thought relationship[19] (which Langacker, 1976, p.355, suggested is like trying to

---

[17]"A linguistic approach that considers social context under certain methodological and analytical circumstances" (Schiffrin, 1994, p. 290).

[18] Emphasizing the need for working with a processual dynamic rather than an hierarchical approach to discourse (Brazil, 1995). See also Chafe's (1996) flow model (pp. 49-65).

[19] Wittgenstein, in a similar fashion, distinguished his line of thought from Whorfianism by saying that "the connection between language and the world is so tight that we cannot isolate the two variables in order to have a theory" (cited in Genova, 1995, p. 211, no. 3).

embrace a cloud) he proposed instead to relate two dynamic entities: thinking and speaking. We are always going to reach an impasse trying to pin down the effects of grammar on world-view or trying to agree versions of linguistic relativity,[20] but we could much more fruitfully adopt Slobin's (1991) reformulation of a "special kind of thinking which is intimately tied to language-namely, the thinking that is carried out, on-line, in the process of speaking". In his own version of Sapir's thesis, he proposed "that in acquiring a native language the child learns particular ways of thinking for speaking" (p. 12).

Grammatical Analysis and the Modal Auxiliaries

The basic premise for this type of investigation is that by studying basic features of language we can see elements of the child's identity in the making. Analysis can uncover "grammatical realisations of dispositions" (Capps & Ochs, 1995, p. 55). To talk about the construction of self or identity is to refer to a grammatical practice rather than to an abstract theoretical concept. Grammar constructs our "particular past, present and possible worlds" (p. 191), and we will see how it is largely via modality in particular that these worlds are achieved.

The language we use in autobiographical or personal narratives displays both our agentive selves (to do with actions, goals, events) and our epistemic selves (to do with beliefs, feelings, wants). These actions and beliefs position us and display our social identity, our self for others (Schiffrin, 1996). The modal auxiliaries are vital to this process. Through studying the advanced grammatical structure (Bamberg, 1994) of the modal auxiliaries, the set of interpersonal discourse functions associated with these forms in autobiography can be described. The aim is to account for how the children use different modal forms to take particular perspectives on events and to express different types of intention, how acts of commitment are tied to the children, how they assign themselves roles, and the ways in which responsibility and agency are distributed. The child's differential use of the modal auxiliaries in autobiographical narrative will indicate the particular "speaker stance" or "self" the child wants to adopt or construct. A detailed linguistic analysis in this context is set up to see whether the child is motivated to make grammatical distinctions based on different perceptions and presentations of the self, given the view that grammar embodies different ways of structuring or viewing the self. A careful examination of the grammar used may disclose important distinctions the child is implicitly making.

All aspects of narrative, form, content, and performance, are important. If it seems self-evident that speakers must take a perspective on everything they

---

[20] See Frawley's (1997) version of linguistic real-time relativism in which Vygotsky has something to offer Whorf.

express, particularly in the case of personal storytelling or autobiographical narrative, even if it is, as Bruner (1990) suspected, old hat to the literary theorist, it is perhaps not quite so obvious just how this happens. There is still a lot to be discovered about how this process works, how the speaker's adopted perspective will in turn shape expression. Grammar in this context is "a set of constructions which are instructions, signposts for the audience to capture the directive(s) that is emitted, not abstract principles of a universalist nature but social know-how relevant for the construction of social meaning" (Bamberg & Marchman, 1991, p. 279). Different intentions are structured into the child's discourse via the grammatical forms used together with their social effects (Gee & Savasir, 1985). As we have seen, children attend to both levels, grammatical and social, in that (to use Slobin's, 1973, well-known formulation) the acquisition of new structures leads them to consider new functions and the development of new functions leads children to seek new forms.[21] In Bamberg's (1994) scheme, form-function relations refer to the function of particular choices of form contrasting with each other in a systematic way. Form is an umbrella term for a range of grammatical morphemes and construction types. Function refers to the role played by forms to convey structured characteristics of events in narrative.

Specifically, in relation to the focus of this analysis, the modal auxiliaries, it is the same form that acquires new discourse functions and new discourse contexts *I can't hear you, You can't be serious*. That means we should see new behavior patterns and new collocations emerging for the modal auxiliaries as the child inserts her or his point of view, her or his subjectivity into autobiographical discourse via the linguistic device of the modals. A word's syntactic behavior reflects and depends on its meaning and differences in collocations suggest a difference in meaning (Wierzbicka, 1996, p. 386). Collocations refer to the words and constructions that the modal auxiliaries co-occur with, in keeping with the Firthian (1957) principle that a word shall be known by the company it keeps.[22] The content (of what is being constructed) and the purpose (for which the content is being constructed), are closely linked by way of the linguistic construction types employed. Children will reinterpret the relation between language structure and language function, in Whorfian terms, the "rapport", in ways that makes sense to and for them. The guiding assumption is that children will "form their own linkages between language forms and language functions" (Berman & Slobin, 1994, p. 127).[23] These type of studies aim to show the interactive development between particular linguistic forms and particular discourse functions, to highlight the discourse oriented, rather than the narrowly semantic, use of these forms.

---

[21] See Berman (1988), Budwig (1989, 1995a, 1995b) and Bamberg (1991, 1994, 1997) on form-function relations within a functionalist-conceptualist approach.

[22] Firth (1957) spoke of the "renewal of connection", the need for constant interplay between theorizing and the linguistic data (p. 199). Use must be studied in order to come to an understanding of the system that lies behind it and in turn understanding of the system behind use contributes to the understanding of use (McGregor, 1997, p. 388).

[23] See Ervin-Tripp (1989) for a similar position.

Fox (1994, p. 25) offered a vivid analogy according to which grammar is like those unidentifiable bits of sponge for children that turn into recognizable objects when soaked in water. The bits of sponge are the presentations[24] and these expand into recognizable patterns of grammar in the water of context. Then, when the sponge is taken out of the water it may shrink into a shape slightly different from its original shape. Her point was that these presentations change through use. Whatever information might be "stored in" the brains or minds of speakers, most linguistic knowledge comes in methods for using those highly underspecified guides to create full utterances in real specified contexts (p. 20). On this view, grammatical structures, created "on the fly are the product of interactional work and not the input to the process. Similarly, meaning is not a static mental form but rather a complex set of methods for construing the world" (p. 48). These grammatical methods are a distributed set of procedures for constructing utterances out of distributed presentations in particular situated occasions (p. 24). Basically, it is a blanket term for the vast amounts of common-sense or knowledge that bring the grammatical instances or re-presentations to life in particular situated occasions of use.

This analysis is built on the premise that to describe, via a form of distributional analysis, the use of particular grammatical constructions, the modal auxiliaries, is at the same time to describe a distinctly organized social practice, which is brought about in part through the use of these constructions. And if "what one does linguistically determines the character of the results produced by one's utterances" (Harré & Mühlhäusler, 1990, p. 149), then a description of the range and "movement"[25] of linguistic options taken in the child's autobiographical discourse should help us to describe the particular character of the results, the self in autobiographical discourse.

---

[24] Remember Shanon's (1993) distinction between presentations and representations.
[25] Shotter (1993) "the function inheres in the word's 'movement' not in its form." (p. 130).

2

Modal Auxiliaries, Subjectivity and the Self

Saying what happened is an angle of saying, the angle of saying is what is important. Heaney (1991)

Any human language primarily functions to allow speakers to take various perspectives/viewpoints on the world. Gee (1990, p. 77)

This section outlines why the modal auxiliaries are a particularly useful grammatical class from which, and with which, to explore the relation between our use of language and the construction of the self. This involves describing the form-function relation of the modals as a way of discovering the child's discursive interests as he or she emplots himself or herself in an autobiographical storyline. Why autobiography? Because as Harré (1983) puts it "the autobiographical belief system of a person constitutes the central core of the psychologically researchable features of personal identity" (p. 42). And because "autobiography is a re-enactment in language of the development of the self" (Eakin, 1974, p. 213). So why use the modal auxiliaries to study this relation?

Back to Formalism Versus Functionalism[1]

This book is part of a movement that is "searching for the relationship between social and interpersonal factors in children's real-life communication and their development of meaning and form in a language" (Guo, 1994, p. 880). A growing number of theorists have abandoned the theoretical framework that has dominated linguistic research since the 1960s. And although coming from different backgrounds with different problems to solve, they all reject the two main tenets of Chomskyan linguistics: namely, the separateness and specialness of language (Chomsky's hypothesized innate mental organ) and the modularity of different types of linguistic information, syntax, semantics, morphology, phonology (Harris, 1989, p. 1).

The modal auxiliaries are analyzed using a functionalist style approach that explains the structures of language in terms of the communicative discourse

---

[1] Functionalist-organizational explanations claim that formal properties have their functional origins in actual communication (Guo, 1994, p. 9). Formal-structural explanations on the other hand define structures and associated constraints. Their key characteristic is that they are not temporal (Shanon, 1993).

functions served. This means the formalist attempt at one-to-one mapping of form to function is impossible, proposing instead "not even a form-meaning mapping but form mixed in with meaning" (Fox, 1994, p. 8). Formal properties are the result of several competing communicative constraints, insofar as "a variety of local pressures conspire on each occasion" (p. 21). Although semantics, pragmatics, and syntax are treated as though they are independent in most formalist accounts, they never are in reality. Hopper (1987) called this type of analysis one of essential unity, where the various meaning components are viewed as systematically interrelated, as manifestations of a particular type of underlying discursive system.

The idea that linguistic forms and their functions ought to be studied simultaneously is not new and yet pragmatic and grammatical development are still rarely treated together. Notable exceptions include Werner and Kaplan (1963) and Ervin-Tripp (1977) who suggested that grammatical development could be related to the kinds of discursive activities in which children are involved. More recently, in the functionalist approach to language acquisition and use[2] theorists like Bamberg (1987, 1991, 1997), Budwig (1989, 1995), Gerhardt (1988, 1990, 1991), and Slobin (1985, 19911, 1994a, 1994b) all share an interest in the way children use particular forms in context, that is, an interest in relating specific aspects of grammatical development with the semantic, pragmatic and discourse functions[3] served by such forms. "It is time to question the generality of the 'unifunctionality' proposal according to which children strive for a one-to-one mapping of form and meaning in the acquisition of grammatical forms" (Gerhardt, 1988, p. 378). We need to examine a wide range of linguistic forms in order to identify the functions they serve, paying particular attention to any distributional regularities between forms and their discursive functions (Budwig, 1989, p. 282).

A Discursive Approach

In order to give such an account of complex grammatical phenomena (in this case, the modal auxiliaries) their discursive purposes must be understood. Most traditional semantic characterisations of the modal auxiliaries typically offer no way of describing "the *internal relation* of the different meaning components" (Gee, 1985, p. 197) which the modal terms are said to harbor. A more discursive approach to the modals, which characterizes them in terms of the social activities they are part of and that they facilitate, provides a way of unifying the temporal, modal, and various other meaning components. The discursive approach gives a better insight into the modals "ethnographically, from the point of view of the

---

[2] Use is understood in terms of the way in which linguistic forms express particular types of discursive intentions that effectively structure the ongoing activity or discourse in distinct ways (Gerhardt & Savasir, 1986, p. 502).
[3] Gerhardt (1988) says we need to distinguish two different factors: different types of discourse or 'discourse formations', and different functions within a single type of discourse. The term discourse function is Foucault's (1972) and indicates a particular type of discourse with distinct structural characteristics that provides a distinct stance for the speaker. See Bruner (1983, p. 32).

speaker who uses them" (p. 198). Children from an early age will take into account what particular grammatical devices do in discourse, as well as their referential function.

The lack of an ethnographic approach to modality is seen as very surprising given its role in expressing different mental attitudes. Ochs and Schieffelin (1989) commented on the fact that linguistics seem to be the only remaining social science that does not have a social constructionist paradigm. This is primarily because the notion of subjectivity as other than a grammatical relation "'is not an ordinary working construct in the linguist's analytic toolbox" (Finegan, 1995, p. 3).

After Benveniste (1971), who said that a language without subjectivity cannot be imagined, "it follows that a linguistics without subjectivity ought to be an oxymoron" (Finegan, 1995, p. 13). The discourse sense of subjectivity has not previously been a feature of linguistic analysis, which concentrated instead on language as the expression of objective propositions (see discussion of Lyons', 1995, position below). But there is a developing interest now in the topic[4], in subjectivity as "a critical facet of language", in language, not just as form or as the expression of propositional thought, but "as an expression, an incarnation even, of perceiving, feeling *speaking subjects*" (p. 2).

The Relevance of the Modal Auxiliaries for Autobiography

Why choose the modals for this debate? Firstly, insofar as the modal auxiliaries are grammatical terms that construct their own activity-context, they are "strategic linguistic tools for the construction of social reality" (Bybee & Fleischman, 1995, p. 8). They are important because of what they do, which is convey interpersonal meaning, indicate subjectivity, express speaker involvement, and signal perspective, all crucial components in the formation and construction of a narrative identity. The modals' most important functions are their interpersonal ones, "language has developed the grammatical category of modal auxiliaries to serve the function of regulating interpersonal relations in social interaction" (Guo, 1995, p. 205). Secondly, as function words they express *layers of meaning*[5] and "capture the grammatical look and feel of a language" (Pinker, 1994, p. 121). Although all languages have function words, the properties of the words differ in ways that can have large effects on the structure of the sentences in the language. Their status as semi-grammaticized forms, as opposed to full lexical or grammatical forms in which the child just follows the conventions coded in the adult model, means that the child is freer to explore or

---

[4] This trend involving analysis of the expression-constitution of self and the representation of perspective or point of view in other than propositional form has even been called a revivified humanistic linguistics (Finegan, 1995, p. 2).

[5] See also Hopper (1991) on the phenomenon of "layering" in relation to grammaticalization and the coexistence of older and newer forms and meanings.

to use the modal auxiliaries to carry out functions important from her or his own perspective. Both the referential and the discourse meanings of these forms are available to the child so patterns of use should highlight the salient factors for the child (Guo, 1994, p. 10).[6]

The modal auxiliaries are learned as part of a complex group of meaningful relations and not just as a set of formal contrasts. Modal expressions, which encode speaker stance, are an important tool used to communicate knowledge and beliefs and to share cultural and social norms with children. They are very important to study in light of recent debates centering on thought in language. A lengthy quote here illustrates these points.

> It may be no accident that many of the world's languages use a single set of devices to express both deontic and epistemic notions. Every society after all must set definitional standards for both knowledge and authority, and language is the primary source of information about those standards.[7] Acquiring a language of modality in part involves a process of socialization of cognition in which the cognitive developments underlying epistemic understandings are themselves influenced by the very language being learned. It may be inappropriate to speak of cognitive prerequisites to the acquisition of the modal system. A more appropriate model may be a dynamic interactive one of mutual influence between language and thought.
>
> (Shatz & Wilcox, 1991, pp. 319-320).

They afford a view of the assumptions, beliefs, and practices expressed as the child develops from an animate being to a social and moral being to a logical being (Guo, 1994).[8] Perkins (1983) made the similar point that the development of modality cannot be dissociated from the child's moral, general intellectual, and social development. For now it is enough just to establish the rationale for focusing on the modal auxiliaries. Each of these points comes up for further discussion. In general, where work in this area has been done, it has tended to concern itself with the gross linguistic devices used in conversation and discourse, for instance, discourse markers, turn-taking, tags, and hedges. But analysis of the discourse functions of utterances does not have to restrict itself to devices with fairly obvious commentary functions. It can fruitfully be extended to even a tiny grammatical pocket such as the modal auxiliaries once we have begun to appreciate "the nondiscrete multidimensional meaning space involved" (Gerhardt, 1991, p. 536).

---

[6] The specific properties of the modal auxiliaries as a grammatical class and why they are of interest in terms of the grammaticalization process will be fully dealt with in the next section.

[7] In fact, as we have seen, language actually *sets* the standards. "Languages are social possessions that partly define who count as 'real' members of the group. As the language becomes a complicated and intricate form only children born into the culture can master it fully" (Gee. 1990). Those who fail to make sense are said to inhabit a linguistic nullity and to exist in a social and political vacuum (Mengham, 1995, p. 84).

[8] But be careful of falling into "language as window on mind" epistemology that discursive psychology disputes (see Harré & Stearns, 1995).

The Modal Auxiliaries, Subjectivity, and the Self

What is the importance of this small, closed, grammatical class for the child's construction of the self in particular? What is a speaker *doing* in an autobiographical discourse context using the modal auxiliaries? The particular roles of the modal auxiliaries as the child adopts and constructs perspectives and viewpoints on events and expresses different types of intentions in relation to the self must be described. Several theorists have claimed that grammar embodies different ways of structuring or viewing the self and that the domain of the self is a linguistically crucial one. Benveniste (1971),[9] for instance, said that concepts such as personhood and subjectivity structure, and are structured by, different grammatical categories, especially those of the person and verb system: "language is marked so deeply by the expression of subjectivity that one might ask if it could still function and be called language if it were constructed otherwise" (p. 225). The issue here is *subjectivity* and how it is dealt with or, more accurately, neglected by linguistics. Generally, the term evokes a grammatical association, as in the subject-object distinction. However my interest is not in subjectivity as a grammatical relation but in "locutionary subjectivity [as] quite simply, self-expression in the use of language" (Lyons, 1995, p. 337). I am interested in subjectivity as the representation of a speaker's perspective or point of view in discourse, "a speaker's imprint" as it were.

> *Subjectivity* is the intersection of language structure and language use in the expression of self, the involvement of a locutionary agent in a discourse, and the effect of that involvement on the formal shape of discourse, in other words, on the linguistic expression of self. (Finegan, 1995, p. 1).

The forms under investigation, the modal auxiliaries, are those aspects of the child's language where modes of commitment and obligation are worked out. As such, they are expressive of *"different speaker stances"* (Gerhardt & Savasir, 1986, p. 503) or what Lyons (1982) called the *"locutionary agent's expression of himself and of his own attitudes and beliefs"*. It might be useful here to briefly mention Lyons'[10] position. It has been very influential on work in this domain and also in relation to theorizing about discourse "as an instrument not solely, perhaps not centrally, designed for communicating ready-made content, but as an *expression* of self and, in part, its *creation*" (Finegan, 1995, p. 6). What Lyons called worlds

---

[9] "It is in the instance of discourse in which *I* designates the speaker that the speaker proclaims himself as the 'subject'. And so it is literally true that the basis of subjectivity is in the exercise of language. Language is so organized that it permits each speaker to *appropriate to himself* an entire language by designating himself as *I*" (Benveniste, 1971, p. 226). Benveniste coined the term auxiliation, that is, the process of the grammaticalization of auxiliary verbs out of lexical verbs (cf. Hopper & Traugott, 1993, p. 25).

[10] When discussing in-depth the concept of modality we see some divergence from Lyons' (1991) position but the point here is to use him as a point of entry to the discussion, in particular to show how he provided the link between the self and particular linguistic constructions. He was one of the few theorists at that time who actually attempted to address this issue in the course of a linguistic discussion.

within worlds underlines the connections being made between the self, discourse and ultimately, the modal auxiliary system. Lyons (1981) started by trying to bring together the three notions of modality, subjectivity, and locutionary agency that he said have not been related as closely as they might have been in most work in semantics and pragmatics. This he attributes to the reassertion of Cartesian rationalism by Chomsky and others, which asserts that "language is, essentially, if not solely, an instrument for the expression of propositional thought" (p. 236). This "intellectualist prejudice", which he says amounts to a total neglect of the non-propositional component of languages, is also at work in standard logical treatments of modality. When "modality is represented as something that holds, as a matter of fact, in some epistemic or deontic world which is external to whoever utters the sentence on particular occasions of utterance, this is what I mean by the objectification of modality" (p. 236). But modality can also be subjective. A speaker can be expressing her or his own beliefs and attitudes rather than reporting, as a neutral observer, the existence of this or that state of affairs. The *subjectivity of utterance* refers to a locutionary agent's expression of himself or herself in the act of utterance and the reflection of this in the phonological, grammatical, and lexical structure of the utterance-inscription.

> Two points need to be emphasized in connection with the notion of self-expression to which I am appealing in this definition of subjectivity. First, I want the term self-expression to be taken literally. The self is not to be understood as being logically and psychologically distinguishable from the beliefs, attitudes and emotions of which it is the seat or location. Second, the self which the locutionary agent expresses is the product of the social and interpersonal roles that he has played in the past, and it manifests itself in the role that he is playing in the context of utterance. The central concepts of epistemic and deontic authority have a social basis. But they are vested by society in the individual; they are part of the self that he expresses whenever he utters a sentence in some socially appropriate context. (Lyons, 1981, p. 240).

Lyons (1981) suggested that the reason why this has not enjoyed much attention except from French and German scholars may be because the notion of subjectivity itself plays a more important part in the Continental philosophical tradition. He contended that there are structural features of all languages which cannot be explained without appealing to it, and that for historical and ultimately social reasons, some languages are more deeply imbued with subjectivity than others (pp. 240-241).[11]

---

[11] To mark subjectivity some languages exploit morphology. Japanese, for instance, uses explicit morphological markers and when speaking Japanese it is impossible not to express one's personal attitude both in relation to the content of the utterance and to the addressee. Other languages, including English, mark it in a variety of more subtle ways ranging from intonation to word order. According to Langacker (1990), subjectivity (in English) is a notion not only of "subtlety" but of "near ineffability" (p. 34).

Some Theoretical Issues in the Linguistic Conceptualization of Modality

At this point I want to consider the relevance of certain theoretical proposals in linguistics for research in the child's acquisition of the modal auxiliaries. The two processes I have in mind, subjectification and grammaticalization, are particularly relevant in relation to the diachronic development of the modals and will form a useful link between the discussion of the specific meanings associated with the English modal auxiliaries and the synchronic acquisition and development of these forms.

Subjectification and Modality

Lyon's (1981) definition encompasses both the pragmatic and the structural components of subjectivity, which means we can examine the difference between unmarked (or off-stage) and marked or inscribed subjectivity in language and how it is achieved both diachronically and synchronically. Subjectification refers to "the structures and strategies that languages evolve in the linguistic realisation of subjectivity or to the relevant processes of linguistic evolution themselves" (Finegan, 1995, p. 1).

According to Traugott (1989, p. 35) subjectification is the pragmatic-semantic process whereby meanings become increasingly based in speaker's beliefs about, or attitudes toward, what they are discussing. Forms can start out expressing concrete, lexical, and objective meanings and, through repeated use in local syntactic contexts, acquire abstract, pragmatic, interpersonal, speaker-based functions. This in effect means that a speaker's consciousness of self is imprinted in her or his linguistic expression of her or his relation to the world, its objects, and its events.

Subjectivity is defined in terms of speaker purpose. An expression is subjective to the extent that it encodes speaker attitudes and discourse-building functions. Subjectification is apparently characteristic of all domains of grammaticalization. Grammaticalization is the process whereby lexical items or phrases are reanalyzed as having syntactic or morphological functions (Traugott, 1995, p. 46) or the process by which an item comes to have a systematic relation to other items. "Subjectification in grammaticalization" is the development of a grammatically identifiable expression of speaker belief or speaker attitude to what is said (Traugott, 1995, p. 32). I am going to be looking at the different kinds of subjectification involved in the development of grammatical markers and the implications for the acquisition and recruitment of grammatical forms.

Three main areas have been the focus of recent studies of subjectivity and subjectification (Finegan, 1995, p. 4): a speaker's *perspective* as shaping linguistic expression.[12]; a speaker's expression of *affect* toward the propositions contained in utterances[13]; and a speaker's expression of the *modality* or epistemic status of the propositions contained in utterances (probably the most thoroughly explored aspect especially as expressed in verbs and more recently adverbs).

Stein and Wright (1995, pp. 29-30) identified five different notions of subjectivity and subjectification. The first two pertain to literary analysis and the expression of subjectivity in literary discourse and are not very relevant here, but their summary of the other three positions is worth going into at this point. First, they mentioned subjectivity in the sense of deictic anchoring that is inherent in all language use and to some extent is encoded in the language system itself. All language usage contains an inbuilt perspective of the speaking ego. The subject slot is the me-now-here locus of viewing. This slot,[14], the one to the left in English, is also the one to which material is being moved that is emotionally salient and enters the speaker's mind for the first time.

Next, subjectivization in the Traugottian sense of transfer into the speaker's mind. This is primarily a diachronic concept. It designates the unidirectional semantic development observed in a great number of grammaticalization processes, that is, when lexical items lose their concrete notional meanings as well as their phonological integrity and become integrated into grammatical paradigms (Bybee, 1985; Givón, 1979; Traugott, 1982).[15] So this treatment assumes an historical, or at least a temporal, context for subjectification.

Finally, Langacker (1990) for whom subjectivity, on the other hand, is primarily a synchronic concept. It is the implicit presence of a speaker in an expression and is the degree to which the speaker is "on-stage." The more overtly or explicitly a speaker is present in an utterance, the more objective that utterance is likely to be. So, seemingly paradoxically, the less marked the language is by the presence of the speaker, the more subjective it will be.

Stein and Wright's (1995) point is that these versions are not unrelated. Carey (1995) also suggested that the models of Langacker (1990) (synchronic, equating meaning with conceptualization) and Traugott (1995) (diachronic, pairing subjectivity and grammaticalization) complement each other in highlighting

---

[12] Especially Langacker (1990) on subjective versus objective construal. If conceptual elements are singled out for conscious awareness by the speaker and given linguistic expression, they are *objectively construed*; if they remain part of the conceptual background of the speaker and are not expressed overtly, they are *subjectively construed*. Kemmer (1995) has a good discussion on the relevance of this notion of "degrees of grounding in the perspective of the speaker" in relation to the semantics-pragmatics of the pronominal *-self* forms and how they involve a viewpoint and subjectivity (p. 32).

[13] For example, Ochs and Schieffelin (1989): "language has a heart" is the way they articulate the fact that language users can and do express affect toward their propositions, also Halliday (1975) and Lyons (1977) who distinguish between the emotive functions of language and its referential and conative functions.

[14] The subject is the unmarked anchoring point for speaker empathy. See also Gerhardt and Savasir's (1986) typological slot which I am arguing is set up by the modal auxiliaries.

different facets of the same process. Both characterize grammaticalization as a unidirectional process involving subjectification. The difference lies in their emphases.

Traugott (1995) stressed the role of function, that is, a form or construction serving an objective function comes to serve more speaker-based discourse functions. Langacker (1990) emphasizes the role of construal: "some aspect of the here-and-now of the speech event can be construed with a lesser or greater degree of subjectivity; the lower the level of awareness the more subjective the construal" (Carey, 1995, p. 84). Both argue the importance of conversational implicature as underlying the process of semantic change.

Grammaticalization and Modality

In philosophy, modality refers to the evaluation of the truth values of propositions (von Wright, 1951). Modality as a linguistic concept is more relevant here, covering "a broad range of semantic nuances whose common denominator is the addition of a supplement or overlay of meaning to the most neutral semantic value of the proposition of an utterance, namely factual and declarative" (Bybee & Fleischman, 1995, p. 2). Modality is expressed within and across languages in a variety of non-mutually exclusive ways, including lexical, morphological, syntactic, and intonational. Although it is possible to express different kinds of modality by any given grammatical device, by and large, different formal categories tend to serve different communicative functions. Full lexical items have concrete referential notions and can explicitly express the subtle modal meaning (Perkins, 1983) whereas the more grammaticalized forms render the semantic subtleties opaque and incorporate more discourse and interpersonal meaning (Traugott, 1982). The process of grammaticalization means that the modals (divided into two different grammatical classes: auxiliaries and catenatives) are semi-grammaticized forms (Bybee, 1985; Palmer, 1986; Plank 1985), in other words, forms located on various historical paths from the lexicon to the grammar. My concern is with the group of semi-grammaticalized free analytic morphemes, the modal auxiliaries.

The development of the English auxiliaries was one of the first topics to draw the attention of generative linguists working on syntactic change. Originally seen as a prime example of syntactic change it is also clearly an instance of the larger process of grammaticalization (Traugott, 1995, p. 45). It concerns a change in the status of lexical verbs such that they become auxiliaries. The development of the English modals is an exemplary case of the historical process of grammaticalization that is the process whereby certain lexical items develop into grammatical formatives (Gerhardt, 1991, p. 533). There is also a semantic shift where lexical items lose their full notional meanings and begin to carry more abstract meanings.

Grammaticalization is the process whereby lexical items and constructions come in certain linguistic contexts to serve grammatical functions and once grammaticized continue to develop new grammatical functions (Hopper &

Traugott, 1993, p. 15). This phenomenon represents a direct challenge to those approaches to language that work with discrete categories and fixed stable systems. As grammaticalized forms, the modal auxiliaries have distinct semantic level meanings, as well as particular pragmatic functions, and the use of modal forms should therefore reflect their ambiguous status. They should exhibit both notional meanings characteristic of their lexical sources and discourse-pragmatic functions characteristic of their rise into grammatical operator status. If it is assumed that source items begin the process of grammaticization at different historical moments and that the development itself is gradual (Bybee & Pagliuca, 1985), then it follows that at any point in time each of the modals should have reached a particular stage of development and should show a particular degree of grammaticalization. The transitional status of modal auxiliaries as semi-grammaticalized forms is interesting because of the correlation between full lexical items and specific referential meanings on the one hand and between grammatical functors and discourse meanings on the other.

Mechanisms of Diachronic Change: Metaphor or Inference?

One very interesting discussion in this area is the notion of metaphor as the major mechanism of semantic change (Traugott, 1989, p. 49). When a lexical source is compared with its grammatical meaning or meanings along a grammaticalization path, a metaphorical relation is often found. This refers to "a shift from more concrete to a more abstract domain with preservation of some of the relational structure originally expressed" (Bybee, Perkins & Pagliuca, 1994, p. 283). The development of modal meanings is often regarded as metaphoric, that is, the schematic mapping of one concept onto another, especially in relation to the development of modal meanings of obligation into epistemic meanings relating to possibility and probability (Hopper & Traugott, 1993). For example, the obligation sense of *have to* predicates certain conditions on a wilful agent such that X is obliged to Y. The epistemic sense is a metaphorical extension of that obligation to apply to the truth of a proposition such that now X (a proposition) is obliged to be true (Bybee & Pagliuca, 1985, p. 73).

Sweetser, based on Talmy's (1988) force-dynamic model, approaches the modals as "sociophysical concepts of forces and barriers", 1990, p. 52). In her view, the key to finding connections between root and epistemic senses of the modals lies in a metaphorical interpretation of force and barriers. Semantic change results from a transfer of the basic semantic structure from the physical to the social domain. This is not to say that physical, social, and epistemic barriers have something objectively in common, just that our experience of these domains shares a limited amount of common structure (Sweetser, 1990, p. 59). It is the speaker's reasoning process that is subject to metaphor (Traugott, 1989, p. 49). There is a structured system of metaphor that relates different sense of modal verbs in which the physical becomes a metaphor for the nonphysical, the mental, rational, social (Gibbs, 1994, p. 159[16]). Sweester (1990) gave some examples: the *may* of permission is understood in terms of a potential but absent barrier, obligative *must* in terms of a compelling force directing the subject toward an act; the force of *must* is directly applied and irresistible, that of *have to* is resistible under certain circumstances. She viewed the epistemic meanings of modals as deriving from the tendency to experience the physical, social, and epistemic worlds in partially similar ways. Similarity in experience allows mapping of sociophysical potentiality onto the world of reasoning. For example, *may*, "in both the sociophysical and the epistemic world, nothing prevents the occurrence of whatever is modally marked with *may*: the chain of events is not obstructed" (p. 60).

There is some debate as to whether the main mechanism of semantic change in grammaticalization is metaphor[17] or inference. That is, metaphorical extensions (e.g., Sweetser, 1990) or conventionalization of implicature (e.g., Bybee, 1994, Traugott, 1995). In Sweetser's version, the image schematic structure of the sense of the modal is maintained during the shift of meaning from the sociophysical world to the world of reason and belief. This shift can be abrupt and results in very few examples of overlap. In the other version (based on Grice, 1975), the context of speech gives rise to conversational implicatures that later become conventionalized and become part of the meaning of the old form (Guo, 1994, p. 871). So inferences that can be made from the meaning of a particular modal become part of the meaning of the modal. At first early meanings imply new meaning, then there are cases where both meanings are used and then the new meaning is used alone. The new meaning gradually becomes the conventionalized meaning (p. 283).

Heine, Claudi and Hunnemeyer (1991) discussed grammaticalization in terms of problem-solving[18] and the need for the expression of certain grammatical functions in discourse. As we have seen, metaphorical transfer involves a sudden shift from one domain to another, whereas grammaticalization takes place gradually. To account for these differences, a second process, pragmatic strengthening, is introduced which is relevant to our discussion. Basically, the suggestion is that different mechanisms of change operate under different

---

[16] Working within this framework Gibbs (1994, p. 349) has a very interesting discussion of the concept of modal tautologies as used to convey new information about the future.

[17] Can any metaphor occur in the process of grammaticalization? Talmy's (1988) version was that grammar is used to encode meanings relevant to the structural and schematic aspects of the cognitive representation evoked by an utterance, whereas the lexicon tends to provide its content (Gerhardt, 1991, p. 531). But, according to Talmy, only certain types of spatial concepts are used cross linguistically in grammatical items, specifically, topological concepts. So when a lexical item expressing a spatial concept is grammaticalized, only the topological concept is transferred. Precise distances between points on a scale or angles in general do not grammaticalize but topological relations on a linear parameter frequently do so, for example, front-back, up-down. Also Quirk (1986, p. 61) noted that our verb forms tend to make us think of time as topological rather than as metrical.

[18] It is telling how often this notion is used in linguistic discussions, for instance, Fox (1994 citing Hopper, 1987) said grammatical structures are "partial solutions to frequently encountered situations" (p. 24). Problem solving is also one of the discourse categories generated in the children's narratives.

circumstances. Metaphor is proposed as the mechanism of semantic change for lexical and grammatical meaning closer to the lexical end of the scale. Inference is proposed as one of the mechanisms applicable to more grammaticized or more abstract meaning.

The rationale for this division of labor is as follows (Bybee, Perkins & Pagluica, 1994, p. 285). Metaphor needs the sort of clear image-schematic structure that crosses cognitive domains and those structures are found near the lexical end of the grammaticalization continuum. As grammatical meaning becomes more abstract and more eroded it is less suitable for metaphor and therefore more subject to the contextual pressures that produce change by inference. The main difference is the perspective (Traugott, 1989, p. 51). The metaphoric process of mapping from one semantic domain onto another is used by the speaker to increase the information content of an abstract notion. Although the process of coding pragmatic implicatures is used to regulate communication with others. So "metaphoric process concerns representation of cognitive categories" whereas "pragmatic strengthening and relevance concern strategic negotiation of speaker-hearer interaction and, in that connection, articulation of speaker attitude" (p. 51). This implies a differentiation between the development of the non-epistemic meanings and the development of the epistemic meanings.

The auxiliaries are an intermediate category in the continuum of boundedness from syntactically relatively free constructions at one end to fused constructions at the other, and this grammatical difference is highly significant in relation to the meanings expressed. When you use modal auxiliaries your utterances are colored by speaker involvement. This means that, on the one hand, referential meaning is not completely bleached out, and yet the auxiliaries are grammaticalized to such a degree that they are also used to encode interpersonal-discourse functions.

When a lexical form is grammaticalized, its meaning may also evolve from propositional to expressive or interpersonal (Guo, 1995, p. 228) and "the interpersonal function in the case of the modal auxiliaries constitutes a crucial part of the meaning of the words and has played an important role in changing their semantic content" (p. 205). This framework should be very useful when describing the developmental patterns in children's use of the modal auxiliaries.

Mechanisms of Synchronic Change

This theoretical debate in relation to mechanisms of semantic change in the study of historical development of language is very interesting and gives a way into the material but I need also to briefly introduce the mechanisms and processes of semantic change at work in a discourse context, that is, synchronic processes. Discourse functions are an important source of semantic change, as gradually "the discourse function saturates the semantic content of the modal resulting in a new semantic meaning" (Guo, 1995, p. 229). There is a complex relationship between discourse functions, referential meanings, and sentence forms. Discourse functions alone, or in combination with sentence forms, shift the focus of the semantic content of the modal, resulting in diluting, bleaching out, or augmenting certain modal aspects (Guo, 1994, pp. 275 & 864).

Guo (1994, p. 865) summarizes the main processes involved in this "semanticization of discourse function" very well. Discourse focus shifting is when the discourse function of the modal utterance deviates from the canonical semantic content of the modal and so shifts the speaker's focus from the canonical meaning. There are two types of shifting. Bleaching refers to the bleaching of the semantic content of modal due to the shift of the focus of the discourse function the modal utterance serves.[19] Or it can refer to cases of diluting where the discourse function of the modal utterance weakens or even obscures the primary semantic focus of the modal resulting in the eventual bleaching out of the original semantic content of the word.   Discourse augmenting (p. 866) is when the shift of the interlocutor's attention may not only dilute and bleach out certain meanings from a word but may also add new dimensions of meaning to the word.

There are two other processes involved. Discourse bridging (Guo, 1994, p. 867) occurs when the goals of two discourse functions are similar and so provide the common ground for a further shift of meaning. Discourse framing (p. 868) means the speaker's intended discourse function imposes the discourse meaning onto the referential meaning. This is the use of a modal in a discourse function in which the original meaning of the modal does not fit the referential content of the discourse situation.   The speaker uses the modal metaphorically and the intended discourse function changes the original meaning of the modal.

Why does this happen, why do speakers make metaphorical mappings or semantic abstractions? Universal paths of language development and patterns of grammaticalization as language-internal factors play a role in change in language but are not the only motivating factor. There are also changes for psychological or social reasons (Myhill, 1995, p. 200[20]) that are the focus of the next chapters. According to Guo (1994), the motivation for semantic change in the modal auxiliaries used by children need not conflict with the processes found in historical development.   In fact it adds an important dimension to our understanding of language change. That is, the motivating forces come from the

---

[19] The development of epistemic meaning is often seen as a kind of weakening. In the context of the development of grammatical markers such as the auxiliaries, this is part of the general claim that grammaticalization involves loss of meaning (desemanticization, bleaching). But it completely ignores the fact that "subjectification involves increasing in coding of speaker attitude, whether of belief, assessment of the truth or personal commitment to the assertion, the development of epistemic and evidential meanings increases coding of speaker informativeness about his or her attitude. There may be weakening of the semantics of deontics but there is strengthening of focus on knowledge, belief and speaker's attitude toward the proposition" (Traugott, 1989, p. 49).

[20] This is discussed at length in the modal analysis section. Myhill (1995) gave an account based on "world view" (e.g., power semantic in pronoun usage has clear parallels in the pre-Civil war modal system). Comradie (1987, p. 179) wrote of an "anti-authoritarian development which has led to a considerable change in modal root meanings."

interlocutor's actions: "it is what they do by what they say at the actional level that matters" (p. 871).

Summary

The aim is to describe how these children situate themselves and others in fields of action in their autobiographical discourse using the modal auxiliaries and to describe the host of linguistic devices that are co-employed to mark various perspectives and levels of involvement.[21] This means setting out to describe how the child's subjectivity and point of view is inserted into her or his autobiographical discourse via the linguistic device of the modal auxiliaries: "not that these forms are the speaker's sole means of adverting to personal attitudes but rather that they function as one means among many" (Gerhardt & Stinson, 1994, p. 162). It is not necessarily the content of the narratives but the linguistic and grammatical means by which the content is communicated that is of interest here. My focus is more on the influence of grammatical categories than on the influence of the lexicon. This implies a view of discourse in which "speakers signal how they want to have a message understood, and *ultimately how they themselves want to be understood as a person* who can be held responsible for what is said" [italics added] (Bamberg, 1991a, p.160).

So how *do* speakers signal how they want to be understood? How do children signal their intentions in the course of autobiographical narrative? According to the viewpoint outlined here, the speaker adopts a distinct stance toward the world that is grammaticized through different linguistic forms such that the speaker is then given what Gee (1985) evocatively calls a typological slot. The speaker's discursive intentions and their grammatical embodiments get called pragmatic operators and are said to structure the ongoing activity (i.e., in this case the autobiographical narratives) in particular ways. The modal element of the utterance, where the speaker is in the process of both describing and constructing, is arguably the element most responsible for this discursive structuration.

The project is to address subtle changes in the organization and reorganization of modal auxiliaries in autobiographical narrative. We can ask *why* these particular forms were used where they were used, that is, try to infer the factors constituting the particular form-function relations. This necessitates the assumption that there are discourse motivating factors that rule the use of the target forms and at the same time guide the development of the constituted form-function relationship.[22] This in turn amounts to an investigation of the function of particular choices of forms contrasting with each other in a systematic way.

---

[21] In the tradition of Bamberg (1987, 1991a) and Budwig's (1985, 1990) studies of the self-reference system; Harré and Mühlhäusler's (1990) study of pronoun systems; Gee (1985); Gee and Savasir (1986); Gerhardt (1991) on the modal catenatives; Slobin (1985, 1994a, 1994b) on passives and the present perfect.

[22] See Bamberg (1994) for a very good discussion on language and the constitution of part-whole relations in narrative.

The ENGLISH MODAL AUXILIARIES and Their SYSTEM of MEANINGS

This section discusses the meanings associated with the various modal auxiliary forms and the syntactic structure or the formal properties of the modals. As function words, the modal auxiliaries express layers of meaning having to do with the truth of a proposition as the speaker conceives it (Pinker, 1994, p. 118). These layers also include negation, possibility and necessity. The characterization used in this study will be somewhat wider than this but what is important is the notion of modal auxiliaries encapsulating layers of meaning.

Characteristics and Behavior of the Modal Auxiliaries

Modal auxiliaries are strongly associated with the verb but in fact they modify the whole clause interpersonally through a scopal relationship (McGregor, 1997, p. 228). The auxiliary is head of the sentence in exactly the same way that a noun is the head of a noun phrase. It asserts something about the rest of the sentence taken as a whole. The basic structure of a sentence contains a modality constituent, specifying such things as negation, tense, mood, and aspect and a proposition, a tenseless set of relationships between a verb and a noun-phrase. In talking about modality what we are basically concerned with is how the speaker wants the nonmodal part of the utterance to be apprehended or how the speaker's beliefs or assumptions are communicated in her or his utterance.

An auxiliary is an example of a function word that is "a bit of crystallized grammar" (Pinker, 1994, p. 119). The mind treats function words differently from content words.[23] People add new content words to a language all the time but the function words form a closed club that resists new members. The set of English modal auxiliaries (*can, could, will, would, may, might, shall, should, ought, must*) can be identified by the following formal criteria (taken from Coates (1983, p. 4) based on the Negation, Inversion, Code, Emphatic (NICE) features of Huddleston, 1976 (p. 333).

---

[23] O'Grady (1987) proposed a taxonomy of lexical items into three logical types based on the number of elements and relations that must be presupposed for that item to work in its intended fashion. Primaries (most nouns) are elements with a "stand-alone" function or meaning and are acquired first. Secondaries (most verbs and adjectives) are items that depend on a relation with at least one primary. Tertiaries (most function words, including therefore the modal auxiliaries) depend on at least one secondary relationship. Function words and content words have different perceptual, semantic, and logical properties and cannot be processed in the same way. (See Frawley, 1997, p. 38 on the features of an IP account like this.) See also Bates, Dale and Thal (1995, pp. 115-116): "each vocabulary type (e.g., nouns, predicates, closed class function words) shows a different growth function and each one has its own season. Grammatical function words may come in later than individual context words because: a) they tend to be short, fast, unstressed, phonologically reduced, i.e., difficult to perceive; and b) most are relational in nature, i.e., their purpose is to set up a relationship between other items in the sentence."

- Take negation directly (*can't, mustn't*).
- Take inversion without DO (*can* I? *must* I?).
- Code, ellipsis-substitution constructions (I *can* swim and so *can* B).
- Emphasis (Ann *could* solve the problem).

and the specifically modal criteria:[24]

- No -s form for 3rd person singular (**cans, *musts*).
- No non-finite forms (**to can, *musting*).
- No co-occurrence[25] (**may will*).

A Linear Analysis

Brazil's (1995) formal characterization of the behavior of the modal auxiliaries from the perspective of a linear grammar as opposed to the constituent-within-constituent hierarchical view of grammar is useful for my analysis. "If discourse can be described in terms of a purely linear apparatus, can grammar, not the grammar of the sentence but the grammar of the functional increments of which discourse is composed, be described in a similar way?" (p. 7). This model, as a linear, real-time description of syntax, avoids making the usual distinction between formal and functional properties. "Purpose-oriented increments of speech" are assumed where "it will be the ability of a stretch of speech to achieve a purpose that will be focal, not its possible status as a sentence" (p. 39). Similarly this description focuses on the discourse purposes of the modal utterances used.

---

[24] The modal auxiliaries are relatively clearly distinguished from main verbs by their lack of surface marking (e.g., for person). Also from the catenatives that are a class of secondary auxiliaries such as *have to, need to, want to, going to*. They are classed as semi-modals despite expressing similar meanings as the modal auxiliaries because they do not have the formal distributional properties of the modal auxiliaries. Whereas the modal auxiliaries do not require <u>do</u> support for standard transformations (i.e., negation, question formation, emphasis) the catenatives do require <u>do</u> support and so function more like main verbs. This means the catenatives are not as grammaticized a construction-type as the primary auxiliaries. From a semantic perspective they can have either a modal or an aspectual meaning (Gerhardt, 1990, p. 50). See also Bybee, Perkins, and Pagliuca (1994, p. 38) on the development of new grams, that is, that it is very slow and also that new grams do not necessarily enter pre-existing closed classes but instead develop their own peculiarities and behavioral properties and form their own closed class.

[25] But there is the interesting feature of modally harmonic forms where the hypothesis is that the appearance of a modal element in a complement is originally motivated by a certain harmony between the meaning of the modal and the meaning of the main verb (Bybee, Perkins & Pagliuca, 1994, p. 214). Lyons (1977, p. 807) uses the term 'modally harmonic for situations where a modal verb and an adverb express the same degree of modality. Coates (1983) uses it to cover all cases of a modal and another word or phrase that express the same degree of modality. The interesting part is that the two elements seem to be in concord rather than doubling the modal effect or having one modal within the scope of the other. Expressing possibility twice neither increases nor decreases the possibility. A nonharmonic combination forces an interpretation where one modal element is within the scope of the other.

Brazil's (1995) discussion of the modals in terms of a linear grammar (i.e., a purpose-driven grammar rather than a sentence-oriented one) suits our purposes very well. The meanings of words and expressions do not derive from a set of relations that exist permanently in the semantic system of which the word is part. Instead, the relations among items is a function of the way speakers use and understand them as having a "this-not-something-else" value that is valid for the particular here-and-now circumstances of their communication. The available set of choices open to a speaker at any given point makes up the "existential paradigm" (p. 249).

Within this framework, Brazil (1995) sets out the following criteria as the distinguishing features of the modal auxiliaries (pp. 113-115).

1. They select for time reference, relating probability time to utterance time rather than event or condition time (*can/could, may/might, will/would, shall/should*) and polarity (*can/can't, may/may not, will/won't, shall/shan't*), an aspect that will prove crucial in this analysis.

2. They select for sense, although the possible existential alternatives for a modal belong to a very restricted class, comprising mainly of other modals.

3. Because their potential for selection is always related to the probability of some event or condition, they are communicatively deficient: progress toward target state is always via a non-finite verbal element (V1). There is no occasion when it is appropriate to say *"She can"* without following it with a V1, for example, *take*.

4. The V1 that follows them has base form (i.e., infinitive). Using a modal verb commits the speaker to producing a verbal element and also one with prospective implications, something that does not apply in a general way to other kinds of verb. The base form of V1 is used whenever independent choice is precluded in this way: "the verb must get what it wants" (Pinker, 1994, p. 121).

Brazil (1995) also discussed specific ways in which we use the modal auxiliaries. For example, the exploitation of differentiated time reference choice to make something more acceptable socially, many instances of which are contained in this corpora (*Would it be possible? If you could give me a lift*) or the use of *shall* and *will* for future with prominence (*I will never forget that, really.*). The main point we ought to take from his analysis is that "used speech exploits the here-and-now values of the linguistic items that speakers make use of" (p. 33), therefore, after Halliday (1973), that the nature of the grammar is, at least partly, due to the nature of the task. This method of analysis rules out an "after-the-event approach" that assumes that the object for analysis already exists in its entirety, just as events and stories do not exist fully formed prior to their telling. Rather, discourse is something that happens now, piece by piece, in time, with the language being assembled as the speaker goes along. Instead of the static concept of constituent structure, Brazil (1995) made use of the dynamic notion of a sequence of states. The focus is on the way people use words to create oppositions: "it is this temporary here-and-now opposition that provides the word with the value that the speaker intends and the listener understands the communicative value of any item is negotiated between participants as the discourse unfolds the this-not-that relationship" (p. 35). This sort of analysis has its earliest roots in speech act theory and pragmatics with its notions of illocutionary force and indirectness. Ultimately however, a standard speech act view proves inadequate "because it ignores the observation of language in use and therefore ignores the pervasive indeterminacy of much language" (Stubbs, 1985, p. 2). Stubbs pointed out that historically, speech act theory has been very ambivalent in its attitude toward naturally occurring language in use. Despite Austin's (1962) formulation of the task at hand as the collection of explicit performative verbs as a guide to illocutionary force, Searle's (1969, 1979) version led Lyons (1981) to suggest that the term *language act* would be more appropriate than *speech act* in order to emphasize the abstract decontextualized view of language as proposed by Searle (Lyons, 1981, p. 172 cited by Stubbs, 1985, p. 5). [26]

A Pragmatic Analysis

I have mentioned how the Searlian speech act has been expanded but it is possible to be even more specific as to exactly how this sort of pragmatic analysis differs from a more traditional speech act theory. Gerhardt (1990, pp. 4-6) has outlined a set of basic assumptions that guide this analysis of the discourse functions of the modal utterances in autobiographical narratives.

1. Context is primary in utterance interpretation (as opposed to speech act theory where the isolated sentence is the primary unit of analysis).

2. Speech acts are not autonomous, as speech act theory would have it, but are components of discourse frames (i.e., functional structures that provide different slots for the component acts of which they are comprised). Utterances are given value within a particular discourse frame.

3. Utterances typically have more than one function (not just a single illocutionary force as in speech act theory).

4. Not all utterances are equally significant, they may be hierarchically organized within a frame.

5. But these hierarchical relations between speech acts do not imply indirectness (as speech act theory suggests). If an utterance is assigned two functions, the contextually based one is not necessarily indirect in the sense of being secondary.

6. Discourse-type is relevant to the utterance function, that is, interpretation of the utterance is sensitive to the particular type of discourse in which it occurs.

---

[26] See also Harré (1993b, p. 231) who, in a paper on what he calls "Wierzbicka's thesis" of semantic universals, says that our account of language-in-use should favour Austin over Searle.

The Importance of Context

One other crucial area requiring elaboration for a description of the modal auxiliaries in this framework is the notion of discourse and discourse context. As the notion of modality is intrinsically and closely related to the pragmatic and interpersonal functions of language and as child language is particularly action and instrumentally oriented and is heavily situated and embedded in the specific speech context, a fuller understanding of the use of modal expressions in child language requires a better understanding of the discourse context in which the concerned modal utterance is embedded. (Guo, 1994, p. 26). Context is interactively achieved rather than predefined.[27] The idea of the situatedness of utterances in actual discourse comes from Gumperz (1982a).[28] He argued that utterances not only carry representational or semantic meaning but also discourse meaning that is the main goal of the speaker for engaging in the discourse. Curiously this fact tends to be ignored by most linguistic studies. The discourse meaning expresses or implies what the speaker actually wants to say or do. According to Gumperz, discourse strategies are determined by different cultural conventions and assumptions.

Guo (1994, p. 9) has redefined context, inspired by the sociological-ethnomethodological approach to the study of discourse "context" of child speech, the "greening of linguistics".[29] Grammatical forms are used as "a constitutive part of the speaker's "normative modes of social conduct" (Gee, 1986, p. 4). In this view, the linguistic expression underspecifies the interpretation. It can locate "fields of possibilities" (Heritage, 1984) but only in a particular context can it have definite "sense" (Fox, 1994, p. 2). Discourse contexts are characterized by the following set of features (Guo, 1994, pp. 9-10).

1. They are constitutive and emergent. Context is not independent of language but emerges as a "field" from the activities of the speakers, the social relations holding among them, the communicative goals, and the language forms used. All factors affect, and are affected by, one another and by acting and interacting together, a social and interpersonal category of practice emerges called Activity Types[30] (Budwig, 1986; Gee, 1985).

---

[27] From the general theoretical background of redefining context in the field of linguistic anthropology, see Duranti and Goodwin (1992).

[28] Also Brown and Yule (1983); Barwise and Perry (1983); Levinson (1983); Schegloff (1982); Sacks (1992).

[29] Wierzbicka (1996, p. 7).

[30] The notion of activity-types used here (Gee & Savasir, 1985, pp. 143-144) is meant to refer to something broader than particular speech acts as worked out by Searle (1969). Speech acts do not always distinguish the situations in which one term rather than another is used and therefore a description based on other distinctions is needed to understand the distribution of the terms under review, including speaker's stance toward interlocutor, temporal and aspectual features, whether the child is narrating future or past events or events in the context, and so on. So, it is not that activity-types are prelinguistically specifiable and as such impose constraints on how children use modals, rather that the function of certain modals is to actually enable certain activities to take place. See also Clark (1996, p. 30) on Levinson.

LIBRARY
COLBY-SAWYER COLLEGE
NEW LONDON, NH 03257

2. The centrality of dynamic and discourse practice. "Static knowledge of social norms, concepts and frames of practices do not have a direct connection with the construction of the context. Rather they are manifested and mediated only via the interlocutor's *opportunistic discourse practices"* [italics added] (Guo, 1994, p. 10).

3. The subjective and interpretive nature of categories in methodology. Context does not exist as such in the objective world but is constructed from the way participants act and react to each other as evidenced by their behavior and their use of language. The researcher's task is to discover these categories and interpret them in a way that makes sense in the situation.

4. The independent nature of the child system. It is very important that it is investigated as a coherent system in its own right, comparable with other systems, and not just as an incomplete and defective version of the adult system.

Types and Categorizations of Modality

What about semantic features or types of modality? In Gerhardt's (1990) words, "the syntactic packaging of the modalized sentence encodes one meaning whereas the interpretation of the utterance with respect to the discourse or situational context conveys another meaning" (p. 1). We need some way of discussing the meaning of modal utterances that does not force a choice between semantic meaning and situated utterance meaning as though the two sources of meaning were incompatible with each other or could actually be discussed independently of each other.

The linguistic approach to modality developed from the philosophical "modal logic" approach. Three major types of modality have been distinguished: epistemic, deontic, and dynamic, which I will outline briefly.[31] Epistemic modality typically involves a statement of the speaker's attitude towards the status of the truth of a proposition.[32] For example, *I don't think that can be true, you can't be serious, he must be out of his mind.* The term root is often used to cover all non-epistemic meanings, that is, deontic and dynamic, both of which are concerned with the occurrence of events or the existence of states of affairs. Specifically, deontic modality concerns permission and obligation or what is possible and what is necessary with respect to some authority or set of moral values. For example, *you can go, you must leave now.* And dynamic modality evaluates the occurrence of events or the existence of states of affairs as

---

[31] Using Warner's (1993) description of the structure and history of the English auxiliaries (pp. 14-15).

[32] Epistemic modality is normally subjective. Objective epistemic modality, which is infrequent and restricted, deals with necessity and possibility within a logical system divorced from the speaker's evaluations (Warner, 1993, p. 14). See Lyons (1982) on subjective and objective epistemic modality.

necessary, important, advisable, possible, desirable and so on within a circumstantial or competential frame of reference. For example, *I can run really fast when I want to.*

There are many different formulations of these categories. Bybee's (1985) categorization system in which she proposed a whole new nomenclature to replace the traditional categories of epistemic and deontic modality will be used here. First to briefly outline some of the other approaches that have contributed to current thinking on modality. Gerhardt's (1991) studies are interesting in that they are pragmatically based. She used the tripartite division of deontic, dynamic and epistemic modality but she cautions that this situation does not accurately reflect the facts. Dynamic and deontic modality "form a multi-feature functional space based on the polarity between the performative use vs. the reportative use of a particular modal meaning" (p. 536). She proposed a developmental path for the modal catenatives as follows: from situated use to implicit use to decontextualized use.

The children in Gerhardt's (1991) study were found to use the forms (*hafta, needta,* and *gonna*) at two distinct functional levels: to represent referential meaning and to help structure frames at the discourse level. At first they used the forms to represent existing physical and social restraints: *I hafta have two blocks; I needta go to the toilet.* Later located in negotiatory frames, these forms acquired discourse meanings: *you hafta let me go first, I'm gonna build a bigger one.* As a function of having occurred in different frames, more general and schematic discourse notions are attributed to these forms, and children start to use them constitutively to achieve certain discourse goals. A continuum is proposed from mapping uses (whose function is primarily descriptive) to constitutive uses (whose function is primarily performative), from descriptive to creative uses, from central to more peripheral uses (p. 540). These represent "critically different directions of fit" (Searle, 1969). Once mapping uses are understood then "constituting uses make sense as a particular type of strategic departure from a more literal use of language" (Gerhardt, 1991, p. 540).

Leading on from Gerhardt's (1988, 1990, 1991) studies, and based on his own pragmatic analysis of the Mandarin modal auxiliaries, Guo (1994, p. 254) has outlined three general principles of development of modal meaning that are useful as a way of leading into our discussion of children's acquisition of the modal auxiliary forms.

First, that modal meanings develop in their core discourse functions first and later spread out to other discourse functions. This is consistent with findings in other domains of development, for example, the acquisition and development of cognitive categories (Rosch) or syntactic categories (Slobin). Children develop the uses of a modal auxiliary first in interpersonal functions and only after they have fully acquired the form in the interpersonal functions do they start to use it in informational oriented functions. (This idea of facilitating functions has obvious Vygotskyan overtones). This developmental pattern is domain specific and has to be repeated in each subcategory of a modal. This pattern is also evident in the narratives in this study. There is much less straightforward reporting and description, and much more use of the modals in their interpersonal narrative functions, than might be expected in the context of monological autobiographical narratives.

Guo's (1994) second principle states that in the development of social and moral understanding and its application, children first focus on the content of the rules, assuming interlocutor's compliance with them. Having acquired the rules, they then focus on the interlocutor's compliance in specific interpersonal situations (p. 275). This is an interesting point to keep in mind in relation to the later discussion of the discourse functions of the modal auxiliaries and children's overall narrative and moral development. Evaluation and establishing of moral and social responsibility forms a very large part of these autobiographical accounts. It will also bear on children's conceptualization of sources of knowledge and epistemic authority. Finally, Guo (1994) discussed the development of modal auxiliaries that represent force dynamics involving two conflicting forces. Children will first use them in socially conflicting situations in which the speaker represents the dominant force and the addressee is the force to be overcome. Internalization of the forces into a conflicting self and incorporation of the conflicts between two people into the lexical item without interpersonal conflicts are apparently later developments (p. 621).

Guo (1994) charted the developmental sequence of the use of modal concepts in interpersonal regulations as follows: from personal desires and abilities to procedural necessities and social-moral taboos; to social-moral necessities; to circumstantial restrictions and requirements; and finally to epistemic necessities and impossibilities (p. 846). He reminded us that lack of application does not necessarily equal lack of understanding but the important point is that developmental trends reflect use. There is "constant action, reaction and interaction between meanings and functions" (Guo, 1994, p. 261).

The Categorization System Chosen for This Analysis

The objective here is not to identify and isolate for each modal a core meaning independent of its context of use, as many linguists are accused of doing.[33] Bybee, Perkins and Pagliuca's (1994) system is used as a point of departure, mindful that the only way to interpret or to characterize each modal is in relation

---

[33] Interpretation of a common interpersonal function for the modals (e.g., Gerhardt, 1991; Guo, 1994, 1995) differs from the standard formulation (e.g., Perkins, 1983) of core semantic meaning in terms of possibility and necessity. The traditional way was to focus on common features that could be extracted from the static semantic meanings of the modals. Sweetser (1990, p. 58): "the polysemy of the modals may lie in the presence or absence of a single feature making the sense more specific". But bear in mind that "semantic features are often a cover term for a vast storehouse for common-sense knowledge about the world which will lead to different contextualizations in different contexts" (Fox, 1994, p.7).

to the host of other factors that characterize the modal utterance, the practice adopted is to assign each modal a set of major meanings (as opposed to a single core meaning) with the rider that the distinctions between them are gradual rather than absolute (Hoye, 1997, p. 23).

Note that Bybee's system does to an extent assume that the modals share a semantic field, which allows initial categorization of that field, which is "that there is some potential of correspondence between the embedded proposition and the situation it represents in a given instance of utterance and that each individual modal encodes its own constellation of potential correspondence" (Klinge, 1993, 1996, p. 36). But it was only through first having coded each modal utterance in relation to temporal indexing, verb forms, psychological subjects, and the like that it was possible to assign the modals to one or the other group. This sort of approach takes into account the semantic complexity of the modals while also allowing for the fact that the various senses described are not necessarily discrete and that meanings often overlap.

The initial system used to analyze the modals (first outlined by Bybee, 1985, and Bybee, Perkins and Pagliuca, 1994) carves the concept of modality into agent-oriented, speaker-oriented, and epistemic modality.[34]

1. **Agent-oriented:** This category includes all modal meanings that predicate (either internal or external) conditions on a wilful agent with regard to the completion of an action referred to by the main predicate.

2. **Speaker-Oriented:** This communicates speaker's stance and includes all directives (commands, demands, requests, and entreaties) as well as utterances in which the speaker grants the addressee permission, utterances that impose or propose some course of action or pattern of behavior and indicate that it should be carried out. This category does not report conditions on the agent but allows the speaker to impose such conditions on the addressee, that is, speech-acts through which a speaker attempts to move an addressee to action, to impose conditions of obligation.

3. **Epistemic:** This refers to the clausal scope indicators of a speaker's commitment to the truth of a proposition. This category applies to assertions, where the unmarked case is total commitment, and also to markers of epistemic modality that indicate something less.[35]

---

[34] This list has been compiled mainly from chapter 6 and Appendix B of Bybee, Perkins and Pagliuca (1994). They also designate subordinating moods as a fourth type of modality, forms used to mark the verb in certain types of subordinate clauses (*we are working now so that we can take the summer off*). This is not dealt with as a separate category here but arises occasionally in the course of how utterance or clause position can affect modal meaning, how the three main modality types are used in subordinate clauses.

[35] A curious phenomenon: "the importance of modal features in the grammar of interpersonal exchanges lies in an apparent paradox on which the entire system rests—the fact that we only say we are certain when we are not" Halliday (1994, p. 362). We can add to this those situations where speakers anticipate being challenged.

I should sketch here why this classification system was chosen and the ways in which it differs from the other tripartite approaches discussed. The obvious difference initially is in relation to the nomenclature adopted, as opposed to the traditional terms of dynamic (agent-oriented), deontic (speaker-oriented) and epistemic modality. But there are also differences in relation to the meanings and boundaries encompassed by each of the categories. In relation to the Dynamic and Agent-oriented categories,[36] although both concern conditions governing the agent (conditions on the agent or actor with regard to completion of the predicated action) the source of the modality in each case is different. The agent-oriented force in Bybee's (1985, 1994) system can be internal or external of the actor, whereas the dynamic category refers to a force coming from or internal of the actor only.

This in effect means the range of application of the categories is different. In particular, Bybee's (1994) agent-oriented category cuts across the dynamic and deontic categories. Firstly, her agent-oriented modality includes directive (deontic) statements that describe obligation and permission (that are still considered to be agent-oriented or subjective in her system as the speaker is involved in eliciting rather than just reporting on action). Secondly, the speaker-oriented category (in contrast to the more traditional deontic category that says the modal force in this category must be external to the agent of the predicated action) includes speech act types (such as imperatives) used by the speaker to impose conditions of obligation. The different foci of the approaches may be characterised in the following way (Dynamic and Deontic versus Agent-oriented and Speaker-oriented):

- Where the modal force comes from, the source of the modal force in the utterance versus how the modal is used by a speaker in the utterance.

- The subject affected by the modal, the target versus the speaker who uses the modal, the imposer of modality.

- How the agent of the verb is affected by the modal versus what the speaker is doing using the modal.

- The actor of the verb in the modal utterance versus the user of the modal.

Overall, I would argue the dynamic and deontic system focuses on a more passive subject, the person as subjected to, or on the receiving end of, the modal force (wherever it originates). The agent-oriented and speaker-oriented system promotes a somewhat more active speaker.

On the basis of these distinctions, evident even in the terminology used by the different systems, Bybee, Perkins, and Pagliuca's (1994) system was used to initially categorize the children's modal utterances. Although a system like this is useful for analysis, it is important to be aware that both agent-based modalities gradually shade into epistemic modality when "the agent referred to loses its

---

[36] What McGregor (1997) called "competential" modality (p. 228).

anchoring in the speaker's agency and control and begins to be the content of the speaker's beliefs" and many systems operate only with the categories of epistemic and non-epistemic or root modality (Bybee & Pagliuca, 1985).

Although pains have been taken to highlight the crucial importance of context, and the role of the grammatical forms and structures used in conjunction with the modal auxiliaries, this is not to downplay the central role of the modals: "there is no reason for describing the modal as a colourless 'shifter' which mainly reflects the sentential elements around it" (Hermeren, 1978, p. 71). After all, although modality in English is optional, "nevertheless the language provides a small set of grammaticized modalities with rigorous grammatical specification of their use" (Slobin, 1996, p. 92, no. 4). It is important to study the modal forms even though as speaker you are not strictly speaking required to avail of these forms, as they will often function indexically to help bring about or structure different aspects of context.

Summary

It is one thing to set out characterizations and categories and to enumerate the subtle (and sometimes not so subtle) differences in how the modal auxiliary system has been interpreted within different traditions but Gee (1985, p. 199) made the point that interpretation itself is often misunderstood in psycholinguistic research. It does not mean just figuring out the meaning of each target word and filing it under pre-established categories but allowing for the possibility of new categories to emerge. So although I start with these pre-established categories as points of reference, the interpretative process primarily involves accommodating new interpretations as they arise. A priori categories often "have more to do with a logical analysis of the way the modals express certain notions which are amenable to truth-functional manipulation" (von Wright, 1951) than with any analysis of they way they actually work in children's speech. What is needed is a thick description (Geertz, 1973) of the use of the modals.[37]

Before going on to discuss specific developmental factors the final word might go to Fox (1994) whose model of contextualization and distributed grammar "takes seriously the omni-indexical nature of language" (p. 32). She said that "grammar or grammatical knowledge is not complete within the head of a single speaker [but] is interactive and distributed in a very deep sense" (p. 33). For Fox, "meaning is distributed across participants, the linguistic expression and other facets of the socially organised environment".[38]

---

[37] In contrast to thin description that merely states facts, a thick description includes information about the context of an act, the intentions and meanings that organize action, and its subsequent evolution.

[38] In perhaps the same way that Bruner (1990) said one's autobiography is distributed across the books you have read, the people you have met, the places you have been, and so on.

A particularly interesting feature of her model is the emphasis on the interaction between grammatical forms, semantic meaning and interactional-pragmatic functions. This invites us "to see specific linguistic instances as the product of interactional work (taken from Schegloff, 1982) and grammatical patterns across utterances as the result of repeated instances of such products of interactional work" (Fox, 1994, p. 31). Fox uses the notion of "work" here to highlight the conscious and unconscious activity that goes into designing and producing an utterance as opposed to most models of grammar that suggest that linguistic behavior is effortless and automatic. So on this view we do not have grammatical knowledge, rather we use grammatical methods (p. 37). If (she cited DuBois) speakers really do "invent a new lexical or grammatical form to meet the exigencies of a particular communicative context" (1994, p. 25), then these traditional modal categories need to be fleshed out, which is done here via an interpretation of the role of the modal auxiliaries. More particularly, an interpretation of the role of the modal auxiliaries from the point of view or perspective of the child using them.

The ACQUISITION and DEVELOPMENT of the ENGLISH MODAL AUXILIARIES: PSYCHOLINGUISTIC RESEARCH

There has been quite a lot of work done on the development of the English modal auxiliaries in child language but little in the way of analyses of particular meanings or meaning systems and the contexts in which they are used. Most studies on the semantics of modal auxiliaries have focused on their referential meanings (Lyons, 1977; Palmer, 1979; Perkins, 1983), on the order of appearance of the set of modals and on the acquisition of the syntactic operations the modal auxiliaries can take. The few exceptions are the force dynamic models within cognitive linguistics (Sweetser, 1990; Talmy, 1988) and discourse oriented studies (e.g., Bybee, 1985, 1995; Gerhardt 1988, 1990, 1991; Guo, 1994, 1995) where the emphasis is on how the child uses the modals in discourse for face-to-face interaction, negation and manipulation.

This section summarizes the development of the modal auxiliaries based on recent comprehensive reviews (Perkins, 1983; Shatz & Wilcox, 1991; Stephany, 1986). The relatively large amount of research, usually starting from totally different premises and more often than not reporting conflicting results, makes it very difficult to be succinct at this point but a useful approach might be to segment the discussion into development before age 5 and development after 5 years of age. The usual bias of attention on the language of preschool children in language acquisition studies in general is also obvious in this area perhaps reflecting the fact that language development after age 5 is so much less dramatic than in the first few years. In Stephany's (1986) summary of work on children's acquisition of modality, the upper age limit referred to in most studies is 3;6, which means that some modal forms are infrequently used or have not emerged at all.

As far as meaning is concerned, the focus on younger children means that epistemic meanings do not feature very largely as the modalized utterances of the young English-speaking child predominantly express deontic meanings. Guo's (1994) data indicates that children use modal auxiliaries fairly frequently by age 3 but the development of form, meaning and function of modal auxiliaries is a protracted process that is not even completed at age 7 (p. 885). Previously the job of the over-fives was seen as mainly building up a vocabulary, it is now obvious (primarily as a result of Carol Chomsky's work in 1969) that children of age 5 still do not know the meaning of certain complex syntactic structures. Hickmann (1987) has shown in her discussion of discourse organization that although the child learns the core grammatical and phonological elements by age 3, a lot of discourse learning carries on well into the school years. Fundamental changes in children's knowledge of language are still outstanding.

Development of the Modal Auxiliaries Before Age 5

According to Brown (1973), the first modal expressions to occur do so in Stage II (Mean Length of Utterance [MLU] 2.0 to 2.75) and are the quasi-auxiliary modals or catenatives (*wanna, gonna, hafta*) followed closely by the various forms of *can* and *will*. Negative contractions are also among the earliest to appear[39] (*can't, won't*) but at first are used as single unanalyzed forms[40] rather than as analyzed phrases with a modal plus negation (Brown, Cazden, & Bellugi, 1969). Modal verbs are at first subject to severe morphological, syntactical and especially semantic restrictions. The initial use of negative modal forms by some children long before the respective positive forms emerge is probably pragmatically based (Stephany, 1986, p. 389). Then the children begin to use them in positive sentences and by 2;5 these forms are used productively in positive, negative and interrogative sentences (Guo, 1994, p. 61). But the forms are basically used in deontic and dynamic senses.

In Fletcher's (1979) study they are used to indicate the child's own willingness and inability, to request permission or to allow or prohibit an action of the addressee but never at this point in reference to a third party. Wells (1985) in a large sample found that by 2;6 only two meanings of *can*, ability and permission, and one meaning of *will*, intention, were being used by half the sample. Shatz, Billman, and Yaniv (1986) analyzed the kinds of constructions in which modal words and concatenatives appeared and found that at age 2;6 the children had a range of modal words but limited "privileges of occurrence" for them. This

---

[39] Although Shatz, Billman, and Yaniv (1986) report children using *can* affirmatively while producing no negative modals suggesting that negative modal constructions, although common, are not necessarily the first forms used.

[40] Some researchers (e.g., Pinker, 1984, p. 261) do not count contracted auxiliaries as instances of modal auxiliaries citing evidence of children's failure to segment the contractions into pronouns and auxiliaries and to use them instead as pure pronouns (Brown, 1973; Kuczaj, 1976). This is not a factor with this age group.

accords well with the description of the acquisition of verb forms and auxiliaries as "piecemeal lexical learning in limited syntactic contexts" (Fletcher, 1979, p. 265).

So modal use begins gradually between the ages of 1;0 and 2;6, often starting with a single concatenative or negative modal form in limited syntactic contexts and with a constrained set of meanings. Then there is a fairly rapid growth in modal vocabulary, but this is not matched by a similar spurt in the range of syntactic contexts available to the child. Kuczaj and Maratsos (1983), based on longitudinal data covering the period from 2;6 to 3;0, suggested that children form a separate grammatical category defined by a single syntactic position for those lexical items that appear in initial position in yes-no questions.[41] In general, first modal meanings center on intention, volition, imminence and ability or often inability (Shatz & Wilcox, 1991, p. 331). Between the ages of 2;6 and 2;11, children use *will, won't, can, can't, shall, going to* and *had better.* Beyond this age a broader range of forms and meanings develop. At age 3;6-3;11 children use these forms twice as much as younger children plus *must, should, would, could, have to* and *got to* (Guo, 1994, p. 61). Modals are used to make predictions and to talk about possibility, obligation and necessity (Wells, 1985). Words become multifunctional and plurilexicality increases, that is, the number of different modals used to express particular meanings increases (Shatz, Hoff-Ginsburg, & MacIver, 1989; Wells 1979). No new forms are added to the list between the ages of 4;6 and 4;11 but their use of *will, won't* and *shall* increase significantly compared to the 3-year-olds whereas frequencies of other forms remain much the same (Guo, 1994, p. 61). Kuczaj (1976) reports that the secondary modals (Sweetser's 1990, distal modals) such as *would* are a later development at around age 5. But in general by the age of 5 most modals are in use.

However, the most frequent forms are still *will* and *can* which is no accident according to Guo (1994). The basic meaning of these two forms expresses notions of personal desire and ability, and it is not very surprising that children of this age should organize their concepts of modality around their desire and ability.[42] By age 3 we see the use of *have to* and *had better* and children begin to decenter their modal concepts from the notions of desire and ability, they "start to be aware of certain objective social institutions and the negative consequences of violating them" (p. 61). Shepherd (1982) argued that increasingly

---

[41] Cromer (1991, pp. 199-200) citing Bellugi-Klima's (1969) study of development of self-reference by the child: the number of auxiliaries used by the child correlated positively both with the mother's use of yes-no questions and the number of her expansions (p. 252). This is interesting in that yes-no questions require the auxiliary to be moved to sentence initial position (e.g., *Can* you do it? *Will* it be fun?). This position, that is, fronted auxiliary input, may be more salient for young children and easier to process. However that also implies that all auxiliaries that could be in that position should be equally facilitated, which has not been found (Shatz, Hoff-Ginsburg, & MacIver, 1989).

[42] "Wants and need are not only among the first concepts children communicate. Concepts involving wants are also among the handful of universal concepts some linguists view as linguistic universals, primes common across all cultures" (Wierzbicka, 1992, p. 119).

differentiated meanings for particular modals develop around this time. The child she studied began to use *will* and *gonna* to indicate distance and level of control. Gee and Savasir (1985) report similar findings with two 3-year-olds who used the forms *will* and *gonna* in a highly complex way to differentiate between undertaking and planning.

Bliss (1988) reported ability and intention as the most frequently used semantic categories for all age groups studied (i.e., 2-, 3-, 4-, and 5-year-olds). These concepts reflect nonepistemic meanings. The epistemic meanings of possibility and probability were rarely used. This supports Hirst & Weil's (1982) claim that semantic constraints guide the development of modals as abstract meanings are developed later than concrete ones. But there are also pragmatic considerations. The topic of conversation in Bliss' study centered around the child, self-related activities and interests were discussed so the notions of ability and intention were obviously more relevant in this context. Modal auxiliaries only begin to appear in abundance after Stage IV, that is, when children have a mean length of utterance [MLU] greater than 3.5. The importance of the modal auxiliaries once they have emerged is reflected by their frequency of use:[43] according to Wells (1979) about 10% of the utterances of a group from 2;6 to 3;6 contained a modal verb, and he reported a marked increase in the use of the modal auxiliaries between 3 and 5 representing one of the main areas of growth in language development over this period.

Summary

Between the ages of 3 and 5 there is a consolidation of the nonepistemic meanings of the modals with an increasing ability to express various meanings with multiple words and to use particular words for more than one meaning. Epistemic meanings start to appear more frequently, but they are still much less common than nonepistemic meanings involving, for instance, action and social relations (Shepherd, 1982; Stephany, 1986). In relation to pragmatic competence, although children as young as 2;0 use modal forms, they primarily use direct imperatives. Directives and imperatives are the most important class of speech acts for which deontically modalized utterances are used, although they are not at first systematically distinguished from declarative sentences on syntactic grounds (Stephany, 1986, p. 390-391).

Children do not start to use indirect request with modal expression until about age 3;0 (Dore, 1979; Ervin-Tripp, 1977; Menyuk, 1969) and preschoolers mainly used *hafta* to state existing norms or to introduce (constitute) norms for the purpose of imposing obligations. Gerhardt (1990) also reported the mapping and half-mapping-half-constituting use as the most frequent modal used at age 3.

---

[43] The core meaning, as used by Coates (1993) in her fuzzy set theory of the modal auxiliaries that includes periphery and skirt examples, represents the meaning first learnt by children as it corresponds usually to the cultural stereotype (Wells, 1979; Perkins, 1983) and yet, statistically, core examples occur infrequently (Coates, 1983).

This indicates that modals are not originated from the pragmatic performative use although they soon become used mainly for pragmatic purposes (Guo, 1994, p. 64).

Development of the Modal Auxiliaries After Age 5

There is a dearth of studies on the modal auxiliaries after the age of 4 or 5. However there are a few worth mentioning. Major's (1974) study using imitation and transformation tasks with children from age 5 to 8 suggests that an adultlike category of modals based on abstract rules is late to develop. Major interpreted the younger children's difficulties in terms of constraints of syntactic development but as the semantic properties, that is, the meaning and situational contexts of the sentences, were not taken into account, the results are not very clear. As Stephany (1986) pointed out, modals present much more of a semantic problem than a syntactic problem for children (p. 390). The fact that when the children in Major's study did make substitutions they did so with other modals, and rarely replaced a modal with a non-modal, suggests that they did have some category knowledge (Shatz & Wilcox, 1991, p. 334).

Coates (1988), using a cluster analytic technique, studied the way children aged 8 and 12 sorted modal sentences according to similarity of meaning. The relative indistinctness of the younger children's system for sorting the modals, coupled with the lack of a cluster for epistemic possibility,[44] again highlights that they do not yet have a wholly conventional system of modal meanings. Hirst and Weil (1982) examined children aged between 3;0 and 6;6 for ability to comprehend differences among modal meanings and found that the greater the distinction in strength between the modal words, the younger the age at which a distinction could be made.

Byrnes and Duff (1989) used similar epistemic and deontic tasks to investigate children's ability to comprehend statements differing in strength of speaker conviction as conveyed by the modal. They found that older children performed better overall but surprisingly that the younger children did better on the epistemic task than on the deontic task. However, the tasks used were widely disparate in relation to the degree of interpretation required of the children and therefore these results do not count as evidence against the claim that deontic meanings are the first to appear setting the scene for later modal meaning development.

Most studies agree on the order of acquisition, that epistemic modal meanings develop later than deontic meanings. One of the main self-constructive implications of this pattern of development, as seen in this study, is that the child can now be reflexive, that is, she or he can take up the position or perspective of onlooker in relation to their own life story. The later appearance of epistemic

---

[44] It may be the case that epistemic possibility cannot be used acontextually. This is discussed later in relation to the findings of the cluster analysis carried out in this study.

meaning is usually attributed to cognitive complexity rather than to linguistic complexity as the linguistic forms used to convey epistemic modality are of the same type as those for deontic modality.[45] Epistemically modalized utterances are mainly concerned with the notion of possibility involving a distinction between reality and some other state of affairs that is based on certain conditions. In Piaget's schema of cognitive development, the notion of possibility as distinct from reality develops in the preoperational stage (2/3 to 7/8 years) where possibility is the potential future (Peiraut-Le Bonniec, 1980, p. 52). At age 7 or 8 children come to have some idea of undecidability but what is sometimes called alethic modality, "the capacity to reason on the basis of hypotheses" (p. 76), is not acquired until age 11 or 12. But the source of the notion of possibility derives from the latter stages of Piaget's sensorimotor period (about 1;6) when the child first engages in symbolic play (Cromer, 1974; McCune-Nicolich, 1981).

The first epistemically modalized utterances typically appear in the second half of the third year in English, about 6 months later than deontic meanings, and are still very infrequent compared to deontic meanings. They become more frequent toward the middle of the fourth year or even later (Cromer, 1968; Kuczaj, 1977). Some early instances are about possible future events, likely present states of affairs or sometimes unlikely future events. Later still we see hypothetical reference, but the conditional mood in most languages is last to develop due to the cognitive complexity of the notions it conveys. Epistemic modality requires a distinction between factual and possible states but for hypothetical reference a further step must be taken. The child must consider simultaneously a nonfactual situation and its relation to some other factual or nonfactual situation.

Perkins (1983) studied the modals used by 6-, 8-, 10- and 12-year-olds. He found that all the age groups used only limited forms. Looking at *can,* he found that permission uses decrease after 6 and that circumstantial possibility and suggestion uses increase (although as he did not study the full set of modals it is not clear if the frequency of subfunctions was compensated for by another modal or whether it represents a genuine decrease in usage of that meaning, see footnote

---

[45] Choi (reported in Heeschen, Perdue, & Vonk, 1988) found a different order of development indicating the possibility that children learning languages other than English acquire epistemic markers early, casting doubt on the cognitive constraint explanation. It is possible that the absence of epistemic modals in early speech is due to differential input. Parents whose language does not mark epistemic modality as a matter of course may use complementizer constructions rather than the modal auxiliaries to mark epistemic modality when speaking to their children. Modals may be reserved primarily for deontic uses (Shatz & Wilcox, 1991, p. 338). Some interesting work has also been done on how other terms with a modal character are being used at about the same time, that is, comparing the semantic and pragmatic components of modals and mental verbs in order to clarify the meanings of the early modals (Bloom & Harner, 1989; Moore, Bryant, & Furrow, 1989; Wilcox & Woolley, 1989). The first auxiliaries appear in children's speech at about the same time as complement-taking verbs (e.g., *want, try*), that is, in Stage II or the third year when simple constructions involving subject, verb, and object have been mastered. Many of the developmental patterns are similar. Children will never misorder either a verb of functional control and its complement (e.g., *I leave wanna*) or an auxiliary and its main verb (*I go can't*) (Kuczaj & Maratos, 1983; Slobin, 1973).

63). Perkins also reported that 6-year-olds use more first person singular subjects than second person subjects and that the situation is reversed for the 8-year-olds. In general we see the modals used for more complex and more subtle interactional situations and social relations between age 6 and 8.

There is no systematic study of the development of English modal auxiliaries with a detailed analysis of meaning and discourse functions but Guo's (1994, pp. 877–879) study of Mandarin-speaking children suggests three important age periods, 3, 5 and 7, and points out some similarities and differences between English and Mandarin. Between 3 and 7 seems to be the main period in which modal auxiliaries develop in form and meaning. By age 3, children have started using most of the modal auxiliaries available in their language but their repertoire is still fairly limited and the predominant use is still in relation to the child's own ability and wishes. From 3 to 5 a fuller set of auxiliary forms is developed and they come to be used for a wider range of pragmatic functions. The frequency of uses of the different forms and different semantic-grammatical categories of an individual form will continue to change and develop up to at least the age of 7. Before 5, children still tend to focus primarily on those auxiliaries that express the notion of personal desires and abilities. After that period the most important change is the "process of decentration from subjective self-involvement to more objective awareness of norms and various strategies in using modals for pragmatic purposes" (p. 65). By 6 or 7, children have learned all the various forms of indirect requests with modal expressions (Ervin-Tripp, 1977). In both English and Mandarin, children at first use modals for norm stating and only later develop the norm constituting use.

Input Studies

One other set of studies is useful to discuss, namely, input studies. Shatz, Grimm, Wilcox and Niemeier-Wind (1989) claimed that parental interactive styles and cultural values[46] may have a significant impact on children's use of modals. They report that German-speaking children use modals to express necessity and obligation as early as 2, whereas their American counterparts speaking English use modals only to express intentions and possibilities. They attribute this difference to the relatively high frequency of modals of necessity and obligation used by German parents.[47] Shatz has even found significant differences in

---

[46] But if cultural differences are a factor, then as Guo (1994, p. 378) pointed out in his study of Mandarin speakers, how is he to explain the fact that these children, coming from a culture commonly believed to emphasise rules and obligations, develop deontic modality later than children whose culture supposedly emphasises individualism and freedom. Maybe this is because children in such a culture would not therefore typically be considered to be in a position to be the speaker or performer of deontic modals.

[47] Although obviously the nature of input itself cannot determine the course of acquisition. Shatz, Hoff-Ginsburg, and MacIver (1989) have shown that children pick up forms that are relatively rarely used, for instance only 2% of the German mothers' utterances expressed necessity, yet the children used it 10 times as often as the American children. Ochs and Schieffelin are currently carrying out further studies in this area in the context of their language socialization enriched model of grammatical development.

development in languages whose cultures would generally be considered quite similar to each other, that is, British English and American English.[48] Gathercole (1986), comparing Scottish and U.S. adults, found that the familiarity of particular lexical items and meanings as exemplified by frequencies in maternal speech has an important bearing on the words and meanings children learn and use frequently. Also a study by Shatz, Hoff-Ginsberg, and MacIver (1989), on the effects of differentially enriched input on the acquisition of English auxiliaries, found that certain characteristics of the input (e.g., fronted auxiliaries[49]) in combination with two characteristics of the child, namely, the ability to carry out distributional analysis (Maratsos, 1982) and the tendency to be somewhat cautious about making grammatical classifications (Pinker, 1984[50]), would account for the observed relation between input and acquisition (Shatz & Wilcox, 1991, p. 340).

We are dealing with a highly complex and irregular part of the English language. For this reason, and because so much of the character of the modal auxiliaries is both language-specific and "defective" we expect them to be difficult to acquire. This may well be the case and they are notoriously difficult for the foreign learner to master, but paradoxically, this does not seem to manifest itself in a high commission of errors by the young child. According to Stromswold (1994) children in fact rarely make errors in the auxiliary system.[51] This turned out to be the case in this study also, the children sometimes made errors with tense markings, gender pronouns, and so on but never with the modal auxiliaries themselves.

Instead, the difficulty seems to lie in acquiring the adultlike generalizations (syntactic and semantic) pertaining to the system: "Children make narrower classificatory generalizations and use heuristics such as the avoidance of plurifunctionality and plurilexicality initially to assign meaning to form conservatively" (Shatz & Wilcox, 1991, p. 348). The plurifunctionality[52] of the modal system, that is, that most modals can express different, albeit related, meanings, has begun to be given due recognition in recent analyses (e.g., by the force-dynamics and pragmatic-oriented analyses as opposed to more traditional logic-based analyses).

---

[48] Take the case of Irish English. As it lacks any formal contrast between simple past and perfect (Harris in Milroy & Milroy, 1993, p. 179) we would not then expect to find this distinction structuring the use of certain modals as, for instance, Gee and Savasir (1986) found with American-English speakers. See footnote 63.

[49] This may function to offset those characteristics of the modal auxiliaries that make them difficult for children, that they are short, fast, usually unstressed, phonologically reduced.

[50]The defectiveness of the auxiliary paradigm must be taken into account. That is, auxiliary paradigms are irregular or defective ones, with no two auxiliary types having exactly the same set of grammatical characteristics, therefore it would be useless for the child to generalize from one auxiliary class member to another (Pinker, 1984).

[51] Some researchers have drawn theoretical conclusions from the existence of an error (e.g., Menyuk, 1969) whereas others focus on the implications of the rarity of errors (e.g., Baker, 1981).

[52] Plurifunctionality rather than polysemy indicates that the range of meanings expressed by particular modals in varied contexts may have pragmatic as well as semantic bases (Gee & Savasir, 1985).

Yet plurifunctionality is supposedly a characteristic that young language learners are busy trying to avoid (Karmiloff-Smith, 1979). If this is true and children do demonstrate an avoidance of plurifunctionality, then according to Shatz and Wilcox (1991, p. 322) this could be seen as a constraint on the acquisition of the modal system (referring to any factor that channels or directs the process of acquisition and as such is seen as a mechanism of development (Shatz & Wilcox, 1991, p. 340).

Constraints on Acquisition

Do any other constraints operate on the acquisition of the English modal system? As the child moves towards the adult system, old constraints cease to operate and a new set come into play. Shatz and Wilcox (1991) proposed a converging constraints model where the interplay of constraints, input, cognitive processing, substantive cognitive, form-function relational,[53] and universal-grammatical[54], "would produce a course of acquisition characterized by early narrow generalizations, limited understanding of meanings, and reorganizations over time, as the system converged onto the adult model" (p. 348). Constraints in this model are presumed to change with the developmental status of the child: input changes but also how the child perceives input data will change; with cognitive and grammatical development, what the child has already learned will partly determine what will be noticed next. In other words, "a major constraint on acquisition is the acquisition process itself" (Shatz, 1987).

It should by now be clear that "the questions raised by considering the development of modality cover an uncomfortably large area of developmental psychology: the acquisition of modal devices cannot be dissociated from the child's social, moral and general intellectual development" (Perkins, 1983, p. 127).[55] The use of modal forms involves knowledge of both natural and social laws. And because the average child's experience of the world, and hence knowledge of such laws is limited, it seems reasonable to assume that the child's use of modal forms will differ from the adult's.

We can predict that the child will not fully master the modal system until relatively late in development. It seems to be the case that even by age 12, the child's system is not necessarily isomorphic with the adult's (Coates, 1988; Pieraut-Le Bonniec, 1974). Related forms like modal adverbs and adjectives

---

[53] For instance, Clark's (1987) principle of contrast which suggests children are not inclined to assign the same meaning to two modal forms or to use a modal to express the same meaning as a mental verb. This could help explain why children sometimes make systematic distinctions between closely related modals (will/gonna, Gee & Savasir, 1985) and why epistemic uses of modals do not occur at the same time as other epistemic constructions in children's speech (Shatz & Wilcox, 1991, p. 343).
[54] Pinker's (1984) auxiliary category to which he claims children assign elements of their language on the basis of semantic information or positive evidence on a case-by-case basis.
[55] And yet he goes on to try to make a case for the validity of his approach that he declared to be "essentially monosemantic" (1983, p. 26) in that he is trying to isolate a single core meaning for each of the English modals that is independent of its context of use.

emerge even later.[56]   Perkins (1983) proposed a theory of development of modality from a Piagetian framework based on his assertion that "the use and comprehension of modal expressions is dependent on specific types of knowledge of the world" (p. 151). He has chosen Piaget's theory as one of the best known and most widely researched but also specifically because it deals with the development of moral judgment that is seen as particularly relevant to deontic modality and the development of rational thought that he links to epistemic modality. This is also very important in relation to the autobiographical accounts in this study.

Tracing the acquisition and use of modal expressions, Perkins (1983) notes that they are first used at the beginning of the preoperational period, when the child is said to be egocentric and therefore unable to consider two aspects of the same situation simultaneously. For some time, only *can* and *will*[57] are used and then only for himself or herself or to allow-prohibit an action on the part of the addressee but not yet in relation to a third person. Even at 6, *can* and *will* continue to be used predominantly in conjunction with the first person singular subject, a trend that declines dramatically from about age 8 on, that is, after the preoperational period.

It is suggested that egocentrism can also account for the infrequency of *must* and *may* in young children's speech, as forms that are not usually subject oriented and are "linguistic devices 'displaced' from the events to which they refer" (Fletcher, 1979, p. 283).[58]   The speech of 8-, 10-, and 12-year-olds sees a dramatic change from I to we as the most frequent subject of modal expressions and Perkins (1983) related this to the development of the child's attitude toward rules.   As modal expressions are "probably the primary linguistic means for talking about and establishing rules and social constraints, it seems quite natural that a change from an individualistic to a co-operative attitude towards rules should be reflected in the type of subject used with modal expressions"[59]

---

[56] Socio economic status (SES) has been proposed as a factor in the development and use of the modal auxiliaries, where middle-class children tend to be slightly ahead of working-class children in their use of modal expressions, also for instance, differences in use of egocentric versus sociocentric sequences (Stubbs, 1985, p. 9). Any differences could be due to a distinction between what has to be made explicit and what can be assumed which has obvious implications for what is conveyed about group membership, an insight of Bernstein's from his work on restricted and elaborated codes that is usually subsumed under the general rubric of social class. See also Corson (1995) for a very good discussion of the lexico-semantic positioning of people from different socio-cultural backgrounds, how discursive relations position people through their vocabularies.

[57] Palmer (1979, p. 100) notes that these are the only modal auxiliaries which may be subject oriented, that is, "may relate semantically to some kind of activity, quality, status, and so on, of the subject of the sentence".

[58] In line with recent models, the explanation for this relative infrequency may be rather that these forms are much more likely to be directed at the child than used by him or her.

[59] He mentioned that the fact that the children in his study were involved in a common task for which a method had to be established would have exaggerated this tendency. My context should occasion a different pattern in relation to selection for subject. He also offered an interesting speculation in relation to his finding of a decrease in the overall frequency of modal expressions in the older age group (Piaget's "codification of rules" stage that coincides with the formal operational period), namely, that the older children would be more aware of the rules of social co-operation for this kind of task and so had less need to talk about new rules.

(p. 154). So, in this framework,[60] basic modal concepts such as nonactuality and relativization are grasped quite early on by the preoperational child but are restricted within an egocentric framework. The secondary modal auxiliaries, which require a grasp of the notion of double relativization,[61] and *must* and *may,* which at least in their deontic sense require an awareness of noncurrent and nonsubjective deontic source, develop later.

Notions such as possibility represent a much higher level of abstraction than the notion of an event being relative to a circumstance (as expressed by *can*). The possible is seen "not as a mere might-have-been or (might-have-done), but as the general structural limits within which the actual must necessarily be situated" (p.157). Complete mastery of the system awaits attainment of formal operational mode. The child's range of uses for each modal will change and increase "as his understanding of natural laws, of socially defined role-relationships and constraints and of rational thought matures" (p. 157).[62] We see this happen even on a moment-to-moment basis in this discourse context.

Universal Aspects

A wide range of studies have been reviewed, including naturalistic and experimental studies, developmental studies, studies of production versus studies of comprehension, studies of the nature, and effects of differential input on modal development, studies assessing the implications of error patterns in auxiliary acquisition. What, if anything, can be said about the universal aspects of the development of modality?

If we start from the premise that cognitive development is fundamentally the same across all cultures, then differences in the ontogenesis of languages must be largely due to structural differences (Stephany, 1986, p. 397). Language development involves a process of grammaticalization of linguistic devices. In the historical development of languages, grammaticalization we are told "consists basically of a process of condensation and coalescence, starting 'from a free collocation of isolating lexemes in discourse' and passing to more and more tightened grammatical constructions through syntactization and morphologization" (Lehmann, 1982, cited in Stephany, 1986, p. 398).

These processes, although not exactly mirrored in ontogenetic development, are nonetheless very important factors in child language development. There is

---

[60] On its own, Perkins (1983, p. 155) realized, Piagetian theory cannot account for a number of factors, for instance, that past tense forms appear later with modal auxiliary verbs than with regular main verbs. To explain various factors he made use of linguistic descriptions and categories, but it remains an interesting theory.

[61] See Brazil (1995) on time reference, the relation of probability time to utterance time and the exploitation of differentiated probability time.

[62] Also Guo (1994, p. 8) said something similar about the modal auxiliaries: that the sort of notions they express may be classified into three categories that characterize human behavior in the progression from animate beings to social beings to logical beings. Through studying the modal auxiliaries he said we can see people's assumptions, beliefs, and practices guided by principles in these three domains.

evidence to suggest that morphological (synthetic) structural devices are acquired earlier than syntactic (analytic) ones. For example, comparing the development of modalized verb forms in the early inflectional stages of Greek and English, we see that the Greek child cannot escape the expression of inflectional categories forming as they do a part of tightly knit lexical forms in Greek. The young English language learner could be said to have a somewhat easier time of it in that she or he can concentrate first on the expression of lexical content leaving modulations of meaning aside for the time being (Stephany, 1986, p. 398). In general, although analytic and synthetic devices are considered to be isofunctional in the languages of the world, there are often small differences that allow certain forms to achieve more differentiated communication than others in particular circumstances (for instance, the Greek subjunctive, in addition to expressing modality, makes distinctions of person, number, and aspect whereas the English form incorporates none of that additional information). But as part of the whole process there is always in languages "a pressure towards the development of new forms which are of a more function-specific character" (Werner & Kaplan, 1963, p. 60).

It has been shown that deontic meanings are expressed before epistemic ones by children acquiring quite different languages so this must be a factor of cognitive development with the egocentric will-do being much more basic for the child than will-happen as we saw with Perkins, aforementioned. In relation to the function of linguistic devices for expressing modality, these provide further evidence that forms are not at first used with their full range of functions. With an increasing differentiation of temporality and modality from concrete actions, the meaning range of the old verb forms shift and new more function-specific form categories will develop.

The ontogenetic order of the development of deontic and epistemic modality (i.e., from deontic to epistemic meaning) is in accordance with evidence from various sources, for instance, Creole and the history of English (Goosens, 1987). Fleischman (1982), studying Romance languages, proposed the meanings of futurity as an intermediate stage in the progression from deontic to epistemic modality. Hirst and Weil (1982) said that children, in accordance with a principle of maximal contrast, first distinguish modals from factuals and that at least the beginnings of this process occur before any differentiations are made within the modal field itself. Differentiation within the modal field also proceeds in an orderly fashion. "The general rule seems to be: the greater the difference in the strength of the two types of modal propositions the earlier this difference will be appreciated" (p. 665).

Summary

The historical development of modal auxiliaries is as follows: main verbs, root modality, temporality, and epistemic modality. Detailed studies on individual modals, such as the English *can,* reveal the following developmental order of modal meanings: mental ability, physical ability, root possibility, permission and epistemic possibility. The general trend from root modality to epistemic modality is found crosslinguistically, in child language and in Creole language.[63]

To explain these similarities between language changes in different domains, in history, in children, in creolization, in language contact, Stephany (1986) pointed to a principle of cognitive development, that "new forms first express old functions, and new functions are first expressed by old forms" (Slobin, 1973, p. 184). However, although this body of evidence shows how the nature of language and the human mind itself may constrain the ways in which language can change and develop, and that children follow the general developmental order of dynamic, deontic and epistemic modality found in historical development, "the search for language universals should not obscure the importance of particulars". We must remember that "any one domain of language change is under many different pressures and constraints, as well as the universal constraints of language" (Guo, 1994, p. 877). We have seen that certain stages of the developmental order may be violated "due to the specific meanings of a particular modal, the grammatical and semantic characteristics of the individual modal and children's different developmental stages of social and cognitive competence" (p. 886). One problem with the majority of studies so far has been the tendency to treat the modal system as though it were a unified whole. An approach that glosses over the differences between the auxiliaries is not likely to be able to satisfactorily account for acquisition.

---

[63] Myhill (1995) did a very interesting study on change and continuity in the functions of American-English modals from principled to interactive (in terms both of the modals used and the functions of modal expressions). The old forms were associated with hierarchical social relationships, and they involved a clear social order and absolute evaluations based on ostensibly universal principles. The new modals are more personal, presupposing more or less equal power relationships between people and they tend to focus on interactive factors. This movement could have a parallel in child language development, with the preponderance of can/will forms in the younger groups and the older children using more interpersonal interactive forms. Myhill (1995) also reported compensatory movements in the increase and decrease of the subfunctions of the modal auxiliaries, that is, he found no case where all markers of a particular function increased or decreased at the same time. This corresponds with Guo's (1994, 1995) findings in relation to the different age groups, where one modal declined or rose in frequency, it was functionally compensated for in some other domain. See also Harris (in Milroy & Milroy, 1993) on Irish English. For instance, it does not have the formal contrast between simple past and perfect which is used in Standard English to differentiate then-time from indefinite since-time (p. 180) but as they point out this sort of comparison is "a matter of swings and roundabouts, what one system lacks in formal complexity in some part of the grammar is likely to be compensated for in some other part" (p. 177). So for instance, Irish English has a more complex tense-aspect system than Standard English although having a simpler strong verb system. "Formal simplicity in a particular area of a grammar doesn't imply a net reduction in the potential for expressing differences in meaning" (p. 177).

3
The Study: A Developmental Linguistic Investigation of Modal Auxiliaries in Children's Autobiographical Accounts

This is a developmental study based on cross-sectional data from three age groups: 5-, 8- and 12-year-olds. These three age groups constitute the main independent factor of the study across the various comparisons made on grammatical forms, semantic meanings, discourse functions, and the development of narrative ability in general.

Narrators

Age 5 was chosen as the starting point in contrast to the majority of language-based studies that deal with much younger children and that presume that by the age of 5, the child's language system is relatively stable with only increases in vocabulary and some of the more complex sentential constructions still to be achieved. However, we know that even at 12 (Coates, 1988), the system is not necessarily fully commensurate with an adult's. Steingart and Freedman (1972, p. 135) have shown that language growth is not uniform and that there are statistically significant increases at at least two developmental points: around age 5 to 7 and age 11 to 13. This type of study is not intended as a demonstration of the ways in which the child's language is different or deficient compared to the adult's, but rather we are interested in the highly idiosyncratic distinctions, perspectives, and functions achieved by the grammatical forms chosen by the child to do the work in her or his autobiography. It was important that the children had a certain level of competence and were using all the modal auxiliaries in their everyday speech and discourse. Different age groups were studied not so much with a view to being able to plot or chart distinct developments in the modal auxiliaries with age but rather because it was thought that different presentations of self might be in operation at these (st)ages, and my primary interest therefore was to see if the children's modal usage could be said to reflect this. The point is not to assess whether or not the children "have" these modal auxiliaries. The focus is on forming a picture of how, at what point, and with what set of intentions children use these forms when engaged in autobiographical discourse. The choice of age groups to investigate was also informed by the many critical functions that research has shown are in place by age 5 in terms of grammatical and narrative development. Around 5 years or so, the child begins to understand that verbal accounts can be structured in different ways to bring about various desired effects that provide a major functional motivation for the acquisition of many grammatical forms (e.g., tense shifts to perform discursive functions). The child has to learn after the age of 5 that there are layers in the interpretation of a sentence that are not immediately apparent from the perceived form of the sentence and that sentences do not always or necessarily mean what they seem to mean.

In relation to narrative development, it is shown how important it is that emotion terms and references to emotional states are used as evaluative stances. A theory of mind is fairly well established so reference to other's and their own mental states should be present in the 5-year-olds' narratives. This ability changes over time from the age of about 5 to adulthood. In the developmental literature on the self, the ages of 5, 8, and 12 are all recognized as important ages. By the age of 5 most children have entered formal education. They have a whole new set of relations and contexts, and they will have been exposed to a particular genre of social life and also of cultural and narrative life, particularly in relation to friends, which for most 5-year-olds are becoming important.[1] At age 5, we are dealing with children who are already very competent speakers and discourse partners. Therefore it is not a question of establishing when certain forms appear but of trying to say something about where they appear and why, and what functions they might serve in this particular discourse setting. The 8- and 12-year-old groups were chosen on foot of Coates' (1988) study of modality that showed differences in these two systems compared with each other and with the adult system. Also the literature on development of narrative ability and narrative style suggests these ages would be fruitful for comparison. Older children, as evidenced in the psycholinguistic research on the modal auxiliaries, are usually neglected in studies of this sort. This is surprising given that the modal system in English is very complex, involving, as it does, some understanding of natural, social, and moral laws. It is almost continuously developing after the initial morphological forms have been acquired. A host of additional factors that led to the selection of these age groups arise in the course of the discussion.

Thirty-six children agreed to participate. All are monolingual Hiberno-English speakers although several have had exposure to other languages, both in school and in extracurricular classes. Children from two schools participated in the study, one of which is a multi-denominational mixed gender school, the other a mixed gender primary school. All the children come from largely middle-class professional backgrounds of above average SES. All children have been

---

[1] Waksler (1996): "since how others perceive one is consequential for one's sense of self, control over who those others are, the company one keeps, takes on great significance for children (as it does for adults). Relations with others can present particular difficulties for children since they may not have sufficient control over these relations to bring about what they see as desirable outcomes. Further complicating such relations are the limits to children's presentation of self evident in their lack of control over their appearance. Children are thus denied resources that adults come to count on in their own presentations of self" (p. 54).

attending school since the age of 5, and all have also attended some form of preschool or Kindergarten. All of the children have siblings. In total, the transcripts of 36 children were analyzed:

- Twelve 5-year-olds (ranging in age from 5;7-5;11, of which eight were girls and four were boys).

- Twelve 8-year-olds (ranging in age from 8;3-8;9, including six girls and six boys).

- Twelve 12-year-olds (ranging in age from 12;1-12;11, six girls and six boys).

Classification Task

This investigated the way the children group the modals in terms of shared meaning using Miller's (1971) and Coates' (1983, 1988) card-sorting method. Each of the set of 13[2] English modal auxiliaries was embedded in the same sentence to reduce contextual interference as far as possible (*I* [AUX] *do my homework*) that was written on a card. The children were given the set of cards in no particular order, having first established that they could read the sentences and that they knew what each word meant. Their instructions were to sort the sentences together into groups, putting those they thought had roughly the same meaning into the same pile. They were told they could make as many piles as they wished and also that they could leave a sentence on its own if they thought it did not fit with any of the other sentences. There was no time limit imposed for the completion of this task. The number of piles made by each child was recorded and which sentences had been placed together, that is, which of the sentences (and therefore which of the modal auxiliaries) the children judged to be of similar meaning. The 5-year-olds were unable to read well enough to complete the task so this part of the study relates only to a group of 8-year-olds (n = 17) and of 12-year-olds (n = 16). The data provided by this task was represented as a similarity matrix that was later treated using a cluster analysis program. The usefulness of this method is that the children's judgments of similarity of meaning, besides being easy to elicit, can be used later as a source of information in relation to their judgment of semantic content.

Interview

Having completed the sorting task, the child was asked, conversationally, if she or he knew what an autobiography or a life story was. Whether or not they said they did, it was then explained to them, that is, to tell someone else all about

---

[2] Including *need to*, *want to*, and *have to*.

yourself, and then they were invited to tell their life story or autobiography.[3] They were told to start anywhere they liked and to tell anything at all they wished. There was no control measure used for this part of the study, the children were simply asked to talk for as long as they wished, and it was not possible or desirable to operate a fixed time variable. Occasionally, a child was prompted to continue in a nondirectional manner (e.g., "can you remember anything else?" or "tell me something else") or if a child asked, as occasionally happened, where they should start the response was simply that they could say anything or start with anything they liked. No comments were made other than to be vaguely responsive in an effort to encourage them to continue. This raises the question of the role of the researcher. "When the researcher's voice is cut out the informant's voice is distorted" (Portelli, 1981, p. 104). You could say that one of the main achievements of this study has been to "intervene in [the children's] lives, asking them to crystallize themselves at this chance moment in time" (Tonkin, 1992, p. 67). However it is very important with a study like this to remember that one's position as researcher should be considered central to the entire process, both with reference to the definition of the problem to be studied and with regard to the way one interacts with the material to produce a particular type of sense.[4] How the material is to be read "reflects on the assumptions made by the analysts about how the interviewer has been interpreted as an audience by the interviewee" (Michael, 1996, p. 26). That is to say, the researcher is an audience of a particular sort and this must be taken into account in all decisions made regarding interpretation and categorization of material.[5] To facilitate the

---

[3] On using elicited narrative material Linde (1993, p. 61) said depending on the type of analysis you want to do, on whether you want to use the data from an interview as an example of a more general social or linguistic phenomenon, you must decide on elicited versus spontaneous narratives. There are some differences, for example, use of the tense system tends to be slightly different in elicited narratives. Wolfson (1978) has shown that the use of the historic present tense is encouraged as a feature of the narrative being performed, that is, being acted out to give addressee an opportunity to experience the event. Also the form of evaluation may be different, in that spontaneous narrative may include a component of negotiation between speaker and interlocutor that the interviewer does not usually engage in, in an effort not to bias data the speaker may give. In the case of a life story, interview data can be used because the life story, as a major means of self-presentation, occurs naturally in a wide variety of contexts (including interviews) and is thus quite robust.

On the specific merits of using elicited rather than "naturally occurring" speech, Johnstone and Bean (1997, p. 223) said "if 'vernacular' speech is best for showing how people's choices are influenced by social facts, public speech is best for showing the ways in which people's choices are self-expressive"; and (1997, p. 226) citing Bauman (1977) "relatively 'performed' speech in which speakers call attention to their linguistic virtuosity is, we think, more likely to reveal how speakers organize diverse sociolinguistic resources than is relatively 'vernacular' speech which may in fact mask the full scope of a person's competence". I would consider the children in this study in the context of the situation I set up to be engaged in a form of performed speech. See also French and Nelson (1985, in Nelson, 1989, p. 301) "when called upon to produce a connected account of an event young children display a command of relatively complex language structures that are not usually found in their interactive speech".

[4] In the sense of listener as active agent rather than passive subject, negotiating their own orientation rather than simply accepting the positions offered by the text (Pope, 1995, p. 47)

[5] Certain discourse categories or discourse functions would be expected to be more pervasive in certain contexts.

generation of autobiographical discourse and personal narratives, parents of participating children were asked to supply the child with some family photographs to bring to school. With the younger children in particular, it was useful to use the photographs as prompts or to give the children a point of reference from which to begin their narratives. This idea came from Calvert (1992), who suggested using pictorial prompts for discourse analysis as a methodological innovation and is based around the child's sense of self being obviously very bound up with family, especially for the younger children, and with a sense of personal continuity over time that could be accessed via the photographs. Most photographs depicted the child in the context of her or his family at different ages.

Recording

All sessions were audiorecorded using a microcassette recorder. It was not necessary to videorecord sessions. The children's speech was transcribed as soon as possible after sessions, usually within hours, so as to minimize any difficulty with hearing the tapes or deciphering words and to maximize any contextual information that could be added from memory. No notes were taken as it would have been very distracting for the children but as soon as they left the room anything of interest or relevance (e.g., overall impressions of the children, their willingness to talk, demeanor, anything that could conceivably assist with the later task of interpreting the discursive activity in which they were engaged) was noted.

Transcription

Despite recognizing that "transcription of oral accounts is not just a problem, it is, properly speaking, actually impossible" (Tonkin, 1992, p.75), transcribing the speech recorded in the sessions with the children was the next step. After Ochs and Schiefflin (1979, p. 4), it seemed reasonable to "abandon the search for a single 'field-wide standard' and to accept it as inevitable that the transcript should reflect the particular interests of the researcher", insofar as any transcription system is necessarily a theory of what the researcher considers to be significant about language and about the stretch of spoken language to be transcribed, about what information is required and at what level analysis will proceed. All the audiorecorded speech of the children was transcribed into series of utterances, using standard orthography, where lines correspond to "intonation units" (Chafe, 1994, p. 53). Intonation units refer to groups of words uttered together in a spurt without a final-sounding pause or drop in pitch.[6] As speech is said to verbalize

---

[6] See Clark (1994, p. 1008) for a list of the 6 properties of intonation units (based on Chafe, 1994, and Gee, 1991, that suggest they are a basic unit of planning. Especially that in narratives intonation units often begin with *and, then, but,* or *so.* This is because intonation units tend to be finite clauses and in narratives successive events tend to be described with finite clauses conjoined with *and, and then,* or *so.* They are not just units of linguistic formulation but represent the way narrators think about what they are describing. They are sometimes called information blocks or idea units.

brief foci of consciousness, each expressed in a spurt of language that tends to contain (in English at least) four to five words, then it should be useful to use the resulting groupings or units to explore the organization of ideas[7] (p. 65). Using these guidelines, utterances (described as "formative units of situations and of joint action", as "real responsive-interactive units" by Shotter, 1993b, pp. 120 & 175) were chosen as units for study rather than the more usual grammatically well-formed sentences. "The utterance is a real social psychological unit in that it marks out the boundaries (or the gaps) in the speech flow between different 'voices', between 'different semantic positions', whether between people or within them" (Shotter, 1993b, p. 121). All the speech was transcribed from the audiotapes onto computer. As this is a study primarily of grammatical forms and their semantic and discourse functions, no actional behaviors or paralinguistic (vocalized but not lexicalized) features were coded. There was also very little phonetic or prosodic detail transcribed other than instances of gross changes of volume and emphasis that could conceivably play a role in the interpretation of the modal.

Three versions of the transcripts were then produced and kept in use during all the stages of coding and interpretation: a complete transcript for each child; one containing each of the child's utterances containing a modal auxiliary accompanied by the two or three utterances proceeding and preceding the target utterance; and finally, a transcript for each child consisting only of each utterance containing a modal auxiliary with no contextual information. All transcripts were then explored for "patterns of representations which by virtue of their internal patterning aim to generate or impart a particular self-image" (Michael, 1996, p. 22).

Coding

Coding differs from transcribing in both content and degree of structuring. It focuses on events that bear a more abstract relationship to each other, that is, on syntactic, semantic, and pragmatic categories and typically involves a tightly specified set of categories. Coding as a process is also quite distinct from analysis itself. The aim of coding is not to find results but to squeeze a body of discourse into manageable chunks. In this sense the categories used for coding are crucially related to the research questions. As coding has the pragmatic (rather than the analytic) goal of collecting examples for examination, it should be done as inclusively as possible. One of the main ideas informing the coding system used in this study is that function does not reside within linguistic forms as such but is constituted instead in the text distribution of a given form (another reason, discussed later, why it is important not to weight modal frequencies). In

---

[7] See also the incidence of self-repairs and hesitations at beginning of units. According to Clark (1996, p. 1011) "These planning difficulties are typical as narrators enter new sections that change the topic and require new perspectives. New sections begin at discontinuities in the experience being simulated".

other words, not all cases of what sounds the same are in fact uses of the same linguistic unit. Any patterns of distribution in a certain kind of discourse context are important and interesting, they should not be presumed to be arbitrary but governed by a kind of logic that it is the job of this type of research to explore. This is not to say that the speaker, the child in this case, sets out to produce certain combinations of features or intends to produce a certain percentage of word classes yet these percentages and patterns are nevertheless produced in the course of their discursive activity and using coding and quantification methods, these unintended consequences can be mined for insight into the child's own categorization system. The coding of utterances in this study was done on the transcript files and proceeded in rounds. At each round, one level of coding took place, all working directly from the written transcripts. Each utterance containing a modal auxiliary was examined and coded for each feature. Coding included the full target utterance, relevant grammatical (for example, case relations between subject and verb, transitivity of verb), semantic (different senses of modals, source of modal force) and discourse information (primarily the categorization system of discourse functions that were generated from the children's speech that is discussed fully in a later section) as well as primary information about the speaker of the utterance. The complete set of transcripts was coded. (See the appendix for the complete manual according to which all coding was carried out.)

The main problem in this sort of research is to decide which linguistic forms are relevant or related to which discourse or narrative function. Items in this study were selected for coding partly on the basis of research in child language and discourse analysis that has shown that "functionally distinct types of narrative are often distinguished through the use of particular constellations of linguistic features rather than the exclusive use of individual features" (Wolf & Hicks, 1989, p. 336). The coding scheme devised draws on a wealth of research in a wide range of relevant areas, for example, research on transitivity, agency, tense, aspectual markings, pronominal systems, verb classes and so on. All linguistic behaviors that in the course of the inquiry were found to be relevant to the selective occurrence of the target forms, the modal auxiliaries, were coded for at this stage. So each modal utterance was coded for a total set of linguistic features that, I would argue, are important for and constitutive of autobiographical narrative. The specific issues involved with each linguistic or grammatical feature coded are discussed fully later, that is, the psychological reality of these grammatical distinctions that determined their inclusion in the coding system. This separation, rather than isolation, of covariables, functions to reduce the data in order to enlarge the view. The idea is not to reduce and abstract from the material to the point where context completely disappears but to compile as complete a picture as possible of the target form, its collocations and its behavior and to build on this information.

Quantitative analysis, word counting, and the like may seem somewhat at odds with the theoretical orientation espoused so far in this book, but there is no reason why studies of this nature should not make use of a combination of quantitative and qualitative methods (Harré & Mühlhäusler, 1990, stated explicitly that what is missing from a lot of research of this type is quantitative material that allows patterns to be identified). The ideal situation to achieve would be a revealing discussion as to what one form rather than another achieves in a particular context while using quantitative data to show that the patterns being described may be general in the language. Quantitative type of analysis is very valuable if it helps us to understand and describe on a psychological level the children's exploitation of particular linguistic devices for particular communicative ends.

We need to keep in mind that the syntax of language, for example, the linguistic features coded in this study as characterizing the modal utterances "are social facts which no-one can bypass except at the price of non-communication (and that is often characterized as insanity)" (Tonkin, 1992, p. 66). And therefore it is crucial to account for these aspects as well as the higher order aspects of the child's language. In light of the fact that the "ideal of linguistic analysis is undoubtedly to achieve a qualitative description of language structure that will shed light on the quantitative properties of language use, especially since diachronically the latter determine the former" (Garcia, 1990, p. 303), the approach adopted here is to use this very detailed account of the systematic deployment and behavior of the modal auxiliaries to arrive at an interpretation of the children's autobiographical discursive activity it is suggested these forms actually help to set up and to structure.

Quantitative Methods of Analysis: Preliminary Treatment

Descriptive statistics were initially obtained for all coded categories. As children of different ages were involved in this study, grammatical categories across groups were compared (e.g., epistemic uses of a particular modal or the incidence of agentive constructions). Comparisons were also made between grammatical categories within age groups. When analyzing some of the subcategories of a specific modal, the frequencies are sometimes too low to apply any meaningful statistical analysis, but they still represent interesting trends and findings. This is not a problem due to the very detailed analysis at a discursive level that accompanies these preliminary analyses. I am ultimately more interested in the particularities of the material than in making generalizations. The fact that a particular linguistic device is used even once in a particular way is important.

The use of a range of methodologies within the scope of this study means that quantitative information can be fleshed out by detailed qualitative analyses that, in this case, amounts to a lot of careful reading and rereading. First, looking for patterns in the data, either in the form of variability (searching for differences in the content or form of accounts) or in terms of consistency (identifying features that may be shared by accounts). This leads to a concern with function and consequence, that is, the formulation of a set of hypotheses about these functions and effects that involves locating the relevant linguistic evidence. So there is no very fixed analytic method as such, instead the idea is to operate within a broad theoretical framework focusing on constructive and functional dimensions of discourse and to try to identify significant patterns of consistency and variation.

Cluster Analysis

Cluster analysis (CA), where the output is natural groupings of cases into categories based on the overall profiles of cases across all variables, is useful for large data sets like this one. A CA was carried out[8] on the correlation matrices obtained from the classification task completed by the 8- and 12-year-olds. A visual representation of the similarity was produced in the form of a dendogram for each group. Keeping in mind that any clusters are, properly speaking, rules of thumb rather than definitive solutions, the next step involves coming up with theoretical labels for the clusters, trying to convey a sense of what type of construct or concept are represented by the cluster solution. In general, clustering techniques are structure imposing rather than cluster seeking, that is, they will find clusters regardless of the particular data used. Not that natural clusters can not be found using these techniques, just that it may impose clusters if the natural clusters are not there. The dendograms for each age group revealed some very interesting and distinct clustering patterns in the children's grouping of the modal forms in relation to meaning that is discussed later (see Figs. 4.1 and 4.2).

General Description of Data

Eight modal auxiliaries and their variants were identified and coded in the corpus: CAN (can't); COULD (couldn't, could've); WILL (won't, 'll); WOULD (wouldn't, 'd); SHOULD (shouldn't); MUST; MIGHT (mightn't); MAY (maybe).

All instances of use of these forms were coded, including a few cases of repetition, that is, where the utterance or part of the utterance was a repetition of the speaker's immediately preceding modal utterance. This repeated utterance was judged to have an independent pragmatic function. False starts and self-corrections or amendments (where an entire modal and part of an utterance was enunciated and then the speaker went on to repair the utterance or to express the utterance differently[9]) are also important in interpreting the discourse activity. It seemed that these types of uses that tend to be labeled uncodable in conventional language-based studies are in fact highly informative and have a lot to contribute to the meaning of an utterance. These types of occurrences can be seen to cluster at moments of uncertainty or of disclosure, for example, which would obviously be very important in this context. A total of 501 occurrences of these modals were found in the transcripts that comprised:

---

[8] Ward's hierarchical agglomerative clustering method (average linkage analysis) was used.
[9] For example, where the speaker replaced the first modal they used with another modal.

- For the 5-year-olds: a total of 11, 939 words, mean = 995 words (range 359 to 1,828 words), 117 modals (mean per child 9.8).

- For the 8-year-olds: a total of 15, 440 words, mean = 1,287 words (range 363 to 2,142 words), 160 modals (mean per child 13.3).

- For the 12-year-olds: a total of 16, 797 words, mean = 1,400 words (range 915 to 2,223 words), 224 modals (mean per child 18.7).

The measure of number of words per transcript was useful in ascertaining that the frequency of occurrence or usage of the modal auxiliaries by these children in this context corresponds with the reported usage of 10% of utterances used or produced in any given situation containing some form of modal expression. When we compare the frequency of occurrence of the modal auxiliaries in this study with some of the major studies done in this area, we see very similar patterns of occurrence that are useful to confirm the generality of these findings (bearing in mind that I do not intend to conduct similar analyses of the meaning of these modal usages).

When comparing modal usage across age groups in this way, the most striking difference initially relates to the number of modal auxiliaries used by the children in the different age groups. Using these raw frequencies of occurrence as the unit of comparison could be open to being seen as a methodological problem. For example, as there was no attempt to control for recording time or for number of utterances, it is possible then to interpret any increase in use of the modals as being due to the older children talking more or perhaps being able to speak faster. This could be corrected, that is, some form of standardized frequencies could be calculated and used for analysis. However within the overall context of this study it is neither necessary nor desirable. Children, after all, can not be relied on or even expected, in the "normal" run of events, to produce the same amount of speech. Adopting a measure of corrected frequencies would reflect the child's modal use only as a proportion of her or his total speech production within a specified time frame and not as an indicator of the importance of modal concepts in the child's discourse in general. The importance of the modal auxiliaries and of modal concepts is reflected in the actual frequency or infrequency with which the child uses these forms within a particular discourse setting. This is borne out by looking at some of the older children's relatively lengthy transcripts that nevertheless do not contain a proportionate amount of modals when compared, for example, with a much shorter transcript from a 5-year-old child. For these reasons it was decided not to use corrected frequencies but to base all further analysis and discussion on the primary data that is, the transcripts themselves and the actual frequency of occurrence of our target forms.

Each child's transcript, as a complex speech act, was taken as the basic unit of analysis. That is, the internal structure, the elements of each transcript are not statistically independent. The framework for the study influenced the analysis considered to be appropriate. There is no need to account for the variability in the length of the children's transcripts, I am primarily interested in what the children answer, what they spontaneously tell in response to being asked for their life story.[10] It is not necessary to try to provoke longer, more statistically significant stories. The analysis is wider also than the modal auxiliaries, they are the starting point, the point of entry for the child, and also for the researcher, but it is played out on a wider scale of verb phase, utterance, discourse function and so on. In general I am looking at the importance of these concepts and stances for the child and as such, some transcripts are simply much more heavily modalized,[11] that is, marked, than others. It is a style, a rhetorical option, and that is why it is being studied in the first place.

Far from being a problem to counteract, the relative infrequency of occurrence of the modal auxiliaries in this context was expected. It is well established that the modal auxiliaries are more typically used in the context of explicitly dialogic, interactive speech.[12] Most of the forms studied here have prior histories in various other types of interactive discourse. But with this in mind, it should be very interesting to study the points or situations in the children's narratives as a particular discursive context where the modal auxiliaries are called on or brought into service. In this study autobiographical discourse is a form of accounting, of persuasion, and therefore properly speaking, is dialogical. Also of course all narrative, especially, as in this case, explicitly elicited narrative monologues, presuppose an audience.[13] I am not interested necessarily in the earliest uses or the first appearance of the modal auxiliaries. The focus is on the range of different discourse functions for which these forms are used in autobiographical narrative.

---

[10] Linde (1993) suggested that it is not very worthwhile to ask children for their life story, but one's autobiography or one's ability to tell a coherent story about one's life does not appear fully formed at adolescence, it is emergent and can be traced. Linde's analysis of the language and narratives used was in relation to one's job or career as the area that defines many adults.

[11] Not just in relation to the modal auxiliaries themselves but modal expressions in general, for example, adverb satellites and so on.

[12] Guo (1994) has shown that the modal auxiliaries are used first for interpersonal functions and only later for information functions. Also the relation of the modals to the future should militate against past personal narratives being heavily modalized but this turns out to be a very interesting aspect to this study, that is, the role of the future in autobiography.

[13] "Narratives seem different from conversations because they seem to be provided by individuals speaking on their own. Narratives rely just as heavily on coordination and the participants as conversations do. It is simply that the co-ordination is hidden from view" (Clark, 1994, p. 1006).

I
Modal Grammar in the
Construction of the Self

The philosophical problem "What is the self?" comes close to being definitively solved by attacking it from a linguistic point of view. Harré (1993a, p. 111)

There has been a tendency to take as metaphysical and/or empirical matters that are in a broad sense grammatical, for instance, the self, agency, intention and so on. Harré (1989, p. 24)

This section looks closely at the range of meanings and functions associated with the use of modal auxiliaries, at how they are used to frame actions, events, and perspectives in the children's autobiographical narratives. How do the children relate the "landscape of action," their agentive selves, to the "landscape of consciousness," their epistemic selves? Bruner (1995) describes how Greimas (1983) proposes an axis:

> extending from inwardness to outwardness, from the subjective to the objective linguistically memorialised in the primitive system of the modal verbs. To *desire* is to implicate little in the world; to *know* what ones desires moves one outward toward the world; to feel one is *able* to achieve *what* one desires is yet another step outward. *To be able*, of course, implies both senses of the term: epistemic and deontic, what one is able or not able to do by virtue of skill and knowledge and what one is permitted or not permitted to do by virtue of the social world. Finally, one acts or *does*, and impinges directly upon the world. Self-accounting must exploit the full axis from desire to action if it is to bridge the gap between the subjective and the objective, between inner and outer. (p. 166)

Self-accounting is the main work of autobiographical discourse. The situations in which speakers manipulate perspective are those in which actions, consequences, and responsibility are at issue. These concepts are centrally at issue as we construct autobiographical narrative and are manipulated and constructed in English largely via the modal auxiliaries. The modal auxiliaries are identified as critical points in the children's life stories, which means it is also necessary to establish the other linguistic forms[1] the children use at these points

---

[1] This is a very difficult area. See Aarts and Meyer (1995) for a selection of different approaches to the analysis of constructions involving auxiliary verbs.

or junctures. The possibility of circularity in this argument ought to be addressed, that is, that the modal auxiliaries are presumed to occur at decisive points in the children's narratives, but that wherever a modal auxiliary occurs is judged to be a decisive point in that narrative. Many different avenues of research have indicated that the modal auxiliaries fit this particular bill.[2]

It is well documented that the modal auxiliaries have a very high informational content (or burden) in English; that because they are related to subjectivity, they must therefore be very important in the telling of one's life story; even the fact of their relative infrequency in this context must suggest that they are being recruited on a highly motivated basis. More practically, modal meaning has been shown to be affected by an incredibly wide range of extra-linguistic factors including, individual difference (Johnstone, 1996), register variation (Coates, 1983; Hermeren, 1978, 1980), SES (Corson, 1995), regional variation (Trudgill & Hannah, 1994), national variation (e.g., see Collins, 1991 on Australian-English or Myhill, 1995 on American-English) and social variation (Labov, 1972).[4] Menaugh, in his sign-based analysis of the modals,[3] summed it up nicely when he said "that we have no way of knowing how the user of a modal is viewing a situation *except* [italics added] through the modal s/he uses to describe it" (1995, p. 199).

Importance of Context for Interpretation of the Modals

The categorization system used to describe how the modal auxiliaries are deployed in this analysis is fully laid out elsewhere. Briefly outlined here is one other of the more interesting ways of categorizing modal meaning that has also been used to inform my reading of the modals in this investigation. Namely, Klinge's (1993, 1996) account of context and modal meaning that gives us a

---

[2] Most of which have already been discussed in the sections on the concept of modality and the development and acquisition of the modal auxiliaries.

[3] "Much of what had previously been judged free variation is in fact significant. Labov showed that meaning does attach to such variation and marks social groups and social circumstances. The notion of linguistic significance was thus broadened beyond semantics to encompass social meaning about language users and the uses to which they put language in their social interactions" (Finegan, 1987, p. 92).

[4] He proposed that for each type there exists a physical analogue in which the likelihood relation between an initial state and an occurrence is modelled as a path between a starting point and a target. A distinctive path analogue can therefore be obtained for each modal. Using this model, he has actually worked out probability scales/figures for the various modals (Menaugh, 1995, see especially pp. 196, 204-206). The characteristics of different modal predictions are compared with established models of likelihood: each modal corresponds to one of three distinct or defined likelihood types: probability, in limited outcome systems (*must, shall, should, may, might*); probability, in unlimited outcome systems (*will, would*); and possibility

system of "preferred readings"[5] for the modals. In keeping with the approach taken in the rest of this book, this discussion is not based on any one system of classification or any one particular theory but is eclectic, based on the findings and results from a wealth of research central to the area. According to Klinge, a recurrent problem in discussions of modality has been the lack of a principled account of how to arrive at an explicit interpretation of an utterance of a sentence containing a modal. In his view, the underlying semantic system is quite straightforward. The differences in meaning that can be assigned to each modal arise from their contexts of use and are to be accounted for in terms of utterance as opposed to sentence meaning.

He favored a monosemic-pragmatic approach[6] and questions the validity of the traditional three categories, epistemic, deontic and dynamic, in which each modal is given several semantic interpretations. This raises the question of whether the interpretations are really of the modals. Klinge (1993, p. 355) made his point very clearly in relation to taking all aspects of context into account. Take the following two sentences: *I will win; I will lose.* In this system, it is not WILL that is different but the connotations of win versus lose.[7] One assumes agency, the other a victim, therefore WILL becomes prediction as opposed to intention. There should be much more emphasis placed on cotext and context sensitivity.

The main attraction of this theory is the series of clues Klinge (1996) provided for interpretation of modal utterances and for giving a "preferred reading". One such clue is the subject of the noun phrase. *You may leave,* for example, will usually get a straightforward deontic reading, as in the speaker grants permission to an addressee. For example, parent to child *you may leave the table now.* But under certain conditions this utterance could be epistemic (*you may leave, if you do we'll reassess the situation*). But given that the you of the sentence usually knows more about their own situation than the speaker, it is not likely that this utterance will ever be taken to be imparting dynamic or volition information to the addressee.

The desirability of the situation represented by the proposition can also give up the meaning. Desirability in this scheme is considered to be crucial for both deontic and dynamic readings. Desirability will occasion a deontic reading. If we oblige someone to do something it is usually because we want it done *you will have to be home by 10,* or if we grant permission it is because the addressee

---

[5] The interpretation of a given utterance that seems to require the least processing effort, the one that first springs to mind (Klinge, 1996, p.39).*can, could*).

[6] Which he contrasts with the traditional polysemic approach. The main distinction is that someone working within a monosemic framework uses context to reconstruct the same meanings that a polysemic theorist would assign to the semantics of a modal (1996, p. 52, no. 1). Klinge's theory of sentence interpretation is in this way "entirely consistent with Relevance Theory" (1996, p. 39). See also Hoye (1997, p. 136) on adverb satellites and modality for a good discussion of what he refers to as Klinge's novel approach to the meaning of the modals.

[7] See, for instance, the work done by McGuire and McGuire (1992) on the psychological significance of word-order regularities and kin pairs. Also Semin and Fiedler (1992) on the inferential properties of interpersonal verbs.

desires that permission *OK, you can have it.* But this does not usually signal a dynamic reading. For example, *she will hurt herself with that* is not understood as her wanting to hurt herself.

Assignment of agent control is important in this context. For a modal utterance to receive a deontic interpretation, *he must resit his exams,* it must be possible to identify the (morally) responsible agent so there must be some correlation between the subject of a sentence and a preferred reading as deontic. Nonhuman subjects of modals therefore will often occasion an epistemic reading, *it must be true.* If there is difficulty inferring agent control, a lot of contextualization is necessary in order for deontic modality to be the preferred reading.

Finally, the temporal indexing of the proposition is a very important variable for interpreting a sentence in terms of epistemic or nonepistemic modality. Situations in the past and present are immutable and therefore judged to be beyond agent control so the preferred reading in such a case would tend to be epistemic. Future time situations on the other hand permit of possible agent control so can therefore be indeterminate between epistemic and nonepistemic. Progressive sentences will also usually receive a preferred reading of epistemic modality. This is because progressive denotes processes unfolding at the time of the utterance so the focus is on the activity element.[8]

So the coincidence of referential situation with time of utterance gives an epistemic reading. But Klinge (1996) pointed out (and we need to remember to treat these only as clues or rules of thumb[9]) that this can also be due to the relative infrequency of situations in which we impose obligation or grant permission to produce some act only to produce the activity-element of an act rather than the final state of that act:

> "And she said 'Oh, CAN you get off because it ruins a person's dive if you're on the diving board'" (JOH8).[10]

Initial Age-Related Trends

The modal auxiliaries CAN, COULD, WILL, and WOULD (and variations thereof) account for over 70% of all the modal auxiliaries used, and the WOULD

---

[8] Both present and past forms of the modals share abnormal frames of time reference and may be used to refer to the present and the future. Generally only the epistemic, as opposed to the deontic, modals combine freely with the perfective and progressive aspects (Hoye, 1997, p. 75). See also Brazil (1995) on time reference.

[9] For example, epistemic modality is normally always held to be in the present but take the statement "*for all I knew he might have done it*". This exceptional past epistemic usage suggests the epistemic modals are not necessarily performative and therefore present (Hoye, 1997, p. 136, no. 7).

[10] The format used to identify examples from transcripts will be the child's initials followed by age. Any underlined word means the word was stressed when uttered.

form is the most frequently occurring form overall (28%).[11] Briefly described are some of the patterns of occurrence before going on to discuss the senses in which the modals are used by the children. Looking at the distribution of the modal variations, the four forms of CAN, COULD, WILL, WOULD are used the most by all three age groups, although when the distribution is broken up into the modal auxiliaries themselves and their variants, some different patterns begin to emerge. The patterns of occurrence can be described in very general terms first:

- CAN features consistently as one of the most frequently used modals for all the children (hovering at around 26% for all groups).

- The occurrence of COULD in this context decreases quite sharply between the ages of 5 and 12, and does not appear among the top five modals used for the 12-year-olds.

- WILL is used much more frequently by the older groups and does not feature in the 5- or 8- year-olds' "most used" category at all.

- The frequency of WOULD in this corpora shows an overall increase with age but peaks with the 8-year-old age group.

- The 5-year-old group does not generally favor the contracted form of WOULD('D) which otherwise features quite strongly in the speech of the 8- and 12-year-olds.

- The 12-year-olds are using WILL('LL) much more frequently than either of the other two age groups.

And of those forms not accounted for by the most frequently occurring category:

- MIGHT, of the four underrepresented auxiliaries, is the strongest, featuring relatively well in the transcripts of the 5 and 12 age groups, but much less frequently in the 8-year-old category.

- SHOULD is not used at all by the 12-year-olds and only very infrequently by the others.

- MUST and MAY similarly do not feature largely at all in these transcripts.

---

[11] One of the themes of this discussion is the attempt to relate what is known from the literature about the diachronic development of the modal auxiliaries with the synchronic patterns and movements of the modal auxiliaries in this study. See for instance Bybee, Perkins and Pagliuca (1994) for a discussion of the rationale for this kind of comparison. But we must be careful: "the point of starting so far back in history is that a number of the processes that can be seen to have happened across time give us a helpful perspective for a suitable framework for analysing modality at any particular point in time, an état-de-langue, which like a single frame of a motion picture gives at best only a partial representation and at worst a misleading representation of a scene" (Matthews, 1996, p. 364). The distribution of the modal auxiliaries for this group of children fits in with, for instance, Myhill's predictions that the older modals, like SHALL, SHOULD, MUST, are dying away in favor of the newer set but this is something that is discussed fully later.

The overall pattern for these modals (even though we are sometimes dealing with very small numbers) tends toward the 12-year-olds being more concerned with possibility, that is, with what might or might not happen or what might be the case, whereas the younger children, especially the 8-year-olds curiously, are more preoccupied with what ought to be the case and what they think should happen but I come back to this point later. Although it may seem to say very little initially, this kind of word counting is essential in order to get at the movement of the modal auxiliaries. It is important to chart the decline in occurrence of one modal and the increased usage of another in such a way that they might be coupled or decoupled.[12] Is it perhaps the case that the functions or set of meanings of a particular modal declining in popularity or usefulness for one group is being picked up or compensated for by a modal on the rise? These sorts of questions can not be answered yet (the caveat "if at all" springs to mind), but pinning down these details allows us to at least address issues and anomalies like these.

The Categorization of the Modal Auxiliaries in This Investigation

It is also possible to look at the different senses in which the modal auxiliaries are used, according to the system laid out previously of agent-oriented, speaker-oriented, and epistemic modality. Overall, almost 57% of these modal auxiliaries used represent agent-oriented modality. Speaker-oriented modality accounts for only 2% of the modal auxiliaries, which is no surprise in the context of narrative discourse (the few instances there are will be accounted for largely within the context of reported speech). Epistemic modality accounts for about 41% of the children's usage of these forms.

Without going into detail at this stage, it seems that by virtue of strictly applying the rules of the categorization system, over one-half of these modal auxiliaries must be classified as agent-oriented modals, that is, as descriptive, and therefore supposedly in some way less subjective (and therefore less interesting). In fact, when you look at their environment and their movement they are actually epistemically oriented or, as I want to put forward in general, have an evaluative function. Also, the situation is somewhat different when each age group is

---

[12]To pick up Shanon (1993) once more, who highlights the importance of the mechanism of coupling and decoupling for cognitive growth. "Specifically, the cognitive system attaches itself to another factor or system, goes along a certain path with it and then dissociates itself from it and stations itself *in a place which it would not have been able to reach otherwise"* [italics added] (1993, p. 275). This as seen later is exactly the process at work in terms of both the synchronic and the diachronic development of the modal meanings. In terms of the meanings accruing to the modal auxiliaries, Bybee (1994, p. 176) has shown that diachronic development seems to be "the *loss of a specific component of meaning* and in relation to synchronic development, we see the *accretion of new meanings* to each form" [italics added]. We are talking about development characterized by decontextualization and autonomy. Shanon (1993, p. 277) said "development progresses from total immersion in the given context and dependence on it towards greater ability to divorce oneself from the context and gain relative freedom from it" and thereby in this context greater facility to use the modal auxiliaries in a wider variety of contexts and ways.

treated separately. In any case, this situation reflects what it is we do in the course of autobiographical discourse, namely, construct for ourselves, both agentive and epistemic selves. The point is that it was never going to be the case that one size or one categorization system fits all. The contribution of my analysis is to establish some point of contact between psychological and linguistic investigations of this sort. It is a framework that working from the bottom up could facilitate a comprehensive interpretation of the self-constructive implications of modal auxiliaries in an autobiographical context.

On breaking these categories down further the agent-oriented root possibility category is by far the most frequently used, followed by modal auxiliaries used in the service of epistemic certainty. And for each auxiliary, the preliminary source of its modality can also be identified. The first observation is that each of the forms seems to be overwhelmingly associated with one particular meaning, with either its agent-oriented or its epistemic meaning (e.g., 89% of instances of CAN are agent-oriented, 66% of usages of WOULD have been classified as epistemic). But the situation is not necessarily so straightforward.

Initial descriptions seem to indicate a simple enough situation. The modal auxiliaries fairly evenly express agent-oriented and epistemic modality and break down into the most frequently used meanings of root possibility, degrees of epistemic certainty, ability, desire, and intention. But the analysis needs to go deeper, to see if any further distinctions in meanings can be revealed, and the best way to do this is to try to marry what is known of the diachronic development of modality with the synchronic patterns in our data. "A real understanding of modality needs a study of diachronic relations" (Bybee, Perkins, & Pagliuca, 1994, p. 176). Linde (1993, p. 223), whose model of the life story as a linguistic unit I make use of later) welcomes the turn to discourse within psychology and linguistics but says that both disciplines tend to miss out on two of the most important dimensions of the term as used by Foucault (1972), namely, power relations and history: "discourses have a history, they have beginnings, they have development and these are linked to historical changes in power relations, technologies, ideas and so on. Discourse analysis within linguistics has up till now been exclusively synchronic". In this context it also seems that the most profitable way to explore the development and movement of the modal auxiliaries across age groups might be against a backdrop of the development of the modal auxiliaries themselves on a wider scale.

Issues of Development and Diachrony

Today's morphology is yesterday's syntax. Givón (1979, p. 413)

First, summarized are some of the main points of the acquisition and development of modality very briefly. By the age of 5, all the modals, including the distal ones, are now in use (one of the main reasons why the age group was included in this exploration). At this time, CAN and WILL are still the most frequently used modal auxiliaries (typically with I as subject), as the children still tend to organize their concepts around notions of personal desire, ability and intention (Guo, 1994). Although my observation, which is discussed fully later, is that CAN and COULD are the most frequent forms used by the 5-year-olds with WILL hardly being used at all. Around 8, children begin to be aware of social institutions and both the consequences of, and the opportunities for, violating them (I show how this is reflected in their developing understanding of authority and moral relations). They make use of increasingly differentiated modal meanings (especially in relation to the source of the modal force), action and social relations (where we is the most frequent subject). This age group first use modals for norm-stating and later develop their norm-constituting use (Gerhardt, 1990, p. 40). Also important to note is the fact that the flip side of being newly aware of social obligations and conventions is that the children are now also increasingly preoccupied with their own rights and position in relation to these conventions and norms of behavior. By age 12, the children's discourse may be organized around centrally epistemic and reflexive notions.

Myhill's (1995) study of modality in American-English distinguished between two main function types: the old types of modality functions that generally involve "a clear social order and absolute evaluations based on ostensibly universal principles" (*my daughter shall marry you; you must always tell the truth*). And the new types of modality functions that "presuppose more or less equal power relationships between people and focus on interactive factors such as co-operation, emotional appeals, advice, apologies, threats. They tend to be interactive rather than principled" (p. 160).

This study shows a similar development takes place with age. This linguistic development could be said to mirror the so-called moral development of the child, and we have already seen how the modal auxiliaries and the child's general intellectual, moral and social development are inextricably intertwined. It certainly parallels quite closely the situation we find here with regard to how the children use the forms, from using modal auxiliaries to express external obligations, rights, and duties to using auxiliaries in a way that expresses a developing concern with, and interest in, the notion of personal responsibility. Our later discussion highlights this point nicely.

Myhill (1995, p. 193) reported that his older modals-*must, should, may, shall*-declined in frequency whereas *can, ought to, got to, have to, gonna and better* increased.[13] This trend holds up for these narratives also in that the four most frequently used forms are the so-called newer modals, *can, could, will, would*,[14]

---

[13] Of which group only CAN is a true modal auxiliary, the others are catenatives and semi-modals. He wonders if this represents a decline in the true modals that may all eventually disappear, to be replaced by semi-modals, interpreted as part of the general drift in English toward analyticity but concludes that the fact that *can* is a true modal and *will, would* and *could* have shown no decline militates against this proposal (Myhill, 1995, p. 199).

[14] Apparently Irish characters in the plays of Howard (1953/1889) and Sheldon (1953/1911) use these newer modals more (see Myhill, 1995, p. 207, no. 3). Perhaps this pattern is a distinctive feature of Irish English. As far as I know there has not yet been a study of the modal auxiliaries in Irish English, although American, Australian, and British English have been studied.

whereas the other older modals are not well represented at all. Typical early modality functions include "strong obligation dictated by social decorum, principles, etc. (*must*); situations where one person controls the actions of another (*shall, should*); statements about generic subjects (*should, may*); situations where the subject has the possibility of benefiting from their own action (*may*); and used to criticise or evaluate past action or present situations (*should*). On the other hand, those functions more typical of so-called late modality include: cooperative versus unilateral or hostile decision (*will* vs. *gonna*); cases in which the subject has the possibility of doing an action for someone else (*can*); used to indicate advice or good idea (*better*, later *should*); preferred future action based on kindness, responsibility, fairness (*ought*); finally, used in the sense of obligation based on emotion (*got to*)". The way these children use the modal auxiliaries in many ways corresponds with this picture of the decline and rise of certain functions or meanings.

The point I want to explore here relates also to the development of various narrative skills and to the child's developing sense of self.[15] It is that neither the central components of self, important narrative structuring devices nor any of the meanings of the modals, await acquisition or development by stages nor depend per se on a certain level of attained maturity. All these components, and similarly all the possible modal meanings, are available to the child all the way along the developmental path or continuum, but only certain elements or meanings are at the forefront at any given time. These aspects of the self and these types of modality are expressed differently at different times by the child and assume different levels of importance and urgency. They do not represent different and discrete stages of development, rather each function or meaning has its own stages of development and its own range of applications for the child.

The problem is to figure out what the old and new modals have in common, whether they fit under the same general functional heading (e.g., root possibility) or whether they represent different stages in a single diachronic process. Myhill (1995) suggested that maybe people, for one psychological or social reason or another, changed the frequency with which they expressed certain types of modality function. This makes sense if functional changes can be shown to form a coherent set, reflecting a single conceptual change, i.e., from modal expressions characterized by principles that are ostensibly universal and absolute (although these may be only the speaker's viewpoint) to modal expressions characterized by temporary interpersonal factors and evaluations that are intended to be relative (emotion, friendliness, advice). (Myhill, 1995, p. 200). The situation is rarely so neat of course. It is not the case that these 8-year-olds can be shown to exclusively make use of principled modal functions whereas the older children concern themselves with the interactive ones, rather that the feel or tone of the transcripts can be assigned to one camp or another.

---

[15] The components of agency, continuity, distinctness, and reflexivity that it is argued are maintained and exchanged through language (see Damon & Hart, 1988; also Linde, 1993). There is a full discussion later.

Myhill's (1995) discussion suggested that "an account based on world-view might be promising" (p. 201). Brown and Gilman's (1960) study of the development of the usage of second person pronouns in European languages supports this idea (e.g., the *tu-vous* distinction in French). They found that the solidarity semantic of the form gradually became more important than the power semantic from which the distinction originated. Originally these pronouns coded power relationships, where the more powerful speaker used the informal to address the less powerful person, and the less powerful person was obliged to use the formal pronoun to address the more powerful person. Later these pronominal forms came to be used more often to index solidarity,[16] where the informal pronoun is used between friends, groups, families, and so on and interactants without solidarity both use the formal pronoun.

Also parallel to this, Biber and Finegan (1994) argued that English has evolved toward being more involved and less abstract. They correlate involvement with oral style and abstraction with written style so there is a general trend toward orality. A drift toward involvement and away from abstraction has also taken place in spoken language itself. According to Comradie (1987), who did a major study of the Dutch modal auxiliaries:

> In broad historical development we seem to be dealing with an anti-authoritarian development: a movement away from the mere exercising of authority or towards a more rational approach in "getting things done with words." In all cases the principle that a communicative act must be expected to be meaningful, seems to play an important part. Using semantically less inclusive or even less performative utterances than the situation seems to require, is a form of understatement that over an extended period of time has led to considerable change in modal root meanings. (p. 179).

The next part of this discussion uses the concept of focal functions[17] to launch the analysis of each of the modal auxiliaries. The data is given in a narrative-like format (as proposed by Gee, 1986) because "careful attention to different facets of the data can be exploited on the basis of one assumption" (p. 12). That a form has been used even once in a particular way to constitute a particular meaning may be of interest and therefore to emphasize only the number of times something happens would lose a lot of information.

---

[16] Although not exclusively, for instance, children might still be required to address an older family member using the formal pronoun.
[17] The focal functions of a modal auxiliary are those functions with which the form is most commonly used (Myhill, 1995, p. 206).

4

A Sense of Responsibility: CAN

CAN

- All age groups primarily use CAN to express root possibility.
- Also CAN to comment on mental ability, especially the 12-year-old group.
- The 8-year-olds use the permission and imperative notions of CAN more than the other groups (a persistent pattern in this data).
- Only the 12-year-olds use hypothetical and predictive CAN.

CAN'T

- The root possibility meaning is the most common use of the CAN'T form for the 5-and 8-year-olds.
- For the 12-year-olds, mental ability CAN'T is most frequent and it is also the second most expressed meaning for the 5- and 8-year-old groups.
- Some uses of the desire function for CAN'T are found in the 12-year age group.

COULD(N'T)

- All age groups use COULD and its negative variant COULDN'T most in terms of root possibility.
- Both 5- and 12-year-olds but not the 8-year-old group use physical and mental ability COULD(N'T) frequently.
- The 5-year-old group use COULD and COULDN'T most overall, over 30% of their modal auxiliaries, whereas the 12-year-olds in this context have little use for this modal.

Overall the root possibility function is the one most associated with CAN (and we'll see with COULD, and their negatives, contracted forms and so on) for this group. There are three points to discuss in relation to this observation based in part on the diachronic literature that has a bearing on the use of these forms in this context. These are the epistemic-root possibility distinction for CAN, social permission, and responsibility.

Epistemic Versus Root

The discussion begins with the ambiguity and difficulties involved in deciding on a categorization of epistemic or root possibility. We have seen that linguistic forms tend to be primarily associated with one or another particular meaning, in this case, CAN used for root possibility and normally MAY to signal epistemic possibility. Initially then this seems to accurately reflect the situation here except for the fact that MAY is hardly used by these children at all and also for the fact that epistemic possibility in this context is largely accounted for by MIGHT and COULD.

So what does this mean? Apparently, the semantic contrast between root and epistemic possibility is weaker than in other root-epistemic pairs[1] so it is that much harder to definitively tell them apart. In addition, where a linguistic form expresses predominantly root possibility, epistemic meanings (here epistemic possibility) are thought likely to develop. Bybee (1995, p. 60) suggested that the crucial difference between forms expressing root possibility and forms expressing epistemic possibility is that the latter involve subjectivity[2] that can act as the criterion for distinction between the two.

Hoye (1997, p. 92) with regard to subjectivity, said that CAN and COULD can be used where neither the attitude nor the opinion of the speaker need be involved. He said examples of CAN and COULD combinations with perception verbs (e.g., *see, hear, taste*) or mental-state verbs (e.g., *remember, understand*) are best accounted for as idiomatic uses or frozen phrases.[3] On the contrary, the instances encountered here, for example:

> "But I CAN'T really remember" (CMcG5, apologetically when she can't continue with a story),
> "But I CAN remember my teeth actually shaking almost and my hands shaking it was so scary" (AW12),
> "And another girl who was about 9, CAN'T remember her name, I CAN never remember names" (SOH12, who uses the phrase repeatedly and states it as one of her defining characteristics),

---

[1] Coates (1995, pp. 151-154).

[2] See also Coates' (1995) addition of subjectivity as a criterial feature to Heine's (1993) semantic feature analysis of the German modals.

[3] Hoye (1997, p. 285) describes "a continuum ranging from relatively 'frozen' units or fixed patterns of modal expression at one extreme to more complex and productive structures at the other". He used *"can't remember"* and *"would probably"* as examples of holophrases like these and said that other less commonly used combinations have "weaker semantic cohesion". In this study most of the instances of *"CAN'T remember"* are not judged to be these simply frozen units although there are a few cases of *"WILL probably"* and *"WOULD probably"* in the transcripts that fit this category.

especially those examples in the 12-year-old cohort, are important discourse markers and markers of subjectivity.[4] They are used at moments of uncertainty as the children become increasingly aware of narrative conventions, of the need to be as coherent as possible and to take cognizance of the notion of recipient design.[5]

There is also a body of work on what is taken, in fact, to be the special case of CAN with perception or sensation words. For example, Binnick (1991, p. 473, no. 111) used the example *I see people over there* "which leaves open the possibility that what is seen is an illusion or that the speaker is in error in some way but to say *I can see* excludes such doubts".[6] And by doing so also introduces very firmly the speaker's position or location. It is a special case of the challenge function of CAN[7] where CAN is being used as a response to some perceived interpersonal challenge or contested ability or even used to challenge and to fix a state of doubt about the ability in question. In other words, CAN in these cases is an instance of epistemic or subjective modality after all. Although CAN and COULD are mainly used in the context of agent-oriented modality (90% and 78% respectively) the argument here is that many of these instances are not really agent-oriented but are special cases of epistemic meaning.

> "I juggled balls on my nose when I was a baby, I <u>COULD</u>" (HOB5).
> "It's a really high-pitched hiss and it CAN be <u>really</u> nerve-racking, if you heard it" (AK12, explaining how for a while he got scared of his pet snake).

However, to go back, the weakness of the distinction between epistemic and nonepistemic possibility does not generally cause too much havoc, in English at least, because CAN is usually reserved for expressing root possibility, and MAY is the form we use when we wish to express epistemic possibility. But taking the sort of historical movements and shifts of meaning I have been discussing seriously, MAY is rarely used outside of formal situations these days, particularly by children, and CAN is usually used in its stead. And so the situation is that CAN has become ambiguous (multifunctional) as a form again. This helps to explain the prevalence of both the form CAN and the meaning root possibility in these narratives.

In exactly the same way, "COULD is making headway as an alternative to MIGHT" (Coates, 1995, p. 63), evidenced here by the fact that COULD and MIGHT were very closely linked by all children in the cluster analysis (see Figs.

---

[4] See also Edwards (1997, pp. 282-283) on claims to remember or forget and actor-narrator accountability.

[5] One of the fundamentals of conversation analysis, that all utterances are recipient designed in that they are specifically constructed on a particular occasion of speaking for a particular audience (Fox, 1994, p. 30). This is discussed fully in relation to the discourse functions of the modal auxiliaries.

[6] Halliday's (1973) assertion, that we only explicitly say we are certain when we are not, only holds if the CAN is emphasized, for example, in response to a challenge. I am indebted to R. Reilly for this insight.

[7] Guo's (1995) mandarin modal NENG. See also Givón's (1982) challengeability scale.

4.1 and 4.2).[8] And indeed COULD and root possibility are strongly linked by the children. In much the same way I will show how SHALL has lost out, as in lost its functions, to WOULD and that OUGHT is simply obsolete for all intents and purposes in everyday spoken language. We can quote Cassirer (1946): "wherever, for any reason, the distinction between two activities loses its importance and meaning, there is wont to be a corresponding shift of verbal meanings, namely, of the words which marked that distinction" (p. 39).

Social Permission

Bybee, Perkins and Pagliuca (1994, pp. 192-193) showed in relation to the development of CAN and MAY (from ability to root possibility to permission, from mental ability to general ability) that "what is lost is the component that requires that the enabling conditions reside in the agent". This is one of the reasons why agent-oriented modality in this scheme cuts across the dynamic and deontic categories and a further rationale for my having chosen to use this categorization system. This means CAN generalizes to include reference to all sorts of enabling conditions, external to the agent as well as internal.

In effect then, a general root possibility sense would automatically include the sense of social permission. Many of the examples of CAN root possibility in this set incorporate this added level of meaning. In diachronic terms, a modal expressing ability would not move directly to the expression of permission without also being able to express root possibility, which is what we see happening synchronically. CAN and COULD are the two most frequently used modal auxiliaries by this group to express the sense of permission.

"And then she said "OK, you CAN use it" (St.JS8).
"I asked COULD I bring in that" (SM8).
"They have to be 3 pages but you CAN have 3 if you want"[9] (JOH8, talking about essays).

Responsibility

The third issue in relation to the use of these two forms is responsibility. Another function of root possibility CAN'T is that when used with the first person subject it gets the subject off the hook for not doing the action: "But I CAN'T really bring all my friends" (JW5, to justify excluding one not very popular child from an outing). This serves an important social function. It presents the situation as though the action is impossible when the truth is that we usually just do not want

---

[8] When I say forms were closely linked, I mean many of the children put these two particular forms together when they were asked to group the modal auxiliaries according to their meaning. So for example, if the majority of the children placed COULD and MIGHT in a pile together that indicates that they considered these forms to be similar in meaning.

[9] A good example of the combination of modal catenative and modal auxiliary.

to do something. We tend to say *"Sorry, I CAN'T help you"* rather than *"I WON'T help you"* if refusing to give money on the street, for instance. Basically it is more polite to intimate that the proposed action is impossible rather than that you simply would rather not do it.

There are also a few examples of the children making requests of the researcher in the course of which CAN is usually preferred to WILL. CAN frames the action as a possibility whereas using WILL tends to focus on, or enquires about, the addressee's intention (Myhill, 1995, p. 187). So when starting a new story or offering to reveal some secret or other, many of the children used the construction "WILL *I tell you?,"* the focus resting squarely on their own intended course of action. On the other hand, "CAN *you turn off the recorder for a minute?"* is more tactful, less direct than using WILL for the same purpose. CAN frames the action as a possibility that the speaker would like to have carried out but leaves the addressee free to decide to do so or not. Often CAN (and COULD) are used in a way Myhill referred to as "other interactively" (p. 185), "I CAN find out for you" (AK12), "where the speaker does or suggests some action for the listener and the main beneficiary is someone other than the subject of the action". His study of the American English modal auxiliaries suggest a trend whereby after the civil war, the root possibility sense became "much more strongly associated with interactive functions (negatives, questions, etc., for example, *may I continue?*) and much less with noninteractives and clauses with generic subjects (for example, *grief may kill a man)"*(p. 186).

It is often stated (e.g., Hoye, 1997, p. 92) that "except for the occasional rhetorical use CAN only operates with an epistemic meaning in non-assertive contexts where it is used for the negation of epistemic necessity as expressed by MUST", "But I don't really think that CAN be true" (CMcG5).

But there are other considerations. According to Antinucci and Parisi (1971, p. 38) many of the so-called nonmodal uses of CAN in these narratives, for instance: CAN of ability, "And I never CAN catch it" (CMcG5); CAN as marker of progressive aspect, "They have to be 2 pages but you CAN have 3 if you want" (JOH8); and CAN as marker of sporadic aspect, "Dad's a bit strict, when he CAN make his mind up" (SOH12), "are in fact special cases of epistemic modality where the speaker expresses a deduction on properties internal to the sentence." These nonmodal or nonepistemic uses of CAN and COULD are very frequent in these narratives and, I argue, are not strictly speaking straightforward examples of agent-oriented modality. Similarly, although Okamura (1996, p. 36) stated that the CAN of ability is not used to talk about the future, "I'm gonna ask for Dr Dreadful on Christmas and you CAN make dreadful things" (NR5), and Coates (1995) made the same point that the only exception to the correspondence between future reference and root meaning[10] is the CAN of ability and examples of generic possibility, for example,

---

[10] One of the conditions of using root MUST, SHOULD, OUGHT (obligation) or root MAY, CAN (permission) is that the speaker believes that the action referred to is not already achieved, in other words, that all core examples refer to a future event.

lightening can be dangerous. Hoye (1997, p. 53, no. 4) pointed out that sentences like *George can swim* could be taken as descriptions of potential future recurrence of similar situations with George as agent rather than simple statements of ability.

In relation to the CAN and COULD of ability, another pattern I noticed at this point is the children's preference for using CAN in the context of mental ability and reserving COULD for physical ability. Are they grammaticizing some distinction of their own via this mental-physical distinction? The uses of CAN and CAN'T with *remember* may have a similar function to the one just described in relation to shifting of responsibility, in which the child is anxious to convey the sense that one could not be expected to remember. This interpretation is supported by the fact that they often try to explain why they can't remember things or to account for not knowing something that they feel they should. It is shown later how important this is in relation to narrative development and the development of interpersonal narrating functions.

COULD is frequently used to assert the child's own physical ability, sometimes in relation to an anticipated challenge, and often in order to show how they are perfectly capable of doing something but wouldn't, "I <u>COULD</u> take his soother but I WOULDN'T" (JW5), or to boost someone else's physical prowess in order to downplay their own culpability in a situation. Having injured someone by pushing them into a swimming pool, this child repeated twice in order to diminish his own responsibility, "That, like,[11] he COULD swim and everything" (IB8).

One other interesting use, particularly given the age of these children, is the rhetorical use of CAN and COULD, of which there are more than the occasional few examples in the narratives. Interesting that is, as in the following examples, if we take the point of view that by speaking rhetorically, "the speaker assumes the role of both speaker and addressee so that the truth-value of the proposition is determined by his worldview and not that of the person addressed" (Hoye, 1997, p. 176):

"My favourite site is something called the Reading room, you CAN tell that" (JOR8, talking about 'surfing the internet'),
"I've already been in two movies so what else CAN I do?" (JOR8, on possible future careers),
"I liked food a lot, as you CAN see" (TA12, showing a photo of himself as a baby),
"Well, where CAN I begin?" (SM12, said theatrically),
"And where CAN I go back now?" (SM12),
"As you CAN imagine, it was very" (SM12, breaks off, after recounting long story about when he thought Mother might die),
"What CAN I say about my DAD" (SM12, to introduce new set of stories),
"She has, like, a, you COULD say, a degree in it" (TA12, talking about his Mother who is a translator).

---

[11] See Haiman (1993) for a very good discussion of the functions of colloquial English *like*

Summary

- CAN is the most frequently used form in the corpora.

- Negative uses CAN'T are less frequent generally and tend also to be used with a more restricted set of meanings.

- The main differences between CAN and COULD are that COULD for this group of children has a wider range of epistemic applications (e.g., epistemic possibility, counterfactuality, inferred certainty).

- CAN, but not COULD, has weak obligation and subjective directive meanings.

- The main differences between CAN'T and COULDN'T is that CAN'T is used to express agent desire whereas COULDN'T more often has an agent permission meaning.

Findings From the Cluster Analysis

Seven of the children left CAN in a group on its own, that is, in their opinion it did not approximate to the meaning of any of the other modal forms (see Figs. 4.1 and 4.2). Otherwise there was a fairly clear-cut distinction between the age groups on this sorting task that fits very well with most of the interpretations and discussion so far. First, for the 12-year-olds:[12]   CAN was tightly linked with WOULD and WANT TO, then with COULD and MIGHT, and only very loosely linked[13] with MAY. In other words, for the older children, root possibility is strongly associated with volition or desire.

> "It's good when you CAN get your own way and you CAN tell them what to do" (KM12).
> "My sister, she CAN get in a very bad mood" (TA12).
> "Mr G CAN be a bit annoying at times" (SM12).

The implication here is not so much that it is physically or in some other root (nonepistemic) sense possible for the agent or subject to carry out the action, rather that they can do, if they want to. This may also explain why CAN is used by this group for mental ability as opposed to physical ability meanings.

The 8-year-olds on the other hand linked CAN tightly with MIGHT, then with COULD and MAY.   That means they coupled CAN more often with its permission senses (and we see how this meaning features prominently for this group) and with its general root ability senses.

---

[12] Only the 8- and 12-year-olds did the classification task.
[13] Loose links in this context means that not very many of the children consider CAN and MAY to be very close in meaning.

"And then see what I CAN do on my project" (SM8).
"My radio CAN only take big tapes" (StJS8).
"She loves her school now but you CAN only stay there for 2 years" (CK8).

COULD was frequently linked with WOULD also (four of the 8-year-olds and six of the 12-year-olds), which brings us back to the issues of responsibility and volition mentioned earlier. But this sort of discussion is getting beyond the scope of this section and is addressed fully in the course of exploring the discourse functions of the modal utterances.

A Sense of Commitment: WILL

WILL

- There is very little use of the uncontracted form WILL by any of the age groups.

- Where it is used by the 8- and 12-year-olds, it is mostly to indicate belief, that is, degrees of certainty or inferred certainty.

Whereas in the case of ('LL):

- The contracted form of WILL('LL) is much more frequent, particularly with the 12-year-olds in the expression of epistemic certainty.

- All groups use WILL('LL) primarily to indicate intention.

- The 12-year-old group use this form in a variety of epistemically oriented ways, mainly centering on the expression of degrees of certainty and levels of probability.

And its negative contracted form WON'T:

- There are no uses of WON'T by the 5-year-olds and overall, the WILL form is hardly used by this age group.

- WON'T was also rarely used by the other groups, except for the occasional agent-oriented use or statement of certainty.

WILL and WOULD as used by the children in this study are generally epistemically oriented (64% and 66% respectively). The main meanings associated with WILL in these narratives are intention, inferred certainty, and certainty. These meanings increase steadily in frequency from age 5 to 12 (it accounts for only 6% of all modal auxiliaries used by the 5-year-olds, in fact even MIGHT is more common at 7%).

The corresponding main meanings of WOULD are desire, certainty and to a lesser extent, hypothetical prediction. The WOULD form shows a similar pattern of age-related increase but is well represented in the 5-year-old category also (20%). It is the most frequently occurring modal auxiliary overall, comprising nearly 29% of the entire set of modal auxiliaries used and featuring among the five most frequently used forms for all the age groups. In this study, the meanings of certainty, desire, and hypothetical prediction are generally expressed by using WOULD; whereas the related meanings of inferred certainty, intention, and probability tend to be expressed by WILL.

WILL: A "Free Floater"

The results of the cluster analysis for the auxiliary WILL confirm what is already becoming apparent, that it is something of a "free floater"[14] evidenced in the fact that the 8-year-olds' clusters revealed no primary or close association for WILL. For the most part, it hovered on the edges of a group containing WOULD, WANT TO, and SHALL and a second group made up of the forms CAN, MIGHT, COULD, and MAY. In the 12-year-olds' pairings, WILL was only very loosely linked with SHALL on first clusters, and it was otherwise in a group made up of SHOULD, NEED TO, HAVE TO, and OUGHT. What does this indicate?

A Sense of Commitment

In the case of the 12-year-olds, regarding the high incidence of groupings of WILL with SHOULD, NEED TO, HAVE TO, and OUGHT, I have interpreted this as firm intention, in the sense of committing yourself to do something you know you should, undertaking to do something you do not necessarily want to do but realize you ought to. There is an "incipient sense of feeling bound to" (Gee, 1985, p. 208). In many cases WILL has more to do with the speaker's willingness than her or his volition (Gee & Savasir, 1985, p. 148).

> "If I haven't finished it, I'LL do some more and then go to bed" (AK12, on homework).
> "If I still like it, I'LL stay" (IGOD12 resigned to another year at a school without his friends).
> "I remember lots of awful days ... if I remember something that's not too awful, I'LL tell you" (SOH12).[15]

---

[14] Hoye (1997, p. 114).

[15] All these examples contain if-clauses about which Bybee (1994, pp. 208-209) has written: A modal must have most of its meaning eroded before it can obligatorily occur in a protasis, since the environment of a protasis tends to bring out the full meaning of a modal. (*we shall get in* = apodosis, *if we queue* = protasis, example from Crystal, 1997, p. 23). So WILL in an if-clause does not signal prediction but willingness. "In order for a modal element to occur in a protasis without contributing

This use brings with it a sense of obligation. Looking across the age groups, this meaning of WILL tracks a developmental path from reliance on, and concern with, externally imposed obligations to a more internally based sense of personal responsibility.[16] This is borne out in the discussion of the discourse functions associated later. In general, I found WILL used very definitely with a high level of commitment by the subject of the sentence, that is, undertaking a plan of action. This study yielded one perfect example of Gee and Savasir's (1985) WILL/GONNA distinction where the child actually repairs the modal in her utterance from WILL to GONNA in order to repair the meaning from co-operative to unilateral decision, from undertaking to planning.

"Hopefully I WILL, I mean I'LL, I'm GONNA ... force my Mum to get me into the Billy Barry School" (AC8, in the context of saying she wants to be an actress).

This is a classic case involving the manipulation or fixing of the source of the control or force generated by the modal. Gee and Savasir (1985) discussed WILL and GONNA in terms of the activity type or discursive practice associated with the use of each form, where WILL involves undertaking, and GONNA is associated with planning and can be distinguished on the basis of level of commitment. "The point of many of the GONNA utterances, in contrast to WILL, is not so much to get things done but rather to organise experiences by projecting them as plans" (p. 206). According to this, "the most notable fact about the use of GONNA is the *rift* it allows between the utterances and its conditions of satisfaction as opposed to WILL which more usually results in intentional satisfaction". According to Myhill (1995) for actions that the subject can control, WILL is associated with cases where the subject is doing the future action for someone's else's benefit and the decision to do the action is in some way co-operative or when the speaker is proposing something. GONNA is used for unilateral decisions made independent of the interlocutor's desires or where the speaker is criticizing or opposing the listener (p. 191).

In general, interactive factors play a major role in the speaker's choice of WILL versus GONNA. WILL is generally used for co-operative actions, proposals, threats, and warnings, which assume some degree of equality of status

---

lexical meaning to the clause it must already have a very reduced semantic content. If the modal element occurs without an element meaning IF then all the conditional meaning is contributed by the modal element itself." This must mean that those modals not used with IF or in protases therefore have "stronger" meaning. She confirms this: "In apodoses modals occur with greater freedom since it appears that most if not all agent-oriented and epistemic meanings are consonant with the main clause of a conditional sentence. So in apodoses, you find forms expressing both probability and possibility (and future) and protases contain mostly the weaker notion of possibility." Note that WILL in all our examples are in the apodosis that Bybee (1994, p. 274) defined as the "main clause where predictions are made that are contingent on the conditions stated in the protasis".

[16] This is not to claim that only the older children are capable of operating at this level: Even 3-year-olds can "construct a type of deontic modality without an external 'deontic source' [Lyons, 1977] which compels the participants to act" (Gee, 1985, p. 208), only that these 12-year-olds are somewhat more likely to be concerned with that type of situation within the context of personal narratives.

and co-operation (or conflict) between speaker and listener. So therefore it is not at all surprising that this function (and indeed WILL overall) is hardly present in the 5-year-olds' scripts.

A corollary of this function is when WILL is used to issue wild threats, in if-clauses or to issue warnings: "If you don't stop, I WI-LL kill you" (CK8); "He knows he'LL get in trouble" (CMcG5). For the 8-year-olds, WILL was also peripherally involved with the notion of obligation but much less strongly than for the older children. For this age group, the main sense is one of personal volition and desire.

> "'Cos Harry WILL keep on going into his room and taking things" (St.JS8).
> "I WILL probably[17] make £100 from my Auntie, I'LL keep it for rollerblades" (SC8).
> "I like swimming and we'LL be going there in a few weeks from school" (SC8).

The overall patterns in the data support the statement that "intention is a generalised agent-oriented sense that can develop out of desire, obligation or movement toward a goal" (Bybee, Perkins, & Pagliuca, 1994, p. 230).

Intention and Desire

The interaction between intention and desire is interesting, both in relation to the forms used to express these meanings and the different ways in which the age groups rely on each of the forms. WILL('LL) is used to express intention by all three age groups (but not just in relation to straightforward agent-oriented modality) and desire is expressed via the contracted modality of WOULD('D). This may be connected with WOULD used as a hedging or distancing[18] device. You are more exposed talking about what you want to happen or what you wish for.

It is also interesting to note that these very personal meanings, when used with first person subjects, that is, to refer to the speakers themselves and their wishes and plans, are more often than not expressed using the contracted forms of the relevant modal auxiliaries. This is a way of inserting distance between the speaker and the statement, especially for the older children who sometimes became self-conscious or embarrassed as they talked about these things. Using the contracted form does not draw as much attention to the subjective element of

---

[17] "WILL + adverb probably/presumably is used to make modalised predictions in the present about some future state of affairs and marks out these modal expressions as potential co-ordinates of epistemic possibility. But unmodified WILL is often used to make a relatively straightforward prediction and less clearly carries the speaker's epistemic judgement of probability" (Hoye, 1997, p. 79).

[18] The discussion of tense later details how exploiting time references can achieve this. Also, although WILL of intention is mainly used for proximal reference, we see WOULD very often used to indicate more distal references.

the statement. Another common device they used in the same area of meaning was to use negation to render the statement more ambiguous.

> "And the other thing I WOULDN'T mind being is" (SM8).
> "And like, I know this WOULDN'T happen but I'D love to be an actor" (PF12).
> "I'D like to be an actress but I don't think I'D qualify for that" (HG12).

They generally did not mind openly stating their desires for things, toys and so on: "I WOULD like Connections" (JOH8).

The WILL of intention prevalent in this study is not so surprising given that "WILL differs from other modals in that its use to mark futurity is grammaticized. That means within the grammar of the language it is a systematic marker or indicator of futurity whereas the other modals simply convey futurity without literally marking it" (Binnick, 1991, p. 465, no. 31). But WILL (and WOULD, where used to express future time as seen from a viewpoint in the past) rarely has simple future time reference. "Futurity is never a purely temporal concept; it necessarily includes an element of prediction or some related notion" (Lyons, 1977, p. 677). In this case the related notions are mainly those of intention or desire. "WILL achieves future reference in virtue of the willingness[19] it expresses (One cannot be willing that something has happened)" (Gee & Savasir, 1985, p. 172).

But Is It Always Future? Back to Commitment

The function of future reference does not necessarily have to imply the distant future. WILL utterances in fact are often used for temporally and spatially proximal activities,[20] that is, those actions carried out immediately subsequent to the utterance or to refer to local or contextualized objects or events and in the service of intentional satisfaction (Gee, 1985).

> "And Daddy video-camera'd it, I'LL tell you why, 'cos she was going like that" (CMcG5).
> "I'LL tell you a bit about a programme I watched" (DPB8).

All these properties set up a particular type of interpersonal commitment, namely, undertaking, in which the speaker adopts a kind of negotiatory stance and "an actual commitment to act seems to develop out of this interpersonal bond" (p. 204). This piece of reported speech is a nice example where the narrator is trying

---

[19] Bybee (1994, p. 255) said the willingness nuance of WILL is a retention of the desire meaning of WILL because it is related to the agent's desires and other modals *shall* and *be going to* do not express this particular shade of meaning.

[20] This is used to show that futurity is inherently a modal notion and that WILL is not a purely future tense marker as some researchers suggest: "This is our first piece of evidence that suggests that the meaning of these terms is not that of straightforward temporal representation but reflects the different social practices that these utterances are part of" (Gee & Savasir, 1985, p. 150).

to show that the speaker is always, at least at the time, fully committed to the action: "After about a month he leaves it and he says 'I'LL get another job'" (CK8, talking about her schizophrenic brother).

In this sense, WILL in these instances are not really cases of (agent-oriented) intention or volition but are used instead to set up some sort of obligation on the speaker. In fact, according to Gee (1985), "intentional WILL has a separate psychological status from the intentional dynamic modals" (p. 216). Intentional WILL retains a sense of commitment as a legacy of its past history. Gee's analysis was based on an interactive play situation. Her interpretations therefore center on joint interaction and negotiation, on "doing", where the actions and events consequent on WILL and GONNA statements can be explored, and it can be ascertained whether the relevant undertakings were followed through. This narrative context is necessarily more involved with "saying",[21] and although WILL, as used in these narratives, is not always relating to the immediate or proximal future,[22] there is the same sense of obligation and personal commitment under construction, the same self-imposed commitment to a course of action.

A second development leads to the meaning of prediction. In fact, the prediction function arises from the intention function. "Intention is the crucial bridge to prediction,"[23] that is, to epistemic modality, and the change from intention to prediction occurs via the inferences that hearers make on the basis of the speaker's utterances. WILL and WOULD are often described in terms of prediction, under which heading related uses are identified. Now there are very few cases in this data of WILL or WOULD being used for straightforward or pure prediction, of the kind, "I WILL have a brother or sister" (IB8), but it is possible to identify usages in the sense of attributions of intention to a third person that in context can function to imply a prediction on the part of the speaker. When intention is attributed to a third person using the WILL form, then the inference of the speaker's prediction also becomes available.

"We can't bring that one home, she'LL get a smaller one for it" (SM8, on trophy they won at school).
"Someday she says she'LL bring me but I think it WILL be a while yet" (AW12).

Also many of the epistemic WILL uses refer instead to direct consequences of the speaker's actions. Gee & Savasir (1985, p. 171) called it the "nascent epistemic (predictive) use of WILL [which] develops out of the activity-type of undertaking the predictive use of WILL [which] seems to emerge from its deontic use" (deontic remember in the sense of intention implying obligation). These uses,

---

[21] Which in her data always selected for GONNA but may well be a function of the different age groups involved.
[22] Gee and Savasir's (1985) original study was with 3-year-olds so although initially when using undertaking WILL to express commitment it is restricted to immediate future reference, with development WILL achieves "more distal imaginary temporal reference" (Gee, 1985, p. 221) as is the case with the children in this group.
[23] Bybee (1994, p. 280).

epistemic predictive and undertaking, involve "a very local sort of causality within which events can be seen as reactions to one another".

> "If I go, I'LL go with a friend" (SH12)
> "You never realise that you'D like that and that next year you'LL be looking back" (AW12).

So tense is always a complicating factor in this context. Epistemic WILL is modal in that by making a prediction, even one that is consequent on the speaker's activities, "the moment of utterance loses its privileged status" (Gee, 1985, p. 222) and the event is therefore less under the speaker's control than the events of an undertaking. However insofar as the speaker may be predicting the results of their own actions, they are not as separate as in other situations. So it can prove very difficult to distinguish between epistemic WILL and future WILL.[24] A probability sense can also develop through the sense of prediction. A future that has reached the stage of prediction can be used to make predictions about the present that can be interpreted as an expression of probability (*"that'LL be her now"*) (Bybee, Perkins, & Pagliuca, 1994, p. 202). The role of futurity in autobiography is a very important aspect at all levels of this study. The future is less a temporal category than a category resembling agent-oriented and epistemic modality with important temporal implications (Bybee 1994) and this will be dealt with fully when the discussion arises on the grammatical feature of tense and the relation of tense and modality.

The final area of meaning in relation to WILL used in this study is that of degrees of belief or levels of certainty. Although it is often the simple present tense form and other nonmodal forms in the present tense that express certainty on the part of the speaker, the WILL-form can also be used to express the mood of certainty.

> "Now we actually do have some importance, but I know next year we'LL have much more" (AW12, talking about being seniors in school).
> "Everyone WILL go to the hall after the church" (MS8).
> "This WILL be the second time we've been in England" (JOR8, of a prospective trip).
> "I haven't forgotten that situation, I WON'T forget it for the rest of my life" (SM12).

In the same way as Halliday (1973) suggested that it is precisely when we are not certain that we feel the need to indicate linguistically that we are, for much the same reason "we cannot think of an event described with pure future will as being as certain as one described with the simple present due to the extra-linguistic fact, our general knowledge about the world, that no future event can be conceived of, as being as certain as one which is already happened or is already happening

---

[24] See Okamura's (1996) discussion on pure future as a primary auxiliary verb rather than a modal auxiliary verb.

because something might interfere with it" (Okamura, 1996, p. 39, no 4.). In fact, in this study, many of the examples of WILL are used to indicate levels of uncertainty.

> "You have to stand up and say "Good Morning" and I don't know if I'LL remember that all the time" (DH12, anxiety about moving to secondary school).
> "She's supposed to be brilliant, so I'm not really sure if I'LL beat her" (SL12).
> "Someday she says she'LL bring me but I think it WILL be a while yet" (AW12).
> "How WILL I start off? (DH12).

WOULD

A summary of the use of WOULD:

- This auxiliary is overwhelmingly associated with its epistemic meanings, particularly with certainty for the 12-year-olds and with hypothetical situations and prediction for all ages. In fact, the 12-year-olds do not use the full WOULD form in its agent-oriented sense at all.

- The possibility and probability meanings are fairly well represented.

- Only the 5-year-olds used WOULD in the context of subjective directives.

And its contracted form WOULD('D):

- For the 12- and 8-year-olds the contracted form of WOULD('D) for desire is the single most important meaning.

- The next most frequent meaning for the 12-year-olds is again epistemic certainty.

- Both 8- and 12-year-old groups make good use of the hypothetical prediction meaning.

- 5-year-olds hardly use this form at all despite the fact that (WOULD)'D is the second most used form overall in the corpus after CAN (although see the following for some relatively sophisticated, if infrequent, uses by the youngest children).

Despite the many sources that report the so-called secondary or distal modal WOULD as shaky even after age 5, this is not at all the case here. In fact both the frequency and the range of uses of WOULD were quite surprising for children of this age.

> "My favourite WOULD be Miss French and Miss Barber" (JW5).
> "There WOULD be noone to mind me" (CM5).
> "And then it WOULD be boy other girl on the end" (NE5, describing class

seating arrangements).
"'Cos my Mum and Dad were going out and I WOULDN'T have them here" (CM5).

And finally trends for usage of the negative form WOULDN'T:

* This is the only form of WOULD that is used to express a meaning of permission (with the exception of one example from the 12-year-old corpus).

* Where this form is used, it is mostly by the 5- and 12-year-olds to express degrees of certainty and to make hypothetical statements

Findings From the Cluster Analysis

This part of the discussion develops from the way in which the children treated this modal in the classification task as there was quite a distinctive pattern to the clusters they formed in their groupings of WOULD (see Figs. 4.1 and 4.2). The younger age group, the 8-year-olds, linked it tightly with WANT TO and with SHALL marking out a close knit bundle of meanings centring around notions of desire, intention, volition, and prediction.

"I'D love to go there again" (JOR8).
"Otherwise I'D be a writer" (JOR8).
"I'D like to make children enjoy doing stuff" (AC8).
"Andrew WOULDN'T hold on, I was the one who had to" (St.JS8, i.e., he did not want to, I had to).

The close link for the 8-year-olds between WOULD and desire, WANT TO, also brought into play for them uses of WOULD relating to when they can't always do as they want. This involved notions of permission and control: "J had to get a lock for his room and Dad WOULDN'T let him" (St.JS8).

They were also using WOULD as a source of authority for their statements and wishes, and to back up personal statements and pronouncements through the device of employing WOULD to shift the authority elsewhere:

"Well, it WOULD be the head drama class of the country" (JOR8, boasting about the class he attends).
"WOULD you like after being on the radio and some man says?" (JOR8, indignant about remark a DJ made when he was being interviewed).

There are also some examples of this trend in the 5-year-old narratives:

"Some of them WOULD have to sit down on the bottom" (JW5, because she wants to go on the top).
"You see, she WOULD have to play with the junior infants" (AG5, reason for allowing a not very popular older sister to come to her party).
"Because then it WOULD be really fair" (CMcG5).

The 12-year-olds produced a different cluster arrangement where initially WOULD was closely linked to CAN and WANT TO, echoing the 8-year-old scenario, but the older children also judged the possible meanings of WOULD to be related to those of COULD, MAY, and MIGHT. In other words, they conceived WOULD as entwined with the concepts of root ability and epistemic possibility:

> "I was holding on to her as if I WOULD never see my parents again" (AW12).
> "I used to run off and my mum's best friend WOULDN'T know where I was" (SM12).

And with speaking hypothetically:

> "And, like, I know this WOULDN'T happen but I'd love to be an actor" (PF12).
> "I WOULDN'T go trying netball 'cos I WOULDN'T be any good" (PF12).
> "It's just like one you bought, one you WOULD buy in the shop" (DH12).
> "But I don't think the priest WOULD be so stupid" (KB8).

The 12-year-olds also engaged WOULD as a means of shifting the source of the statement but in quite a different way to the younger children. This time they are using it either as a way of providing some distance between the utterance and themselves, that is, of boasting without seeming to:

> "Some people WOULD think I'm nice like, that I'm grand, others WOULD probably think that I'm a bit arrogant" (SM12, clearly does not mind this assessment).
> "It WOULDN'T actually be that much more difficult" (AW12).
> "You never realise that you WOULD like that" (AW12).
> "But if we win it, I think it WOULD be a fluke if we did 'cos there's only 4 of us but if we win" (AW12, hastily amends impression).

or in order to hedge or mitigate their statement:

> "My Mom likes swimming as well but my Dad WOULD probably be better at it" (RL12).
> "I don't really get on well with her any more, I WOULDN'T mind if she didn't go to Muckross" (RL12).
> "Mike is moving to Churchtown which I WOULD actually be a bit jealous of 'cos they're opening a new petshop but" (AK12).

Past tense modal forms in general are more marked for tentativeness or indirectness than their present tense counterparts (Hoye, 1997, p.81). A good example is a 5-year-old complaining of being given out to for leaving her seat in class by trying to undermine the rule that everyone remain seated: "You COULD be going to get something" (EF5, despite the fact that she wasn't).

One other interesting trend was the use of the contracted form WOULD('D) particularly to talk about desires and wishes for the future. This also helps explain why use of this form was especially popular with the 12-year-olds, as the 5-year-old narratives, for instance, are on the whole much less future oriented. Again it seems likely using the shortened unstressed form created a sense of distance and made the proposition seem somehow less subjective.

"I'D like to be an actress or a singer or a dancer" (AC8).
"I hope I get into vet cos I'D really like it" (AK12).
"I'D prefer to be like my Mum than my Dad" (KM12).
"I like Art but I'm not very good at it, I'D like to be good at Art" (SOH12).
"I'D, I think I'D like to stay in primary school" (DH12).

Only the 12-year-olds used WOULD to indicate epistemic certainty with any degree of frequency and really only the most straightforward initial interpretation of the utterances lend themselves to this. The most interesting analysis of these modal utterances is at the stage of analysis of discourse function.

"So she said 'Tommy, now don't do it again', like, that WOULDN'T stop him or anything" (HG12).
"He'D really slag you, I've never known someone like that" (AK12).
"I CAN be real annoying sometimes, I'D say" (RL12).
"She'D know if you took her hairbrush and put it back" (SL12).

One other use of WOULD is when "the overt expression of future appears to resemble that of past habitual meaning" (Bybee, Perkins, & Pagliuca, 1994, pp. 156-157). WOULD in Old English is the past tense of WILL and WILL can still be used for characteristic behaviour (e.g., *water will boil at 100 degrees*). There are some examples of WOULD used for relative future in the past in this study, but this does not so much parallel the characteristic use as much as it is used to express the sense of having gone through the action on many different occasions in the past:

"And they WOULD keep on doing this and it WOULD be Saturday morning" (AW12).
"But it WOULD be just a sum-up of everything we were going to do this year" (AW12).
"We WOULD play hurley and Gaelic in the fields in Tipperary" (AK8).
"This is what my friends WOULD say to me but he's being mean to me as well" (RL12).
"I've never really been away by myself before so it WOULD seem very strange" (AW12).

The relatively frequent use of this meaning may be because the older children in particular are very future-oriented. To say "we WOULD hear" or "we WOULD sing to them" makes the situation habitual or ongoing or even present in some way. There is a sense sometimes that the children are presenting schemas or idealized typical events rather than particular memories: "We WOULD play hurley and Gaelic in the fields in Tipperary, and we'D play rugby with our cousins, we, em, we'D visit another uncle, em, we'D" (AK8). The use of grammatical habituals like this in tandem with other forms and constructions help also to establish and express a sense of continuity of self.

All these aspects are discussed fully in the next sections. Some of the main findings are anticipated here in relation to wider interpretations of the discourse functions here. For instance, later it is shown that WOULD has a consistently different distribution across discourse functions in the 5-year-old narratives. WOULD is used for problem solving only by the 5-year-olds, for reporting by the 8- and 12-year-olds but not by 5-year-olds, for prescribing at 5 but only very rarely for this function at ages 8 and 12, and whereas it is the main form used to mark agency by the 8- and 12-year-olds, it is hardly used for this purpose at all by the 5-year-old group (who tend to use CAN instead).

SHOULD and MUST

There are only 10 instances of SHOULD, including its negative form SHOULDN'T, in the entire corpus, and the 12-year-olds do not make use of this form at all. Almost all of the uses are either speaker-oriented or constitute some form of "deontic comment" (Matthews, 1996, p. 373, although within the categorization system in use here they would be classed as agent-oriented subjective directives). These types of utterances do not necessarily directly try to effect change in the real world but instead function to merely comment on its being at odds with the desired world in some way.

Obviously, within the context of narrating, only reported speech can have this function, but in so far as these forms are used to express what the speaker thinks ought to have happened or wanted to have happen in an ideal world, they are more epistemic or evaluative than performative. For instance, the SHOULD of recommendation, what Matthews (1996) called *futureate potentialis*:

> "That's what Mommy said we SHOULD do at my party, even K's little sister" (JW5).
> "Em, you SHOULD say 'COULD you go get?'" (DPB8).

And "backward looking *irrealis*" or a speaker's comment on a failure to act, which accounts for many of these cases, usually in relation to someone else's failure. This SHOULD is used to criticize or correct the subject of the utterance, either regarding a past action or their present situation.

> "But she SHOULDN'T just go home that way" (VMcG5, when his minder went home while he was out with parents).
> "She didn't actually come, she SHOULD have still come" (St.JS8).

"My Mom is afraid of the water 'cos she fell in the water but I don't think she SHOULD have" (St.JS8).

SHOULD can also be used to talk about general principles applying to generic subjects but the children in this group seem to make more use of WOULD for this function. However given that SHOULD is more tentative and interactive than it used to be and that the most common function now is its future good idea function (Myhill, 1995, p. 178, e.g., *you really don't think I SHOULD go?*) I would not expect this form to be used much in this context.

The major distinctions within obligation have to do with the strength of the obligation, whether it is strong or weak. Cases like these set up situations only of weak obligation that is interesting diachronically.[25] Bybee, Perkins, and Pagliuca (1994, p. 186) outlined how a sense of destiny is another sense closely related to obligation and that is often conflated with it, in relation to situations destined or prearranged to happen. In Old and Middle English both SHALL and SHOULD were used in the context of both moral and physical obligations and inevitabilities. In Middle English, SHALL was used more frequently in the first person to make promises and state intentions, but SHOULD continued to be used primarily in the third person to report past destiny and inevitabilities. In modern usage, SHOULD is used mainly for weak obligation because now it is used in present time without this sense of destiny and with more of a sense of personal obligation.

"Yeah, that's what we SHOULD do, that's what we have to do" (JW5).
"I kept saying 'I think we SHOULD go faster and we SHOULD go more'" (St.JS8).
"I mean, the parrot thought that he SHOULD not live in the palace" (CMcG5, anaphoric he).

As weak obligation markers they compare the actual state of the world with an evaluation system stating the way the world ought to be or should be, where the basis of the evaluation system for SHOULD is based on social role, personal characteristics, and *post-hoc* evaluation (Myhill, 1995, p. 177).

There are also very few cases of MUST. SHOULD and MUST are often treated together. According to Salkie (1996, p. 385) one way to pin down the difference between them is to distinguish between inference and prediction. Inferring something is not a linguistic act but a mental one: First you make the inference, then you may or may not choose to report it in words. Making a prediction, on the other hand, is a linguistic act that cannot be performed without uttering certain words. MUST therefore reports an inference whereas SHOULD is used to make a prediction. Of this very small number of cases most of them report on an inference of one sort or another.

---

[25] As there are only a few relatively straightforward cases I need only note that "since both harmonic and non-harmonic uses remain, the analyst of the synchronic situation faces the difficulty of determining whether SHOULD is meaningful in complement clauses or not" (Bybee, 1994, p. 218).

"But I can't find it anywhere, it MUST be upstairs on the attic" (JW5)[26].
"And I MUST have fallen asleep on the way" (VMcG5).
"It MUST be you just don't know what paper is" (HOB5).[27]
"But then I got a pair of earrings from this woman for Christmas so she MUST have thought I had them pierced" (SOH12).

One other use in evidence is what could be called a performative use: "And also, my favourite, which I MUST remember, was when I was, when I went to America" (JOR8).

It is possible also to distinguish between emotional GOT TO and principled MUST. MUST is less subjective than GOT TO[28] but it is nonetheless subjective. Using MUST does not imply the speaker is objective or indifferent to what happens, he or she may actually be very concerned that the event under discussion will take place. As in this case, where the speaker wants to tell about this holiday but has already recounted a long list, has moved on to another topic and when he remembers this one needs to find a way or a reason to include it. So he or she presents himself or herself as being obligated by some sort of social principle or rules of conversation and this allows him or her to get the point across. (Myhill, 1995, suggested that the hypocritical nature of such rationalizations may have something to do with why this usage is disappearing). Furthermore the principles referred to are basically of a social nature; they do not follow from strict impersonal reasoning. "It is the emotions themselves and the concern of the interactants with satisfying the emotional needs that obligate the event" (p. 170).

This context of autobiographical narrative would not be expected to occasion many instances of MUST obligation uses that rely on "the establishment of an asymmetrical relation between participants such that the obligation is created by someone who is external to the one carrying out the action" (Gee, 1985, p. 209). These uses in fact "are nearly mutually exclusive from MUST as inferred certainty" (Bybee, Perkins, & Pagliuca, 1994, p. 201) which is the most frequent meaning in this study.

---

[26] It is interesting to note that at this age, and there are even some examples in the 8-year-old narratives, that the children still make mistakes in relation to pronouns, tenses, and in this case, locative prepositions, but there were no erroneous uses of any of the modal auxiliaries. On the contrary even the 5-year-olds used the modal auxiliaries in very sophisticated nonroot ways. What does it mean that the children do not make mistakes with the modal auxiliaries but do in just about every other grammatical feature? The fact that L2 learners always find them difficult yet typically do not have problems with pronouns or tenses and will often continue to make mistakes when fluent for all practical purposes otherwise must be revealing. Why this differential error pattern? Are the children less sensitive to their multifunctionality, but then how can they use them in such a variety of situations and contexts?

[27] This is a good example of incorrect use of tense and pronominal forms with the appropriate modal. This utterance is in relation to someone else's story about drawing on the wallpaper when very young and she is trying to explain why they might have done it.

[28] Myhill (1995, p. 169). The differences in subjectivity between MUST and HAVE TO are relevant also and are discussed in relation to how these two forms were dealt with in the classification task.

MIGHT and MAY

A summary of the main findings:

- The most basic pattern here is that the 8-year-old group make very little use of the form MAY.

- 12-year-olds use it almost exclusively to express epistemic possibility.

Both MAY and MIGHT are basic to the epistemic system and serve as coordinates of epistemic possibility. They are supposedly interchangeable as forms but Coates (1983, p. 147), based on evidence from child language research and research into dialects and the like, said that "MIGHT is superseding MAY as the main exponent of epistemic possibility" which is indeed the case in this study.

> "My Mummy MIGHT get me a Gameboy on my birthday" (NR5).
> "She said she, they MIGHT be coming over next year" (KM12).
> "I think it MIGHT also have been for grommets, I'm not sure" (SOH12).

Although all cases perhaps ultimately could be glossed by some statement of possibility, there are more complicated uses by virtue of other elements in the utterance (which are fully discussed later so only receive a cursory mention here), which led to them being categorized as having the meaning of intention or desire:

> "I MIGHT get one from the guy in the shop" (JW5).
> "So we decided we MIGHT come back tomorrow so we did" (NR5).

of inferred certainty:

> "I think he went back, he MIGHT have gone back after and leaved it when everyone was asleep" (JW5).

or counterfactuality:

> "I MIGHT have done that but I don't think the priest WOULD have been so stupid" (KB8).

or used to express hypothetical situations or make predictions:

> "And then I just thought it MIGHT be 9" (DPB8, recounting the process of working out a square root).
> "There's me, I'm just finished reading a book 'cos I thought I MIGHT be interested in books" (TA12, showing a photo of himself as a baby holding a book).

There is only one use of MAY, an idiomatic or formulaic use, "I'D like to be answering all the phones going 'Hello, MAY I help you?'" (HG12), which underscores how formal it is now considered to be and explains how little it is used in these narratives. All the rest are cases of MAYBE that should be included because in context they contribute an epistemic meaning or flavor to the utterances and are usually used with other modal forms (both harmonic and nonharmonic). Also taking into account the curious enough situation that MAYBE itself is nowhere near as frequent as one might expect. Basically, the word space between MAY and BE, which was "structurally bogus" anyway, has disappeared as with, for instance, ANYWAY and ANOTHER (Sinclair, 1991, p. 110). There are only seven utterances containing the form MAYBE and for that reason alone they are interesting to consider.

> "MAYBE this time I MIGHT be lucky" (AW12).
> "MAYBE I COULD be a nurse or a babysitter" (AG5).

Some General Conclusions
Based on the Cluster Analysis

To sum up, suggested here is a set of concerns for the two older age groups based on their spontaneous modal utterances but also on the clusters found in their groupings of the modals. Simply put, the shorter and tighter the link between cases (modal auxiliaries in this instance) in a dendrogram, the closer in meaning the items are judged to be. Similarly, if the analysis for one group produces ten clusters compared to the second groups' three clusters, this could indicate a restricted set of relations or meanings for the second group compared to the first. Even a quick glance at the dendograms shows that the links in the 8-year-old groupings are shorter and the clusters much easier to pick out, than those produced on the basis of the 12-year-old groupings of the modal auxiliaries.

Overall the 8-year-olds seem to have much more definite groupings or clusters of the modals. This is the case at the expense of the subtleties the 12-year-olds have factored into their system. If the children, for instance, take into account only the root or nonepistemic meanings of the auxiliaries then it should be easier to assign them to groups. In that case you would expect a small number of quite contained clusters, which turns out to be the case in relation to the 8-year-old system. There are three fairly definite clusters that presumably correspond to three circumscribed areas of modal meaning. Namely, those meanings associated with obligation, ability and intention. The 8-year-olds have fairly definitely assigned most of the modal auxiliaries to one or other of these three groups.

Except, that is, for WILL and HAVE TO. These, in fact, form exceptions in both age groups. In the 8-year-old system, these forms are only very loosely assigned to any group. The 8-year-olds either can not decide on a main or dominant meaning for the forms or have decided that they do not belong with any of the other modal auxiliaries in terms of meaning.

The 12-year-olds on the other hand have classed WILL and HAVE TO together (i.e., they appear in the same cluster, albeit not very closely or tightly linked). A possible explanation for this pattern may lie with something that I

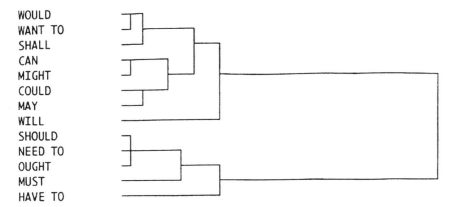

Fig. 4.1 Dendogram produced using Ward's Method of Hierarchical Cluster Analysis for 8-year-old classification of modal auxiliaries (n = 17).

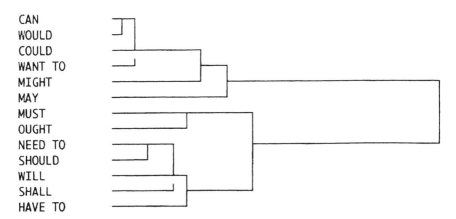

Fig. 4.2 Dendogram produced using Ward's Method of Hierarchical Cluster Analysis for 12-year-old classification of modal auxiliaries (n = 16).

have already discussed. WILL and HAVE TO are put together by these 12-year-olds because they have connected these auxiliaries via the meanings of intention and responsibility, in short, undertaking.

This, by the same token, could be precisely why the 8-year–olds, who do not make this connection in their classification scheme, nor do they express intention and responsibility modally very frequently, have difficulty in assigning the forms definitively to one or another of the groups and that results in them being left free floating, as it were.

Apart from these cases of WILL and HAVE TO, three clusters or groupings can be picked out for the 8-year-olds. However, within these three groups or clusters there seems to be little differentiation of meaning according to the source or locus of control, which amounts to a bias in favor of the nonepistemic meanings of the modal auxiliaries. In other words, the modal auxiliaries have not generally been assigned to groups based on what is taken to be the source of the modal force of a particular auxiliary. All modals expressing each gross concept (i.e., their root or nonepistemic applications), for example, desire or possibility, are thrown in together.

Briefly, the tightest links for this age group, connecting those modal auxiliaries considered to be closest in meaning, were WOULD and WANT TO, CAN and MIGHT, and SHOULD and OUGHT, which are all fairly obviously motivated choices. The highest agreement was reached for the HAVE TO and MUST combination and for WOULD and WILL, which means these two particular forms were put together in a group most often by the most number of children. The 8-year-olds' HAVE TO and MUST pairing in particular is important, in light of the observation that the 12-year-olds were much more likely to put WILL with HAVE TO. This reflects the commitment meaning shown to be in operation for the 12-year-olds. But it is revealing here also in light of the 8-year-olds' overall clustering patterns that do not seem to reflect distinctions based on the source of the modal force. The difference in strength and level of obligation between HAVE TO and MUST inheres crucially in the (non)involvement of the speaker, where to use HAVE TO presents the obligation as not necessarily coming from the speaker. The 12-year-old clustering of WILL and HAVE TO reflects this ambiguity nicely.

On the other hand, if the 12-year-old cluster system at first glance seems somewhat more chaotic, with more indistinct groupings and clusters, close inspection reveals a level of method to their madness. There seems to be a much greater effort after meaning reflected in even the most unusual pairings. Bearing in mind that these, and most 12-year-olds, can be very sophisticated in their use of the modal auxiliaries in a conversational or narrative context, it would not make sense to dismiss any of these patterns as erroneous. It is because the 12-year-olds are more aware of the multifunctionality of the modals and more skilled in the use of these pluriforms, that they have, in turn, more difficulty with the task than their 8-year-old counterparts.

Within the 12-year-olds' clusters, it seems to be the source of the element of control associated with the modal, (absent in the 8-year-olds' system), which drives the selections and pairings in this instance. In particular, three clusters of meanings can be defined: one group of auxiliaries whose modal force is under the speaker's own control, whether due to ability or volition but not necessarily only internal control; a group of meanings relating to a modal force that is clearly externally controlled; and a set that refers to internally controlled but self-imposed modal force.

Taking a closer look at the composition of the clusters, they could be said to reflect the separation of epistemic and root possibility. First there is a cluster that comprises CAN, WOULD, and WANT TO very tightly linked. These modal auxiliaries can be used for situations that are under one's own control, within one's ability, and often dependent only on whether one wants to carry out the action or not. COULD and MIGHT are loosely attached to this cluster, introducing situations that are somewhat less certain, but still not necessarily out of one's control. They are still indicative of, or related to, levels of ability. Finally, both these clusters are very loosely attached to MAY, which probably acts to bridge the two sets of meanings in some way, being ambiguous in its root and epistemic senses.

The next cluster is somewhat more deontically or speaker-oriented in its modality consisting of MUST and OUGHT very loosely linked. This pairing reflects externally imposed obligation, impersonality and a concern with sources of authority. The third main cluster is also about obligation but this time the obligation seems to arise or originate with the speaker or the subject of the modal. SHOULD and NEED TO are very closely paired and this time the obligation or force arises from a sense of personal commitment freely undertaken or of responsibility assumed. SHALL is on the fringes of this group, in the sense perhaps of committing oneself to a (not necessarily desirable) course of action. Even more on the outskirts lies WILL and HAVE TO, the undertaking use, where the comixing of meaning arises here as a result of WILL indicating a definite commitment but one not necessarily arising out of any personal desire. The MUST and OUGHT cluster is very loosely aligned with this one. Overall, compared to the 8-year-old group (and in contrast to Coates', 1988, study that reported exactly the opposite age-related trend) the links are very weak between modal auxiliaries and the clusters very indistinct. This suggests less agreement in their meanings, that is, more discourse oriented meanings. This fits with my overall thesis that the 8-year-olds' narratives are on many levels more straightforward than either the 5-year-olds' or the 12-year-olds' narratives.

Other Modal Elements

Modal elements frequently combine and interact dynamically, there seldom being one carrier of modality operating in isolation within the clause. Different realisations of modality do combine having a cumulative effect on the modality expressed. Hoye (1997, p. 3)

It has been asserted several times now that modality cannot be adequately accounted for by focusing on the modal auxiliaries alone, and to this end the next chapter is a full discussion of other relevant linguistic elements in the targeted modal utterances. But it is also important not to discuss the auxiliaries in isolation from other modal elements in the utterance that may be functioning synergetically within the same environment. There is a wide variety of ways of injecting contrasting or additional modality into an utterance in English. For example, by using emphasizers, intensifiers, focusing subjuncts, items that themselves express modal meanings of likelihood (POSSIBLY, PROBABLY, CERTAINLY) and items that carry no particular meanings themselves but reinforce and focalize the verb head to which they are attached (JUST, WELL). Using other modal forms in a clause in addition to the auxiliary can help to interpret or sharpen the modal element.

Overall there are relatively few different modal elements used with the modal auxiliaries in these narratives (only about 13% of the modals have any form of modification, directly attached to the auxiliary that is) that may be a feature of child language generally. Coates (1988, p. 425) said the modal adverbs and adjectives are even later than the modal auxiliaries to develop. But you could also argue that it is a style: Taking into account all the examples given so far, it is often the case that the same children are using the same forms over and over. Also the transcripts with the most modal auxiliaries tend to be the most heavily modalized or marked overall.

Modal coloring, or what could be called an epistemic quality was found frequently supplied in this narrative context by a range of mental verbs, for example:

> "We DECIDED we MIGHT come back tomorrow so we did" (NR5, disharmonic or contradictory modal elements).
> "And I was THINKING I'LL draw an X on it" (DG5).
> "Someday she says she'LL bring me but I THINK it WILL be a while yet" (AW12).
> "I THOUGHT I MIGHT be interested in books" (TA12).
> "I used to[29] THINK I'D LIKE to work as an artist or something" (SM8).

What is an issue is *how* the modality is encoded. As speakers we are generally motivated to give prominence to our own point of view and the most effective way of doing that is "to dress it up as if it was this that constituted the assertion (explicit [subjective] *I think*), with the further possibility of making it appear as if it was not our point of view at all (explicit objective *it's likely that.*)" (Halliday, 1994, p. 354).

> "But I THINK it WOULD be better if some of them sit on their laps" (JW5, so she can sit in the front of the car).
> "Because then it WOULD be REALLY fair, WOULDN'T it not?" (CMcG5, to justify sneaking some toys for herself).

---

[29] USED TO can form part of the marginal modal set or it can be used as an auxiliary of tense and aspect (Hoye, 1997, p. 74).

"You NEVER REALIZE that you WOULD LIKE that" (AW12, creating distance via general statements from what he liked to do last year).

Sometimes these constructions work so that the speaker's version of the world is not so much offered as imposed on others. Adverbial modification of the modals makes identification of the speaker with, or as, the source of authority much more explicit. The modal and its adverb points to the speaker in such a way that the modal operation itself becomes the focus of attention rather than the content of the utterance (Hoye, 1997, p. 66; See Kress & Hodge, 1979, p. 127f).

REALLY is by far the most versatile and one of the more commonly used emphasizers and freely combines with all modals: "as a disjunct it makes explicit the speaker's view that what he is saying is in fact true" (Hoye, 1997, p. 161) and Greenbaum (1969, p. 144) concluded that "it is often difficult to distinguish between the disjunct and the intensifying [emphasizing] functions of this item." In this study, REALLY is used quite frequently, for example, with CAN'T and COULDN'T as an intensifier:

"'Cos I COULD be REALLY busy (CmG5).
"He'D REALLY slag you, I've never known someone like that" (AK12).

or as a delimiter, in which case it tends to be unstressed:

"But he COULDN'T REALLY kiss me" (JW5).
"But he COULDN'T REALLY trick him very well" (CMcG5).
"But I CAN'T REALLY remember" (CMcG5).

However REALLY, when used with CAN and COULD in this study is more consistent with the earlier point that many of the uses of these particular modals are challenge-type uses. Especially if we take REALLY's counterpart CERTAINLY into account, which would also often be used in these sorts of combinations and situations but which is not used at all in this study. Like REALLY it collocates with all modals but, unlike REALLY, conveys "straightforward affirmation of truth without there being the implication that an assertion is being made in opposition to the contradictory notion of non-truth" (Hoye, 1997, p. 162). In other words, it does not do the job REALLY does in fending off imagined or anticipated challenges to the assertion being made (both aspects tend to be stressed).

"And I COULD REALLY hear them" (CMcG5, when it seems impossible that she could have).
"And he COULD REALLY ACTUALLY see him" (CMcG5).
"'Cos he REALLY CAN do it very well" (CMcG5, stressing how good her father is at tennis to explain why he always wins when they play together).

There are also some mitigating adverbs used, that is, adverbs used to mitigate the speaker's claims in relation to himself:

"You see, having snakes I COULD KINDA spot them" (AK12, when noone
else could see them in the zoo).
"And it WOULDN'T ACTUALLY be that much more difficult" (AW12,
about always getting highest marks in extra tuition assignments for
scholarship exam).

NEVER, as a negative amplifier or an intensifier, and CAN are frequently paired
in these narratives:

"That's why I won and I NEVER CAN catch it" (CMcG5).
"My dad NEVER CAN catch it" (CMcG5).
"I CAN NEVER remember names." (SOH12).

but NEVER also appears with some of the other modal auxiliaries:

"And then we were in hysterics, I'LL NEVER forget that really" (SM12).
"I was sure that I was going to say there and that I WOULD NEVER see my
parents again" (AW12).

In nonassertive clauses EVER replaces NEVER although an element of
temporality remains. But there are two examples here of EVER used in an
assertive clause, although one is a rather idiosyncratic, typically childish use:

"They were big gerbils, the biggest ones you COULD EVER get" (JW5).
"I don't think 5th and 6th WILL EVER REALLY get on" (AW12).

ONLY and JUST, both of which are found in this data, are called attitude
diminishers, in that they "imply that the force of the item concerned is limited,"
or downtoners, in the sense that "they scale downwards from an assumed norm"
(Hoye, 1997, p. 174).

"My radio CAN ONLY take big tapes" (StJS8).
"I only told three 'cos I COULD ONLY remember three" (CK8, sins at
confession).
"She loves her school now but you CAN ONLY stay there for two years"
(CK8).

In the next set of examples JUST is a focusing subjunct that acts to draw attention
usually to whatever constitutes the 'new', rather than the given information, in
the utterance. The fact that these clauses were generally signposted in some way,
including delivery in a different pitch, deliberate presentation of the utterance as
outside the main text or delivery just before the speaker left the topic altogether
for a new one as an aside, fits with this interpretation.

"And I COULD JUST walk around" (EL5).
"He CAN JUST get the parachute" (DPB8).
"And they WOULD JUST look at me" (JOH8).
"You CAN JUST eat it normally "(JOH8).

But looking closely, the position of JUST after the modal means it is reinforcing not the force of the auxiliary but the action of the other verb in the clause. Compare these with the next example of a subjunct emphasizer, JUST, used to reinforce a negated modal, CAN'T, where the point of interest or the focus really is on the fact of the subject's inability rather than what it is he is unable to do: "He JUST CAN'T come to terms with it but he is fat" (SM12). Emphasizers can be placed then either before or after the modal but in cases of special emphasis will tend to precede it.

Overall, as many elements as possible should be considered. Using two or more different indicators of modality in an utterance does not necessarily mean just doubling up on or reiterating the same modal theme as the auxiliary. Each element can add a whole new dimension, either by virtue of modal concord or of cumulative modality. Ochs and Schieffelin (1979) called them lexical touch-offs. When speakers have not organized their discourse, the use of one lexical item may trigger another lexical item having a complementary or opposite meaning. However this situation is often problematic in terms of analysis or interpretation because "when two or more modal elements are present in the same clause the synergy produced often permeates the whole construction and it is simply impossible to identify the precise locus of modification" (1979, p. 289).

Summary

The modal auxiliaries used by the children in this study and their meanings in relation to the type and source of the modality expressed have been described. The auxiliaries CAN, COULD, WILL, and WOULD (and variations thereof) account for over 70% of all the modal auxiliaries used and the WOULD form is the most frequently occurring form overall. CAN features consistently as one of the most frequently used modals for all the children (hovering at around 26% for all groups). The prevalence of the form CAN (and the meaning root possibility) in this study is explained in terms of the status of CAN as an ambiguous, multifunctional form.

Overall almost 57% of the auxiliaries used represent agent-oriented modality. Speaker-oriented modality accounts for only 2%, and epistemic modality accounts for about 41% of the children's usage of these forms. The agent-oriented root possibility category is by far the most frequently used (and I have argued that many of these instances are not really agent-oriented but are special cases of epistemic meaning) followed by modal auxiliaries used to establish epistemic (un)certainty. The overall patterns for the modals tends toward the older age group being more concerned with notions of possibility, that is, with what might or might not happen or what might be the case, while the younger children, especially the middle age group, are more preoccupied with what ought to be the case and what they think should happen (e.g., the 8-year-olds use the permission and imperative notions of CAN more than the other groups, a pattern evident across many aspects of the data).

The overall finding is that no self-contained categorization system is likely to prove adequate to the range of meanings associated with the modals and further, that we are not dealing with distinct or discrete stages of development for the modal auxiliaries. Rather that each function or meaning has its own stages of development and its own range of subfunctions and applications for the child. The analysis showed quite clearly that although the younger children are often using the modals in quite complicated constructions, their use of the auxiliaries is not yet associated with as wide and as flexible a range of discourse oriented meanings as those of the older children.

II

The Grammar of
Autobiographical Narrative

Sentences, not words, are the essence of speech just as equations and functions, and not bare numbers, are the real meat of mathematics. Reference of words is at the mercy of the sentences and grammatical patterns in which they occur. Whorf (1956, pp. 258-259)

We must be wary of treating grammatical considerations too formally, syntax is soaked in semantic presuppositions and meaning-making is a form of translation. Bruner (1995, p. 24)

Human conduct is a text and the inter-relationships among its parts are semantic rather than causal. Harré (1988, p. 4)

This section explores some of the additional linguistic structures selected as constitutive of autobiographical discourse, in order to describe "the nature of the verbal processes involved in the practical authorship of oneself" (Shotter, 1993b, p. 189). This involves a type of variation analysis not usually used in psychological studies on language, what Schiffrin (1994) called an approach to discourse "based within a socially realistic linguistics" (p. 290). It involves describing patterns of speaking in context, in this case, in the context of a child asked to engage in autobiographical discourse, as a function of both linguistic and social factors. Both grammatical structure and discourse function are explored, which allows the integration of different aspects of language that most developmental psychologists interested in self-development have usually considered separately. Previous research suggesting that language plays a central role in the child's construction of self brought us to this point but the fact remains that little is known about this process.

A Grammatical Perspective on the Self

All the linguistic forms chosen for this study play a central role in constructing narrative insofar as they make it possible to situate narrative events in time, in space, and in relation to each other. Similarly, these are the forms that make it possible to situate or position the self in discourse: temporally, socially, and morally in relation to others. Bamberg's (1991) "'third' point of orientation from which events can be seen as having something in common" (p. 279) is very interesting. His point was that referring to events requires a perspective (his *tertium comparatonis*) from which they are viewed as related. In this book, the argument is that it is one's sense of a core self, however fragmented or piecemeal in the case of the 5-year-old children, that constitutes the third point of orientation of autobiographical narratives or discourse. The idea of the self which we all have, the belief we all share that our life story is something that can be "told" (with varying degrees of skill and sophistication) is what these narratives and utterances have in common. Self is the vantage point from which the autobiography is told, and this is broken down into its component parts later.

This perspective is represented at the linguistic level by the choice of many different devices, lexical and grammatical, which is why so many grammatical features are treated in this context. Bamberg and Dammad-Frye (1991, p. 701) suggested that these devices interact at the level of their evaluative function that Labov (1972, p. 366) described as "the means used by the narrator to indicate the point of the narrative, its *raison d'être*, why it was told and what the narrator was getting at". But evaluations occur at many more locations than Labov originally indicated.

The linguistic forms that construct an evaluative stance cannot be specified simply. Evaluation is indicated by a wide range of linguistic structures and linguistic choices. Nor, we will see, can the discourse functions of utterances simply and exclusively be defined as, for example, evaluative or constitutive. But before going into detail on specific structures, a model like Linde's of the life story as a linguistic unit, as an oral unit of social interaction is very useful for situating this discussion. She said that part of the interpretative equipment furnished to us by our culture is the idea that we "have" a life story and that any normally competent adult has one "which incorporates things like 'what events have made me what I am' or 'what you must know about me to know me' where knowing a person specifies a range of linguistic and social activities and relations by the knowers." (Linde, 1993, p. 20).

This model is particularly relevant here because it sets itself the question of why narrative is so effective in creating and maintaining the self and describes three characteristics of the self that are specifically maintained and exchanged through language (p. 100).

The first quality supported and maintained by language is continuity of the self, particularly continuity of the self through time, so there is a relation but not necessarily a complete identity, between the self then and the self now. According to Linde (1993) this is established in narrative by one of the most basic text-structuring strategies in English, namely, the narrative presupposition of event sequence, which is marked by verb tense (p. 110). And maybe even more importantly, the knock-on effect of triggering narrative presupposition, in addition to facilitating temporal sequence and temporal continuity, is that it also provides causality: "Establishing adequate causality is one of the most important tasks for the teller of a life story [it] permits the creation of a self whose past is relevant to its present, since events in the self's past can be interpreted as causing present states and events" (p. 111).

Second, our sense of ourselves as separate and unique but related to others (Linde, 1993, pp. 111-113). This aspect is established linguistically on several levels[1] and in several ways but at its most basic level is brought about by person systems or pronouns (a universal feature of languages) that formally establish distinctions between discrete persons. But at a different level this also happens as a function of the fact that "the act of narration itself is a relational act" (p. 112). The narrator is in a relationship with the addressee, but at the same time, the narrator is indicating her or his relationship with the protagonist, this time the self of the story, and to all the other characters in the narrative and the relations between them. This can be seen in more detail in, for example, discussions of positioning theory, but for now it is just important to note the profoundly relational character of narrative activity.

But "not only must the self be related to others, it must be related properly. As soon as the self is seen as existing in relation to others, that relation must be some particular relation" (Linde, 1993, p. 123). Narrative "is crucially involved with the social evaluation of persons and actions: it is always involved in the question of whether an action (and hence an actor) is expected or unexpected, correct or incorrect." (p. 123). We have already seen how important a role the modal auxiliaries play in this type of evaluation and also how important these concepts are in the children's narratives.

The third quality of the self given to us by language is reflexivity or the ability to treat the self as other, where "the very act of narrating creates the occasion for self-regard and editing" (Linde, 1993, p. 105), for adjusting and creating distance between self-now and self-then, as we saw achieved by the judicious use of some of the modal auxiliaries. This primarily refers to the moral evaluation of the self. The judgments and evaluations we make in the course of our narratives are not just about other people and situations, we also must reflect on and judge our own actions that will require the related but not identical narrator and protagonist mentioned earlier. "Narrative is an extremely powerful tool for creating, negotiating and displaying the moral standing of the self part of the hidden point of any narrative is to show that the narrator knows what the norms are and agrees with them" (p. 123). The case of first person narratives is especially interesting because the nature of the evaluation set up means that "the speaker is always moral, even if the protagonist of the narrative is not" (p. 124). The child-as-

---

[1] It is interesting to see at just how many levels this plays out. Take, for instance, Hoye (1997) on modality, politeness and the concept of face (see Goffman, 1967), which incorporates the idea of the self as different but related. "There are two aspects to face; a positive one which affirms the individual's right to self-determination as an independent agent and a negative one which stresses the individual's need for approval and freedom from the imposition of others. In interpersonal communication positive and negative face are constantly at risk. Any kind of linguistic action which has a relational value is potentially face threatening. To counteract the risk, speakers pursue different politeness strategies to address their positive or negative face wants by lacing their interaction with appropriate doses of politeness. The linguistic strategies associated with positive face emphasis what the participants have in common with each other or refer to desirable attributes in the hearer. With negative face the strategies suggest distance by emphasising the individuality and independence of the participants" (Hoye, 1997, pp. 129-130).

speaker at least is always moral, because in the course of recounting how you may have behaved badly or in trying to justify or account for your actions, you are also of course indicating that you know you were wrong and that you share the norms of the addressee now even if you didn't do it at the time and so on (p. 124). This evaluative function is a crucial part of the later discussion of the discourse activity occasioned by the children's narratives.

Which Grammatical Features Are Important in This Context?

Within this complex matrix of relations, the narrator's grammatical choices affect not only the speaker-event (referential) relationship but also the speaker-addressee (pragmatic) relationship. In other words, not only what we talk about but also how we talk about it, that is, how we want (what we talk about, here the self) to be understood is communicated. The speaker's "set of 'on-line choices' will inform how the reference to an event is to be understood with regard to an overarching global theme" (Bamberg & Reilly, 1996, p. 337) and in this case, that overarching theme is the child's presentation of self, as author, as character, and so on.

In this study, the more important functions associated with autobiographical discourse involve areas like agency, responsibility, evaluation, accounting and so on and in that framework, it is not just the relationship between speaker and utterance, between the child and what she or he says, that is important but also the relationship between speaker and hearer where the utterance should be treated as "the actualisation of that relationship" (Guo 1994).

Bruner's (1995, pp. 167-169) account of what is involved in autobiographical discourse could be used as a starting point for an investigation of which grammatical features might be important. In this account, the discourse of witness, interpretation and stance[2] are combined "to create an account that has verisimilitude and negotiability". The discourse of witness, mimesis, refers to our accounts of events in which we were participants (in one way or another), and this type of discourse makes most use of the past tense, of verbs of direct experience (*see, hear*) and tends to be marked by declarative speech acts.

Bruner's discourse of interpretation, diegesis, on the other hand "creates 'facts' to fit its needs, it organises the detailed constituents of witness into larger-scale sequences and places them into evaluational frames" (p. 168). In relation to its grammatical shape, it is, he said, more subjunctive than mimesis, it focuses on paths not taken, so it feels retrospective and counterfactual, it uses epistemic verbs like *know* and *believe*, and it is usually in the present or timeless tense. Finally, he described the "autobiographer's posture toward world, self, fate, and

---

[2] Tonkin (1992, p. 82) in her study of Liberian oral historians: "in oral art, the participants are perhaps especially conscious of the magical power of mimesis and diagesis, which both represent and re-present the past", which is not to suggest that the children in this study are conscious of employing these techniques, nevertheless, there is evidence of the different positions.

the possible" as stance (p. 169), which is apparently without intention and is linguistically marked by seemingly uninformative markers like some of the ones we have just discussed (JUST, EVEN, ONLY).

Even this very general foray into the area throws up a host of factors that will have to be considered: tense markings, verb type, so-called discourse markers, and so on. A large part of the work of a project like this involves identifying and selecting the relevant linguistic features in this context, those linguistic forms that display and construct one's subjectivity in their speaking, as it were. Especially in light of the fact that "*every facet of an utterance* [italics added] responds to the specific pressures of recipient design" (Fox, 1994, pp. 30-31), that is, "are specifically constructed for a particular listener (or group of listeners) on a particular occasion of listening".

The concept of recipient design is important at every level of development; modal, narrative, self, and so on. Tonkin (1992) also brings up this issue: "a narrator who is asked to narrate must consider the occasion, the audience, even when giving a monologue. Strictly the narrative is a kind of dialogue. *On these formal grounds alone the structure also contributes to the meaning* [italics added]*" (Tonkin, 1992, p. 67).

All linguistic structures have meaning then, that is their raison d'être (Tomasello 1992a) after all, but it is important to guard against being too simplistic when analyzing linguistic choices as having particular meanings. Choices have a range of meanings "dependent on the context in which they occur and the presuppositions which the researcher brings to bear on the interpretative process" (Mills, 1995, p. 149). Any one particular linguistic form or some combination or collocation of forms "does not stand per se for one versus the other narrative orientation, it is a complex interaction of form-function relationships" (Pope, 1995, p. 187). This work can serve also in the capacity of a checklist of the more relevant grammatical forms in this context, those by which language prefigures a place for the Subject (Kerby, 1991), in order to draw up a profile of the areas that could be sourced in an examination of how the self is constructed via language. Work of this kind is difficult to report in summary form, this sort of analysis needs to be done at length, and sometimes even using single examples, so the case made in this book is primarily theoretical rather than empirical.

Outline of Grammatical Forms for Study

Having started with an analysis of the set of modal auxiliaries, this section profiles the following sets of forms, as recruited by the children in their autobiographical stories. Starting from the idea of grammar as the solution to a problem, in discussing each grammatical feature, I want to ask what "problem" is being solved, what discourse context is achieved by being able to differentiate and shift between tenses, aspects, and so on. This involves describing the social or discourse function of these linguistic subsystems:

- The systems of tense, case, and aspect, which help to establish causality and the continuity of self.

- Verb groups, which, through their agentive features and the indexing of the semantic role of the speaker, help to establish reflexivity and an evaluative stance vis-à-vis the self.

- The pronominal indexical system, which helps establish the distinctness and relatedness of the self.

- and finishing the grammatical analysis by exploring, in the last section, the set of discourse functions or discourse activities set up by all these grammatical features in tandem with the modal auxiliaries.

5

A Sense of Location

TENSE: ACTING OUT OR ACTING INTO?

Past, present and future are all in the Present for me. Subjectively, my Present is not like one dot on the dotted line of time, a dot distinct from the dot that preceded it, distinct from the dot that will follow. On the contrary, this directly experienced moment flows without a break into the future and it contains its past. What has already happened gives meaning and content to this Present; what is foreseen gives meaning and content to this Present. Fingarette (1996, p. 44)

Time is one of the essential things stories are about. Portelli (1981, p. 162)

There are many reasons why tense plays such a vital role in this context, including perhaps the most important one, as elaborated in Linde's (1993) model, that tense and temporal connectedness is vital for establishing a sense of continuity and of causality, as a central component of the self. This theme appears over and over again in the literature. For instance, Kerby (1991) asserted that apart from bodily identity, temporal connectedness best accounts for our initial sense of personal identity. Modell (1993, p. 3) said that "to speak of narrative is simply to emphasise the temporal, that is, the historical, nature of the self." According to Taylor (1989):

> Another basic condition of making sense of ourselves, that we grasp our lives in a *narrative*. In order to have a sense of who we are, we have to have a notion of how we have become, and of where we are going. But narrative must play a bigger role than merely structuring my present. What I am has to be understood as what I have become. My self-understanding necessarily has temporal depth and incorporates narrative. (1989, pp. 47-50)

When we ask someone to talk about themselves, to tell their autobiography or life story, we expect their narratives to be firmly set in the past, yet even with children we find the curious situation that a substantial part of their story is not past-bound[1] and that the speaker or autobiographer is "a kind of point" (Davies &

---

[1] This trend is borne out by, for example, Bruner (1990), who reported that 33% of the Goodhertz family's autobiographical discourse was in the present tense. And Gerhardt and Stinson (1994): "the very idea of narrative draws attention to the fashioning of experience in the present rather than the uncovering of memories from a buried past" (p. 152).

Harré, 1991, p. 11)[2] pivoting in time within their narratives, both "to select the span of time involved and also an orientation to this span of time [the] focus may be as much on the speaker as on what is being described" (Tonkin, 1992, p. 79). We experience the multidimensional time of narrative wherein "the past is purposefully deployed to change the future" (p. 66). On a linguistic level, it is thought that the self-reference and temporal reference systems develop over the same period of time as they are both essential to the construction of self within a temporally organized social world (Nelson, 1989, p. 305). And the modal auxiliaries are understood as being used to pick up on some of the earlier idiosyncratic contrasts made by children in relation to these systems.

The tense system is a very good source of information on the grammar-discourse relation because tenses are shifters (in the same way as, for example, pronouns). Their meanings are relational. Tense places an event in time in relation to the speaker. The narrator, the narrative and the audience are fused at this moment of time in a particular perspective and in relation to all those other moments (Tonkin, 1992, p. 67). The category of tense is not just a grammatical category but a pragmatic one as well[3] (Fleischman, 1982; Gerhardt & Savasir, 1986; Lakoff, 1970). In many ways tense, hence time, exists only as a function of language: "We cannot help asking at this point-how can such differentiae exist prior to language? Do we not, rather, realise them only by means of language, through the very act of naming them?" (Cassirer, 1946, p. 24).

What do tenses do, and what is the narrator doing when she or he uses different tenses or shifts between tenses in the course of a narrative? A feature of a well-organized narrative text is the appropriate use of tense and aspect, that usually involves choosing a tense that is then consistently favored throughout the narrative (Berman & Slobin, 1994). For instance, the simple past tense can be used "to characterize past, though potentially normative qualities" and the simple present "to signal the atemporal, hypothetical character of the situation" (p. 131).

Young children are not very good at doing this. Even at 5, children are less than systematic in their choice and use of tense markers (there are even some errors made with tenses by the children in this study). In that the discourse or the "extended function of tense shifting is motivated by the thematic organisation of the narrative as a whole" (p. 134) the 5-year-old children's narratives often seem quite disjointed and unmotivated. The "why-tell function"[4] is not always immediately apparent and their overall stance, for example, is not always obvious

---

[2] But see Holland and Skinner (1997) who from a neo-Vygotskyan and Bahktainian perspective argued that discourse theory disregards development. "We disagree with discourse theory in anthropology and psychology that too readily equates identity with subject positions in discourse and practice (for example, Davies & Harré, Harré & van Langenhove). The individual must be recognised as having a history-in-person, that is, identities are developed over time in experience" (In Tudge, Shanahan & Valsiner, 1997, p. 198).

[3] Ochs (1994) pointed out that particular temporal dimensions are even socioculturally linked to affective stances, for example, in English the temporal dimension of the present moment 'now' may help to constitute a stance of affective intensity: "NOW look what you've done" (p. 419).

[4] Bruner (1990, p. 71).

or consistent. Where the children should be making a "narratively motivated choice" (p. 601) in relation to tense, they are sometimes using developmentally earlier locally motivated or managed choices.

Local, minute-by-minute shifts means the story is not really being globally organized in relation to particular discourse functions. Children are capable of this by age 5, but there is still a lot of room for refinement, for instance, to acquire the rhetorical flexibility necessary to select a tense to perform as an anchor for the narrative and then to use aspectual distinctions to make other contrasts. In other words, the child of 5 is less able to keep the overall project, as it were, or story in mind that is then used to structure particular episodes, vignettes and events. It is all part of the process mentioned earlier of forming a "representation of the listener" (Fox, 1994), of "creating and attending to a 'co-text' in the process of narrating" (Berman & Slobin, 1994).

But this criterion of well-formedness according to the consistency of choice of tense need not be too rigidly applied to autobiographical narratives. Telling a life story is not, after all, a straightforward retelling or recounting of a story, of something that happened, but involves trying to capture or to give an account of your life/self that involves future and present scenarios as well. Tense shifting is a legitimate device for switching temporal perspectives within an ongoing narrative (Bamberg, 1987;[5] Schiffrin, 1987) and telling one's autobiography is an ongoing narrative.

And in that the main interest is in how the children tell their stories, then as Weinrich (1970, p. 36, cited in Bamberg, 1987) pointed out "since it is the communicative situation that is to be analysed, it is not relevant whether a fact is situated in a moment previous to present time, but in the way the speaker looks back to it." It is well recognised that tense forms have as much to do with expressing the speaker's point of view on an event as with expressing temporal relations per se.[6] "It is the speaker's subjective perspective that he or she imposes onto the narrative as a whole by use of tense alternations" (Bamberg, 1987, p. 113).

Weinrich (cited in Bamberg, 1987) gives three categories according to which each single tense form used can be described, which will be briefly summarized here: (a) "discourse mode" or "Sprechhaltung" by which the speaker indicates how she or he wants the message to be understood, that is, reveals her or his attitude to the message, either via narrative mode (using simple past, pluperfect, and conditional forms to mark this particular subjective attitude) or via the discursive or reporting mode (which uses present tense, perfect and futures);[7] (b) the "Sprecherperspektive" or discourse perspective, this time the focus is on the

---

[5] Bamberg did a major study on German tense markings and alternations in narratives.
[6] See Gee (1985, p. 224) on Benveniste (1971).
[7] Bamberg (1987, p. 180): "the narrative mode or remote tense (Joos) is a more distanced, more general perspective towards the communicative situation in contrast to the discourse mode (the unmarked tense group). Even at 3;6, children can be consistent in their choice of tense form, usually opting for the unmarked tense so characterizing their perspective towards the discourse mode as 'reporting' or 'discursive'."

situation being described[8] and there are three options available, zero perspective (using present tense), retrospective (which involves using perfect tense), and prospective (the future tense); and (c) *"Reliefgebung"* or discourse grounding, the speaker here is giving information as to how her or his utterances should be interpreted meaningfully in relation to each other. This description is reminiscent of the earlier discussion on the different levels of relations involved in the reflexive evaluation of the self and relates to positioning theory that deals with a very similar tripartite system of connections between the narrator, the audience, and the relations between these and the characters and events within the narrative.

Finally, the relation between tense and modality itself is very complex. The systems of tense, aspect, and modality are in fact often treated together,[9] and it can be very difficult to pinpoint where one system starts and another ends. Temporal categorizations of pastness or futurity necessarily involve various modalities (e.g., obligation, volition, belief) "which qualify the relationship between speaker and hearer as well as between speaker and message, rather than the world of processes and events" (Bamberg, 1987, p. 108). There is "time inflected and made rhythmic by the human being who inhabits it" that we can call modal time or "experiential",[10] and there is also "a time that is flat, uniform, a continuous succession of temporal points with measurable distance between them, chronometrical time" (Bowie, 1993, p. 13). I am interested here in modal rather than chronometrical time in the children's telling of their story.

In some cases it can be hard to distinguish whether it is in fact the modal auxiliary or some other marker that is introducing the temporal element to the utterance.[11] The fact that the modal auxiliaries themselves select for time reference (CAN and COULD, MAY and MIGHT, WILL and WOULD, SHALL and SHOULD) confounds the relation. But Brazil (1995, p. 113) said, regarding the element of time reference, we should think of the modal as relating what he calls probability time for an event that has not yet happened to utterance time.

We can also consider the tenses used in relation to the distance set up between the narrator and what is being told and also between the narrator and the audience. The ability to use tense to distance yourself as a speaker from your

---

[8] This is similar to discussions on foreground and background distinctions (e.g., Givón, 1979, Hopper, 1987, Langacker, 1990).

[9] "Straddling the fields of syntax, semantics and morphology are the grammatical categories of tense, aspect, voice and modality" (Aarts & Meyer, 1995, p. 12).

[10] See Ochs, Schegloff and Thompson (1996, p. 20) on kairotic time that is the time in which grammar operates, which is directional, meaningful, or meaning-implicated time.

[11] "For instance, English does not allow the future in an if-clause: the use of WILL there is purely modal" (Binnick, 1991, p. 390). There is serious debate as to which category the modal WILL belongs to: Some linguists (e.g., Hornstein, 1977, 1990) assume this morpheme is ambiguous between a modal and a tense; others say all occurrences of WILL are modal, it is never a tense (e.g., Jespersen, 1924, Yavas, 1982); and Comrie (1995) for instance said the evidence is inconclusive although he did also say that he thought it possible to have future time reference without modality where definiteness is involved. However Enç (1996) has shown that definiteness is compatible with, and therefore does not preclude, modality. As indicated, the area is a very difficult and a hotly debated one.

material is newly available around the age of 5 (Bamberg, 1987). The modal auxiliaries, in particular the so-called distal forms, are a very important device with which to do this, with which to exploit the system, for example, by creating a strictly fictional shift in time perspective to be diplomatic or to distance yourself from your sentiments.[12]   Speakers may use the differentiated time reference choice to make requests or suggestions more socially acceptable (Brazil, 1995, p. 116): "COULD *you give me a lift?*" or "*I thought you* MIGHT *be able to help me out...?*". Notice this is using the past tense as more marked for indirectness, in combination with using CAN rather than WILL as a further measure of politeness, deflecting attention from the addressee's intentions with regard to your request and focusing instead on establishing their ability *apropos* the proposed action.

Perhaps this is where the modals really enter this discussion, when considering the extent to which the children's narratives are involved either with "the 'telling' of what is absent (past or future tenses, retro-[13] or prospective experience and events) or the 'showing' of what is understood to be present or constant (present tense, circumspective evidence and events)" (Pope, 1995, p. 73).

Three different categorization methods are used to explore the tense or temporal system being used within the children's narratives. First a crude measure dividing up the target utterances according to simple past, present, and future orientation (suspending for the moment all the problems with this sort of approach and the vast body of literature and research on time, temporality, tense and so on, even the sort of research that suggests there is no such thing as future tense). The situation in these narratives is that over 38% of all the modal utterances are future oriented, whereas past and present references amount to about 31% each. When broken down by age, much the same situation holds, with some differences. Mainly there is a reversal of trends for the 5 and 12-year-olds with the majority of the youngest group's utterances in the present and past tense whereas the older group make more future-oriented modalized statements. The tenses are fairly evenly represented in the 8-year-old narratives but they too use more futurized statements.

A system based on simple or nonsimple tenses is also used. All modal utterances were categorized according to the marking of the duration or the type of temporal activity referred to, rather than as a marking of when the activity (or event or thought) took place. Simple and conditional uses accounted for the vast majority of all utterances (88% together), with the 5-year-olds using the simple tenses most often and the conditional tense showing a steady increase in frequency between the ages of 5 and 12. The other three systems of aspect were only very infrequently used with the exception of the present historical that constitutes a relatively high 7% of the 8-year-olds' modal utterances.

---

[12] See Brazil (1995) for a very good discussion of this facet of the system.
[13] "Between the ages of 5 and 9 the most important narratively-motivated temporal functions to develop are retrospection (reference to an earlier event which is reinvoked because of its relevance to the current point in plot development) and simultaneity" (Berman & Slobin, 1994, p. 604).

Finally, a rather more elaborate breakdown of the temporality indicated by the modal utterances in this context is drawn up. And in relation to the modals themselves, we can find out which modal is used primarily to express particular temporal arrangements. For our purposes here, we can run briefly through the patterns:

- The simple present is the preferred tense of the 5-year-olds (but is almost equal with the future conditional and the simple past).

- For both 8- and 12-year-olds, the future conditional tense is the most frequent.

- The 5-year-olds use the simple past almost as much as they use simple present, but this tense shows a sharp decrease in frequency between the ages of 8 and 12.

- The frequency of the simple future tense on the other hand shows the opposite development, from hardly being used at all by the youngest children to being the third most used tense by the 12-year-olds.

- The 8-year-olds of all age groups make most use of the past conditional tense, consistent with trends in relation to their preoccupation with what should have been, what others did wrong, didn't do, should have done and so on.

- Overall the future conditional tense is the most used by all age groups, perhaps not what you would expect in the context of autobiographical narratives but nevertheless a consistent feature in this study.

- The present historical is the only other tense that shows an interesting pattern, even though the numbers concerned are small, with the 8-year-olds in particular making use of this device.

Predicting the Future

The status of the future of the verb is at the core of existence. It shapes the image we carry of the meaning of life and of our personal place in that meaning. Steiner (1975, pp. 138-139)

Narratives of personal experience have one face toward the future. Ochs (1994, p. 132)

Even given the fact that reference to future events and states is a crucial aspect of the meaning of the modals (Coates, 1995) it is still surprizing in the context of autobiographical discourse to find that the future tense is used in more than a third of all the modal utterances and that the future conditional is the most used tense overall. But maybe not, if we agree with Fleishman's (1982) assessment that the crucial factor of future and the futurates[14] is "the 'present relevance', the 'go-future' connected with subjectivity and specifically with speaker involvement" (Binnick, 1991, p. 389). The future actually forms a very important part of one's autobiography and the focus on "memories of one's own past as a locus of self-identity" is now thought to be "too narrow in omitting one's plans for the future as a source of self identity" (Snow, 1990, p. 236). Heidegger (1973) even designated that-which-is-to-come (*Zu-kunft*) as the home territory of human existence, of *Dasein*.

The future tense is very rarely used for making subjectively neutral or factual statements or for posing objective questions about the future (Fleischman, 1982, p. 129). Futures, as we have seen with the modal auxiliaries, commonly appear in utterances involving likelihood, inference, lack of knowledge, wishes and desires, intention and volition, obligation, and command. The use of the modal auxiliaries within autobiographical narratives means that the stories children tell "are not only reconstructions of past experiences but preconstructions of future experiences as well. Stories may imply or make explicit what will, might, could or should (not) happen next. They draft lives in progress, allowing interlocutors continually to (re)create their past, present and future selves at once" (Ochs, 1994, p. 108). The most important areas of future reference in this study relate to intention, including desires and uncertainty, what we call using the future to work through the narrative.

Intention is an important aspect of the meaning of the future, but it is a very general term, and we see that it takes quite different forms in relation to the different age groups involved. Plans for the future account for a large proportion of the future statements used here. Briefly, plans for the 12-year-olds mainly pertain to what they want to be or what they want to do when they grow up:

"I'D like to be an architect" (TA12).
"I hope I get into Vet 'cos I'D really like it" (AK12).
"I'D like to be a doctor or, I don't know,
just help people or be an ambulance driver" (IGOD12).

whereas the younger children, especially the 5-year-olds, engage in more short-term planning, for example, birthday and Christmas presents.

"And I WOULD sit in the middle and the others WOULD have to sit down on the bottom" (JW5).
"I WOULD like Connections" (JH8).
"I WON'T really miss my Mom, you see, the games WILL cheer me up" (StJS8).

"What counts is not the way I will or will not feel in the future. What counts is the impact on me now of my present expectations about that future. We do often

---

[14] Which refers to the present, present progressive, and present perfect used for future and future perfect.

take into account how we *will* feel about something in the future. Yet what is truly fundamental is how we feel about it now" (Fingarette, 1996, pp. 67-68). This helps to explain the case for the 12-year-old children in this group in particular. It is the impact of their plans and intentions for the future on their present feelings and situation that is important. Frequently for the 5-year-old group the future modal utterances relate only to things they want to get or that they have been promised, straightforward planning activities of near-future activities, parties and the like. Whereas with the older children, the 12-year-olds in particular, the futurized modal utterances are often in the service of a working-through of something that they are anxious about:

> "She knows what secondary school and college are like, and I'LL have that headstart of, sort of,
> to know what it'LL be like" (AW12, speaking about his sister),
> "It gets really embarrassing but not in the play next year 'cos I'LL know everyone there" (DH12, on acting),
> "You have to stand up and say "Good Morning" and I don't know if I'LL remember that all the time" (DH12 on going to secondary school),
> "If we ever, like, if Mum CAN'T collect us we'LL just go to my Granny" (SL12, this child often worked out similar scenarios in this way as they came up),

or when it is in relation to what they want to be or do when they are older, it is frequently in the context of worrying about whether or not they will be able to achieve this or if they are good enough. Lacan remarked that "the tense structure of the European languages seems to know something important about the fragility of the subject's wishful constructions and the imperfect and future perfect have a special eloquence on this theme."[15]

> "I'm always worried that I've forgotten something that I'LL need" (SL12).
> "She's supposed to be brilliant so I'm not really sure if I'LL beat her" (SL12).
> "When I grow up I want to be an actress but I don't know if I'LL be able to" (SL12).
> "And, like, I know this wouldn't happen but I'D love to be an actor" (PF12).

On this "working through" theme, Ochs (1994) said "story coherent future time references are integral to the story in that they give meaning to its events, they further the construction of the story itself using future ramifications to help shape what they see to be the point of the story's past events" (p. 107). Often, the 12-year-olds' future utterances are in order to convince themselves of something, to allay their anxiety about some future event, in a meaning that I argue is a corollary of the undertaking or commitment meaning of WILL discussed earlier:

---

[15] Cited in Bowie (1993, p. 34).

"But if it still like it, I'LL stay" (IGOD12).
"I have to go right down to the bottom again and work up but I think it'LL be fine" (HL12).
"Eight others from our class are going, so I'LL be fine, but I'd say it'LL be real different" (RL12).
"If I haven't finished it I'LL do some more and then go to bed" (AK12).

Everything in the future is necessarily uncertain, insofar as it has not happened yet, it is not yet a reality. Claims about the future are always weak compared to claims about the past because our predictions and expectations can be changed by intervening events (Comrie, 1985). Uncertainty is an inherent property of the future.[16] Here there is a very explicit marking of uncertainty via the future tense in particular by the 12-year-olds. The 5-year-olds tend to be much more concrete in their use of the future tense and you could roughly characterize their non-use of WILL and their disproportionate reliance on WOULD, in terms of a preoccupation with conditions and justifications whereas the older children tend to be much more projective in their futurity. The 5-year-olds are using WOULD mainly for prescribing and problem-solving functions whereas the older children, the 12-year-olds in particular, are using the form in relation to issues of agency, especially intention, statements of desire and preference and theory of mind type statements (all these discourse categories are discussed fully in the next chapter). This observation fits with Benveniste's (1968)[17] distinction between what he called the "intentive future" and "the future of predestination." The former is based on the speaker's own volitional activities and refers to totally independent future events or to events not previously formulated. The predestined future reference involves what has been laid down in the past. What is projected of the future is something predetermined by the past, either the recurrence of a prior event or the fulfilment of a plan. Heidegger (1962)[18] suggested that a property of our species is that we have human cares, and these cares lead us to conceptualize the present in terms of the past and future, the past in terms of the present and future and the future in terms of the past and present. Obviously the 5-year-old's set of cares is very different to the adolescent's particular set of cares and anxieties, and this is what we see reflected in their respective turning to past and future. Narratives about the past are always in some way about the present and future as well. Sometimes these narratives open up novel possibilities for the shape of our lives to come. In other cases they touch off a concern about the present or future.

But when the modal auxiliary does not have its own temporal meaning (e.g., in an IF-clause or conditional situation) but is instead purely modal, there is the

---

[16] According to Yavas (1982) the ontological difference between the past and the future justifies treating WILL as a modal even if its function seems to be to specify a future time (cited by Enç, 1996, p. 348).
[17] (1968) cited in Gerhardt (1988, p. 373).
[18] Cited in Ochs (1994, p. 190).

curious phenomenon whereby things are now very certain indeed. The modal in this case is often used to indicate almost absolute certainty where in its more temporal use it was associated with uncertainty:

"So I said "Mark if you don't be quiet, I WILL kill you" (CK8),
"It said "people WILL be prosecuted if they tap on the glass" (AK12),
"If I go, I'LL go with a friend, but if I'm not, I'LL probably go to the Boyzone one in December" (SOH12),
"But if she finds out, she'LL go mad" (AW12),

and again certainty, even though the action of the verb associated with the modal is conditional on the rest of the utterance.

"He WON'T be able to go for a while 'cos he's doing his leaving" (SM12).
"And he CAN'T, like, you WON'T ever do him, Dad, he's always in the right, he's perfect" (HG12).
"He didn't tell cos he knows he'LL get in trouble" (CMcG5).
"Because then it WOULD be really fair" (CMcG5).
"I mean, if I liked it, I'D try" (TA12).

The future conditional form was heavily represented in all age groups but in several different ways. In keeping with the overall tone of their narratives, the 8- and 12-year-old children used this tense a lot in relation to long term plans and goals:

"I'D like to be an architect" (TA12).
"I'D like to be an actress" (HG12).
"Otherwise I'D be a writer" (JOR8).

In relation to the working-through function outlined for the future tense in general, there are examples like:

"I mean it COULD be handy for quite a lot of things" (TA12, on Irish which he hates and hasn't worked at and about which he is now worried).
"If Mum CAN'T collect us we'LL just go to Gran's" (RL12).

And the outlining of plans, mainly short term:

"Maybe we CAN play hide and seek" (SOH12, plans for her party).
"I have it in her book so I COULD get it photocopied and stuck in my project" (SC8, on Enid Blyton's autograph).
"There's two things I'D like to find out about" (DPB8).

The Conditional future was also used to express future in the past, usually in the context of reported speech or in relation to their own or others' thought processes, so-called theory of mind uses:

"But I said "If you CAN'T get me Barbie, get me Cindy" (JW5).
"He thought he COULD get in to the palace" (CMcG5).
"When I was a baby she brought me so her friend Ann COULD see me"
(EL5).
"But when it comes to interviews I get real shy so they think I WOULD be
shy in front of the cameras" (PF12).
"So she said "Now Tommy, don't do that" like, as if that WOULD stop him
or anything" (HG12).
"The earliest really he'D be back WOULD be about 9 or 10" (AC8).
"I thought I'D be there for ages" (SC8).

Perhaps Bruner (1990) can have the final word here: "The self as protagonist is always, as it were, pointing to the future. When somebody says as if summing up a childhood, 'I was a pretty rebellious kid', it can usually be taken as a prophecy as much as a summary" (p. 121).

Understanding the Present

The 5-year-olds in this study make the most use of the simple present, and the 12-year-olds seem to need it least. The main theme here is the habitual, the usual, or the canonical. Children are using the present tense to comment on the taken-for-granted of their experience. They use it to talk about what they see as the essential constitution of the things in their environment and to remark on what is unremarkable. When the simple present tense describes an event the speaker feels to be unusually or absolutely certain of at the present moment of speaking, then the simple present tense is modal rather than temporal. To say something is temporal means it refers to two different points in time, the moment of speaking and some time prior to it or some past time and a time prior to that and so on. The simple present does not refer simultaneously to two points of time but is actually unmarked for time, undated.[19] It is used to describe general conditions primarily, and we see that the discourse category of reporting is the most common in all age groups.

"You CAN get sausages, you CAN get burgers, you CAN get chips" (EF5).
"You CAN write in letters" (DPB8, on a TV programme).
"And now I just realised that you CAN have a TV and everything in my old
room" (HG12).

The present tense is often used for indicating expected or desired events that can be very revealing in the context of autobiographical narratives, in the sense that it can tell us something about the areas in the child's life that are characterized

---

[19] For a very interesting discussion see Fleischman (1991) on discourse as space and as time (esp. p. 297 no. 14, the historical future of narrative discourse as epistemological cheat). Also Okamura (1996) and Quirk (1986).

for them by regularities. The absence of any explicit tense or aspect meaning in the simple present, leaves it open to absorb the meaning inherent to normal social and physical phenomena, and this meaning, if described and broken down explicitly, consists of habitual occurrence and behavior as well as ongoing states (Bybee, Perkins, & Pagliuca, 1994, p. 152).

The function of present tense narration is often to convey an illusion of immediacy and instantaneity, quashing any suggestion that the outcome is knowable in advance. The use of present tense narration severely restricts the possibility of any temporal movement outside the present moment. "The outcome, both linguistically and thematically, is a complete closing of meaning: there is no interpretative task for a reader to perform, no inference undrawn" (Stephens, 1996, p. 65).

"I have their phone numbers so we CAN hang around normally" (PF12).
"It CAN do everything that a dog does" (JW5).

The simple present downplays subjectivity or, at least, does not overtly display subjectivity and uniqueness the way other tenses can. It plays down the distinctness of any one event and also therefore the speaker's personal agency. It is used for routine events, for decontextualized events that makes it available for encoding generic normative meanings.

The fact that the simple present tense and the future (especially the future conditional) are the two main tenses used means it is the notions and concepts conveyed by the use of these modal rather than temporal tenses that together constitute the children's subjectivity in their narratives. It is interesting that when asked to speak about themselves autobiographically, to tell their life story, that such a large part of that story takes place in relation to what might be the case in the future and what is considered typically to be the case at the moment.

Interpreting the Past

Any representation of pastness is identity-constitutive and can be elaborated into an identity support as well. Tonkin (1992, p. 135)

If the present is about the unmarked, and hence the unremarkable, about the way things are and most importantly the way things are expected to be, the opposite is true of the past tense. Whereas the simple present is marked by zero in many languages as the default situation, the simple past never is because it always expresses an explicit temporal relation.[20] The events have always occurred prior to the moment of speech.

"They were big gerbils, the biggest ones you COULD ever get" (JW5).
"And I COULD really hear them" (CMcG5).

---

[20] See Bybee, Perkins and Pagliuca (1994, p. 152ff).

"I was really shy and I COULD do reading very well" (SC8).
"The memory is, that I was so small that I COULD fit in a basin in front of the fire" (AW12).
"I had the chickenpox when I was a baby and my mother COULDN'T get them away" (NR5).

According to most categorization systems for the modals, an epistemic reading is preferred for past-tense situations because the situation, event, or state is now out of the speaker's control. You can only comment on something in the past, you cannot effect any changes.[21] In this way the simple past is like the simple present. The simple present works to say the way things are, whereas the simple past mainly narrates what happened. The simple past usually recounts specific events where the speaker is often the agent. You need to add either perfect or progressive aspect to move away from this default situation.

A temporal device sometimes used in narrative to make it more dramatic, to make things more vivid and more present for the audience is when events in the past are narrated using the present tense, what is called the present historical tense.[22] Over 4% of all modal utterances in this study were present historical and almost 7% of the 8-year-old's utterances were of this type, particularly with regard to the auxiliary WILL.

"And he says 'Ah, I WON'T tell you anything'" (KB8)
"So we say 'we probably WON'T be in the same school' and next of all we're in the same school" (IB8).
"So I find he's not there so I say 'Oh, I'LL let you go then'" (JOR8 his hamster).
"And I was thinking 'I'LL draw an X on it'"(VMcG5).
"So after about a month he leaves it and he goes "Oh I'LL get another one"'(AC8).
"She trots up the stairs: 'I'LL never believe you again', And I'm, like, 'God' and she goes 'you're a liar' and like, she just says that but she doesn't, she does believe me, I know she does" (SM12).

This device, shifting the past to the present, allows the speaker to make the objective subjective in some way. It makes whatever it is you are talking about currently relevant by shifting the background to the foreground of the narrative. In the reverse movement, it is possible to render the subjective objective, as we have seen already the modal auxiliaries used by the children to distance themselves from their sentiments, for example. Shifting the nonpast, that is, what

---

[21] Pope (1995, p. 73): "A thorough-going transformation of the verbs from the simple, universalising present into the simple non-progressive and thereby 'closed' past".
[22] Wolfson (1978, p. 236) did a study of American-English autobiographical tales on what she called Conversational Historic Present (CHP) which she concluded could be seen "as an index of professed commonality between speakers and its use may provide insight into the way speakers view themselves and their relation to others." Tonkin (1992, p. 81) used this point to indicate how deeply social relations enter into the linguistic form of discourse. Binnick (1991, p. 388) also thought the historic tenses probably have discourse functions, for example, demarcative ones.

the child is currently feeling or experiencing, into the past signals much less speaker involvement, more distance. Volitional control over emotions and feelings is also weakened by talking about them as taking place in a hypothetical world. "The past is objective where the present is subjective" (Binnick, 1991, p. 390).

> "X is moving to Churchtown which I WOULD actually be a bit jealous of 'cos they're opening a new petshop" (AK12).
> "I've never really been away by myself for more than a week so it WOULD seem very strange" (AW12).
> "Some people WOULD think I'm nice like, that I'm grand" (SM12)

Using the Perfect and Progressive, Treated With Aspect

In addition to indicating when something took place, a speaker will often mark her or his particular viewpoint using aspectual distinctions. An event can be presented as imperfective, from inside an ongoing event, or as perfective, from outside an event that is either already concluded or that has yet to begin. The speaker's point of view can be either from inside an event, as the experiencer, or can position both speaker and listener outside events, looking in as it were. The perfect (*have -ed/-en*) and progressive (*be + ing*) aspects are more marked than their simple counterparts.

The pattern here is that the younger children, especially the 5-year-olds, make comparatively more perfective statements than the 12-year-olds. This fits with the development of narrative in general where, as the child gets more proficient in telling stories and recounting events, she or he makes more use of aspect as an anchoring device. In general, the perfect functions to indicate some kind of casual relation when referring to past events and on a wider scale to signal that a past event is still relevant to the speaker.

> "They COULD have given me big bites " (CM5).
> "And em, I COULD have been in a film" (JOR8).
> "It COULD have been hibernating" (AK12).
> "But he COULD'VE eaten in the morning they found out" (IGOD12).
> "And that's how he WOULD have been with his right hand writing" (SM8).
> "And she didn't actually come, she SHOULD have still come" (StJS8).
> "And I MUST have fallen asleep on the way" (EL5).
> "I think he went back, he MIGHT have gone back after and leaved it when everybody was asleep" (JW5).
> "I was going to be, I MIGHT have been in a film" (JOR8).
> "She MUST have thought I had my ears pierced" (SOH12).
> "I think it MIGHT also have been for grommets, I'm not sure" (SOH12).

If it is not referring to the past then the use of the perfective usually means some prediction or logical consequence from the subjective point of view of the speaker.

"Then we're minding my little cousin 'cos she'LL just have had a baby and
she'LL be tired" (SL12).
"You actually look back and wonder how COULD you ever have been that
age and been interested in that " (AW12).
"'Cos she used to read in school here 'cos she WOULDN'T, she COULD get
given out to in her school" (SL12).

The progressive represents the speaker's point of view as imperfective, from
inside an event, which therefore includes reference to both event time and
utterance time. It means that the speaker is affected in some way by the activity
or event described and describes some aspect of internal experience (Gee, 1986).
Events have temporal contours and progressives focus on the internal contours of
events. The semantic meaning is one of temporary duration but the discourse
meaning is something like instability.[23] It is used in describing situations that are
seen as episodic, hence less stable or constant, as somehow lacking in the
intrinsic permanence of the simple tenses.   Whereas simple forms encode
certainty and permanence, the progressive (-*ing* form) involves uncertainty and
change.
    It is very interesting that there are so few examples of progressives in these
narratives as the progressive is the first of Brown's (1973) 14 grammatical
morphemes to be acquired.   This further supports a discourse motivated
analysis.[24] If the children in this study are not using it very much, then they are
not using it quite deliberately. It has been well documented that nonuse of a form
does not have to suggest any incompetence in relation to that form.   The
distribution found makes sense in a narrative context as the progressive is
typically used to effect some sort of interchange with an interlocutor and the few
instances in this corpus did have the quality of being somehow more directed at
me and more requiring of some sort of response than most of the rest of the
narrative sequences. It can work to draw in the interlocutor in order to complete
the transaction in some way. It sets up an open text in the same way the use of
the simple present works to close off the text. Use of the progressive like this can
be seen as a bid to negotiate what is being spoken about, for example, "You
COULD be going to get something" (EF5, protesting at class rule that says
everyone must stay seated, she had been given out to for getting up without
permission).   This could be read almost as a challenge rather than as a
straightforward description of an event. If the progressive relates to instability,
here it relates to this child's knowledge that her version is likely to be overridden.
If the simple present relates events that are highly regular and recurrent, the
progressive on the other hand is used to negotiate events, to change things, and

---

23"The judgement of temporariness is less about duration and more a modal statement about the
probability of a given state continuing" (Goldsmith & Woisetschaeger, 1982, p. 83).
24 Frawley (1997) talked about the metafunctions of tense and aspect where the contrast between
simple present and present progressive is connected to speaker stance: "The former implies that the
information is fixed and decontextualized, the latter indicates that the information is mutable and
contextualized" (p. 202).

to show how things could or should be otherwise. The element of instability is the speaker emphasising the "negotiatory, up-for-grabs status of the information" (Frawley, 1997) being conveyed.

> "I CAN be real annoying sometimes, I'D say" (RL12)
> "We'LL be getting a little Tibetan terrier" (EF5).
> "I MIGHT be getting drums for myself" (PF12.
> "I like swimming and we'LL be going there in a few weeks in school" (SC8).
> "I'm not afraid to try new things but I WOULDN'T go trying netball" (PF12).
> "We'D be swimming around the place" (EF5).
> "My sister MIGHTN'T be going to High school next year" (SC8).
> "She'D be teaching like the toddlers and us at the same time but it's better now" (RL12).

This reminds us of one of the reasons for targeting the modal auxiliaries in the first place, namely their privileged status as "negotiatory forms of speech *par excellence*" (Gerhardt, 1988, p. 357).

VERBS: ACTING OUT OR ACTED ON?

The first reason for exploring the verbs that co-occur with the modal auxiliaries is that, as the modals are communicatively deficient, they always occur with a verb in its base form.

> *You SHOULD always that way.
> *I CAN never.
> *He WILL quickly.

Only when the verb is implied, that is, understood to be deleted or elided for conversational purposes or for brevity, does a modal occur on its own.

> I WILL [do it later].
> Yes, you CAN [go].
> No, I WON'T [ruin it].

Verbs have a special place in language[25] and in many ways it is the verb that is at the core or the heart of any utterance. It is not a good idea to attempt an interpretation of a modal without also taking into account the verb in the utterance. Verbs are relational terms *par excellence* in that they link the noun phrase arguments that refer and they indicate when (tense) and how (aspect) an action has been carried out. The situation for acquisition is complicated by the fact that the actions verbs pick out are transitory. Once completed they are no longer present for contemplation or analysis, unlike object categories or nouns.

---

[25] See, for instance, Clark (1996) and Tomasello (1992).

Actions must be grasped as they occur, which is one of the reasons why nouns, as opposed to verbs, are usually the first few words to be acquired by the child.[26] There are three relevant aspects relating to the verbs used with the modal auxiliaries, including: the transitivity of the verb used; the semantic roles the child assigns himself or herself in relation to the verb; and the level of agency that can be assigned to the range of verbs used.

Verbs and Transitivity

First, the different patterns of transitivity in the children's narratives that are "the prime means of expressing our internal and external experiences which is part of the ideational function of language" (Wales, 1989, p. 466). As a system, transitivity is thought to be very close to "real life."[27] It tells us who did what and to whom and it is very important in constructing and describing the narrator's views of the world.[28] By making transitivity choices, the narrator assigns different roles to the participants and characters in the story and creates in each case a distinctive worldview. High-transitivity markings[29] tend to be common in first-person narratives, but these are not just stylistic or rhetorical devices, they are part of the narrator's representation of the characters. For example, as victim of circumstance or as someone actively in control.[30] Transitivity in discourse is part of the construction of agency (Duranti, 1997, p. 336).

Briefly, a transitive verb can take a direct object (*he saw the dog*) whereas an intransitive verb does not take an object (**he went a car*). Lots of verbs have both a transitive and an intransitive use (*we walked for at least a mile* and *we walked*). To use verbs transitively implies some carry over or extension from one participant to another.[31] Intransitive usage means no extension to another participant, the verbal processes are presented as self-sufficient (Pope, 1995, p. 34). The subject of transitive verbs is usually the agent that means that acts that affect another's state will generally be encoded by transitive verbs (*she*

---

[26] This is the case for English and for many other languages (see Gentner, 1982), but there may be cross-linguistic differences (e.g., Choi & Gopnik, 1993, reported a verb spurt in Korean prior to a noun spurt).

[27] See Knowles and Malmkjaer (1996, p. 78ff) for a good discussion of the issues involved. Also Slobin (1985) who proposed transitivity as one of the basic categories underlying children's early grammatical constructions.

[28] Halliday's (1973, 1994) work is very useful here also.

[29] In Bamberg's (1997b) scheme of transitivity (with the animate actor in the subject position): my brother bit me = high; my sister moved away = medium; my sister lives far away = low. When coding the modal utterances in this study for transitivity, I just wanted to see whether the sense of agency conveyed in a particular unit was high or low, so I did not use any of the more elaborate classification systems available, for example, Hopper and Thompson's (1980) 10 parameter coding system for transitivity.

[30] Romance novels and romantic scenes in fiction are a perfect ground for transitivity analyses and have been widely discussed in the context of feminist stylistics, for example, Mills (1995).

[31] From Hopper and Thompson's (1980) system combining language typology with discourse analysis.

kissed the baby). On the other hand, for instance, inalienable actions tend to be encoded with intransitive verbs (*she dances*).

This section explores whether the children tend to use transitive or intransitive verbs with the modal auxiliaries. The transitivity of a given modal auxiliary and its accompanying verb was classified according to the number of participants in the events represented linguistically. A narrator may choose to focus on one of several participants or include them all, or to represent an event from the perspective of one participant rather than another and in this way it is clear that when a speaker chooses a verb she or he implicitly chooses to represent the event from a particular point of view.[32]

The main distinction is between transitive and intransitive verbs. Choice of a transitive verb allows presentation of an event from the point of view of the agent. An intransitive verb allows several options depending on the verb: An event can be presented from the point of view of an agent that is simultaneously the object affected as in *Kate laughed*; the agent of the action with no affected object as in *Kate was eating*, or from the point of view or perspective of the object and the action affecting it as in *the door opened.*[33] Some verbs offer both options, some only one, so the options for conveying different perspectives on a scene will depend on the particular language spoken. The picture for all the age groups in this study is very similar. The majority of the verbs used with the modal auxiliaries are used transitively (almost 63%) and most of those with their direct object. Also the category of intransitive verbs appearing most frequently was from the vantage point of the agent as the object affected by the action of the verb.

A transitive event involves a wilful (and therefore usually human) actor whose actions have (either permanent or temporary) consequences for a patient (i.e., the entity undergoing the action or movement) or for a state of affairs. But even if the children in this study are mainly using transitive verbs, this does not mean that the child himself or herself is always the actor or agent involved. Nor is the child necessarily even involved, that is, as a participant, in the story at all. But just the fact of mentioning someone else and what she or he did, by introducing a new character, the child is doing more than just passing on information. It is all part of the process whereby personae for themselves, and for the people and events connected with them, are constructed. But if the children themselves are not always the actor or the protagonist in their stories, then who is?

The grammatical person used with intransitive verbs is fairly consistent across age groups but the more interesting question is which grammatical person is used in conjunction with the transitive verbs, that is, who is the subject or agent when the children are using these agentive type verb constructions? There is an increase in first person-transitive statements with age, where a relatively small

---

[32] There is a huge body of research in this area starting from people like Joos (1964, p. 140): "the event is not mentioned for its own sake but for the sake of its consequences" up to, for example, Clark (1990) on verbs that encode locative relations that help mark speaker perspective.

[33] "It is not the form-based transitivity *per se* which is relevant to passivization but rather the semantic quality of affectedness of the patient" Fox (1994, p. 6 citing Bolinger, 1975).

number (just over 11%) of the 5-year-olds' transitive statements are actually in the first person. The 5-year-olds refer most to the actions of a third person using transitive verbs, which is reflected also in the large number of their modal statements from which they are absent altogether as either actor, recipient, or experiencer. Basically, a lot of the time the youngest children are talking about other people. The 8- and 12-year-old children on the other hand make most reference to first person actions and events and also to generic or "everyman" scenarios, what one would or could do in certain situations, what options or courses of action are available and so forth.

The grammatical system of transitivity sets up two types of situation. First, it helps to constitute or identify the social agent in the narrative, those whose actions are noteworthy or make a difference of some kind. Secondly, as it deals in causal agents, it works to assign responsibility for actions. The consequences of the act, and the intentions of the actor even, are singled out by the narrator via the choice of verb. In other words, use of the transitivity system can help to establish a moral world within the narrative.[34]

Verbs and Semantic Role

The narrator's transitivity choices construct the different roles she or he wishes to assign to the participants and characters in the story. This also reveals something of the way the narrator views her or his own position in the world and her or his relation to others, that is, to the other characters in the narrative. I have pointed out the preponderance of transitive verbs used, which means the children are primarily making reference to actions undertaken or carried out by wilful agents. If we also look at the semantic case relation between the surface subject of the modal utterance and the verb of the utterance, this is reflected in the 91% of cases in which the subject is the actor or experiencer of the main verb.

The dominant case role of the subject in these narratives is that of actor or agent. The subject of the verb is primarily a volitional causal being. But the surface subject of the child's modal utterances is not necessarily himself or herself. The situation is entirely different if we this time look at the child's own semantic role within each modalized utterance. In fact the child is actually absent (as the subject of the verb but not totally obviously) in almost 36% of all their modal utterances, which means that over a third of the modal auxiliaries used by the children in the context of autobiographical discourse are used to make statements about, or to otherwise comment on, events and people other than themselves.

This echoes some of the surprize earlier when it was revealed that only one third of the targeted utterances were actually situated in the past tense. In fact, if

---

[34] Duranti (1994, 1997, pp. 195-197) had a very interesting discussion of the construction of ethical and political positions via these forms in the ritual speech of leaders in a Samoan village. He discussed the correlation between grammatical forms and political stature in a community as evidenced in more powerful members using a type of discourse higher on the transitivity scale than the discourse of less powerful members.

we look at the semantic role of the child in her or his own discourse, together with the temporal distribution, an interesting pattern emerges whereby the child is absent from many of their stories that are situated in the past and in the present moment and is, relatively speaking, more present or more of a presence in their future projective statements. The child is an agent or actor more often when she or he is referring to future-time events than when she or he is telling stories and events from the past. This is the case for all age groups but is much more prevalent in the 12-year-old children's narratives. The meaning of this cannot be pinned down obviously but maybe it centers around a perceived lack of control experienced in the past when the child was younger and the feeling that it is possible to exert control over one's future.

We can track how the child assigns semantic roles to himself or herself in the modal utterances used in autobiographical stories (where, it is my argument, it is the modalized utterances in this context that are most indicative of point of view and subjectivity). This can reveal the degree to which, and the contexts in which, the child portrays himself or herself as an agent in control of events, relationships, and other areas in their lives. Is the child placing himself or herself in the position of agent (who acts on entities) or experiencer (as an entity acted upon by an agent) or in the place of recipient (representing the endpoint of action or experience)?

Looking more closely at the patterns across ages, as already mentioned the most striking finding is that overall almost 36% of the modal utterances do not feature the child directly at all. The highest figure in this regard is for the five year old children (a massive 44%), which is not that surprising given their tendency to talk more about family, extended family and possessions than they do about themselves[35] and also their tendency to give often lengthy accounts of what appear to be, at least on initial analysis, fairly unconnected and not very typically autobiographical events. The figures for the older children are also very high but show a small decline between the ages of 8 and 12 (35% and 32% respectively). This decrease also suggests a developmental dimension whereby the older children focus more on events and stories in which they directly participated in some fashion and also, as we see, show an increased interest in explaining and exploring their own motivations, emotions and thoughts.

Overall, the child is cast as agentive subject, as a causal agent who volitionally carries out particular activities, in only 20% of all modal utterances. Interestingly this time it is the 5-year-olds who cast themselves most often as agent or actor (26%). Again this reflects the youngest children's preoccupations, that is, with action stories, with asserting what they can do or are able to do, with recounting what they did at a party and so on. But it may also be a function of their reliance, in the main, on a very straightforward SVO word order, a strategy that tends to

---

[35] In the conclusion I discuss how all these features cohere on the wider level of the construction and presentation of self and relate this to the systems of possession (self-as-owner), action (self-as-character) and description (self-as-narrator) and the different preoccupations of each age group. Also this finding contradicts Engels (1995) who said that as children get older, their personal stories are in fact more likely to include material on other people reflecting an increased interest in the social world.

make the 5-year–olds' narratives sound more like a list of unconnected, unmotivated events and scenarios than a motivated organised whole. This global quality is much more evident in the older children's narratives, especially for the 12-year-olds, and is largely due to their positioning themselves as experiencer (i.e., in relation to mental experiences) almost 35% of the time. Overall the 12-year-old children in particular are much more introspective. The 5-year-olds only refer to themselves as experiencer in approximately 19% of their modalized utterances. The 8-year-olds as a group position themselves most frequently as either the patient or the recipient of the action of the verb (almost 21% of the time compared to 11% for the 5-year-olds and 15% for the oldest age group). That is, frequently this group of 8-year-olds present themselves as being on the receiving end of the actions of others and usually also in relation to actions or events they find somewhat less than desirable. Overall, the middle age group comes across as being the most concerned with asserting their rights in certain situations, especially situations involving ownership of toys and so on and also what they are, or are not, permitted to do, which often then translates to them being at the receiving end of a prohibition. A frequent complaint is that "it's not fair," that is, the actions taken toward them, of which they are the unwilling recipient.

Verb Classification

Despite the fact that the child is not always, and indeed not even frequently, casting himself or herself in these personal narratives as actor or agent, this does not mean that there is necessarily a complete lack of agency or control implied. The last area to look at is the verbs used with the modal auxiliaries in terms of a classification system that categorizes them hierarchically according to levels of activity, and hence according to levels of agency, involved. Verbs in English can be divided into categories depending on the kind of activity to which they refer. In addition the participants involved can be identified in ways that indicate the process and whether they are performing it or having it done to them.

The most basic distinction is between dynamic and stative verbs and involves looking at how the difference between events and states is linguistically catered for or signaled. This distinction highlights the dynamic nature of events and shows that events are typically highly transitive situations in which an actor performs an action that has some effect on an object. But of course not all utterances in a narrative refer to events. We would expect a lot of talk about feeling states and thoughts in the context of autobiographical narratives. In particular, the 12-year-olds are much less preoccupied with events and actions than the other two age groups, in which only 45% of the verbs used are classed as dynamic compared to 65% for the 8-year-olds and over 75% for the 5-year-olds.

Breaking this distinction down further, even references to states show a bias toward the 12-year-olds being much more interested in talking about internal states (almost 31% of the verbs used make reference to some internal state or feeling) compared to the tiny fraction of verbs used in this manner by the youngest group (5%). The 8-year-olds fall in between at almost 19%. This initial classification (based on, for instance, Quirk, Greenbaum, Leech and Svartvik's original 1972 classification of verbs) between dynamic (58%)[36] and stative (38%) needs to be fleshed out. To do this I made use of Schlesinger's (1995) taxonomy of verbs.[37] There are 11 categories in all:

1)	activity-specific	(*write, throw, slice*)
2)	activity-diffuse	(*abandon, work, learn*)
3)	momentary	(*jump, kick, knock*)
4)	transitional, intentional	(*arrive, stopover, leave*)
5)	transitional, non-intentional	(*die, fall, lose*)
6)	process	(*deteriorate, mature, grow*)
7)	stance	(*lie, sit, stand*)
8)	mental-stimulus	(*impress, please, surprise*)
9)	mental-experiencer	(*think, hear, suppose*)
10)	relational verbs	(*depend on, deserve, need*)
11)	bodily sensation	(*feel, hurt, itch* in their intransitive use)

Basically this model starts from the dichotomous distinction between static and dynamic but then subcategorizes the verbs according to the levels of activity involved within each separate category. Classes of verb coming at the top of the list are those in which the subject of these verbs may be said to engage in an activity and the lower down you move in the list, the less activity can be ascribed to the subject. Verbs in the lower-activity classes are State verbs and their subjects will therefore be attributees. High-activity verbs will usually appear in event predicates, and their subjects will be agents. So verbs do not just differ in relation to the level of activity of the subject but also with respect to the degree of agency of the subject. Schlesinger's (1995, pp. 192-193) verb hierarchy therefore reflects a gradient of agency.

The resulting distribution when the children's verbs were classified according to this scheme is interesting. Overall, activity verbs and mental verbs are best represented, but notice the reverse patterns across age groups. The 12-year-olds use mostly mental experiencer verbs followed by verbs referring to specific activities. This trend is exactly reversed for the 5-year-olds who are responsible

---

[36] These two figures correspond to the percentage of all the verbs used in conjunction with the modal auxiliaries for all age groups together.

[37] Another interesting model is Semin and Fiedler's (1992) Linguistic Category Model (LCM), which is a taxonomic model of interpersonal verbs. They look at the causality implicit in interpersonal verbs and ask whether interpersonal verbs might also mark other features of interpersonal relationships in a systematic way, for example, what and how interactants feel toward each other, how they relate to each other, what the inferred duration of an event or state is and so on. Certain features of social interaction are said to be preserved in interpersonal verbs. See Edwards and Potter (1992, pp. 97-98) for problems with this account.

for the majority of the specific activity verbs. And although the next most frequent category of verbs they use is also that of mental experiencer, this accounts for only a very small percentage of the range of verbs they use. The 8-year-olds are somewhere between the two positions, a familiar location by now as we have seen for many of the forms and functions explored. They seem to use both categories of verbs equally, and we can perhaps presume that they are on the way to a usage more like their older counterparts, that is, that they are tending toward being more focused on explaining motives, ascribing thoughts and feelings and states of mind both to themselves and to others in the course of their narratives.

We can be more discriminating in relation to the level of agency associated with each verbal element. Schlesinger[38] proposed a further classification of the verb categories whereby each category of verb is assigned to one of five groups, according to the agentive features that can be associated with each type of verb. The three features involved are cause, control and change. In particular, control, as the prototypical property of agentivity, is relevant to this discussion.

Take an example, *the woman drank her coffee.* In this utterance, the subject is an entity in motion (i.e., there is an element of change), who causes the activity, and who also controls it. Change is when motion or some sort of change of state is involved. The feature of cause refers to any source of an activity, event or situation, when an entity makes something happen.[39] And once an event has been caused, then it is possible to be in control of it, to steer the event in different directions, to stop it and so on. Usually when talking about people, cause and control typically co-occur, but conceptually they differ. Control implies volition and intention (or at least purposefulness, for instance in the case of a computer) whereas these are not necessary in order to be able to assign cause to an entity. Neither is it necessary for there to be awareness for there to be cause. So inanimate things and animate entities other than humans can have cause but not control. Describing each category of verb according to the presence or absence of each of the set of features of cause, control and change, Schlesinger (1995) came up with five groups of verb type. In Group I, the subjects have all 3 agentive features (1, 2, 3, 6); in Group II, the subjects have only cause and control (4, 5); Subjects in Group III have only change (7, 8); Group IV subjects have only control (9); and finally in Group V the subjects have no agentive feature at all (10).

If we apply this to the verbs these children used and try to describe the characteristic features of the classes of verbs we get quite definite patterns. The two most important groups for all ages are Group I and Group IV, but these have an inverse relationship with age. There is a steady decrease in the amount of Group I verbs[40] from the ages of 5 to 12 (falling from 65% to just over 26%) and

---

[38] See Schlesinger (1995, p. 30ff) for a full discussion of this system.
[39] Cause can be assigned to subjects of transitive or intransitive verbs: *she kicked the ball/* or *she jumped up.*
[49] Made up of momentary, activity (specific and diffuse) and transitional (intentional) verbs.

the exact opposite pattern for Group IV verbs[41] where from just over 13% for the 5-year-olds, the figure rises to over half of all the verbs used (53%) for the 12-year-olds. The two groups, however, both converge on the notion of control. It is important finally to note, taking into account the fact that the subject of the verb, as we already saw, is not necessarily the speaker and therefore not necessarily the source of control or change, this situation is also reflected in the frequency with which the subject of the Group I and Group IV verbs is actually the child himself or herself. For the activity verbs of Group I, the 5-year-olds cast themselves mainly as actor or agent. In relation to mental experiencer verbs, this time it is the two older groups who see themselves in this role.

PRONOUNS: SPEAKER OR SPOKEN ABOUT?

There is no getting away from the passionate attachment to self, that I-beam set down in the dead center of the world and holding the whole rickety edifice in place. Banville (1993, p. 26)

It takes years of labour to put together an 'I'. When that's done it's also too late. Keizer (1996, p. 239)

This section focuses on how the children refer to themselves and position themselves via the device of the personal pronouns in their autobiographical narratives. Pronouns are shifters, referring not to any object or entity but more properly to a highly specific moment.[42] Pronouns convert language into discourse, into specific concrete acts of giving voice. An exploration of the children's personal indexing is no simple counting exercise given that the I of "*I have a brother,*" "*I can never remember names,*" and "*I was born in 1991*" shifts according to what elements of identity the speaker is hoping to index (or establish) on this instance of use.[43] Overall, and unsurprisingly, the first-person singular pronoun is the most popular (over 54% of all utterances), especially in the narratives of the 8- and 12-year-olds. Third-person pronominal forms are the next most frequent, particularly in the discourse of the 5-year-olds (35%).

A more detailed breakdown revealed with whom the narrator is empathizing, whose point of view the pronouns help to plot. Two particular patterns of usage of the pronominal forms were striking in these narratives. Namely, discursively motivated shifts of pronoun, and cases of explicit positioning via pronominal choice.

---

[41] Consisting only of mental (experiencer) verbs.
[42] See Benveniste (1971) on pronouns and intersubjective communication.
[43] The suggestion is not however to use the pronouns to simply read subjectivity off language. That "would be little more than a mincing step into the dead-end of radical Whorfianism" (Frawley, 1997, p. 202).

Pronoun Shifts

First, I noticed how the children frequently made "expressive shifts"[44] by changing or switching pronouns midcourse and this almost always in the direction of increased genericity, starting from first-person position, I or inclusive we and then switching to impersonal you or neutral it. This tended to happen either midutterance or in the course of a stanza on a particular topic to accomplish a variety of ends, including to achieve maximum distance from one's statements, in the course of appealing for support from external sources or in order to provide a stamp of authority and also when looking for empathy via identification. Take this extended passage:

"I think in May I'm going to Disneyland but I MIGHT go hostelling for my birthday and ponyriding 'cos it's not really too far from the hostel but I CAN'T really bring all my friends 'cos we don't have a really big car but I MIGHT bring 3 of mine, my best friends, but I think my, it WOULD be better if some of them sit on their laps, my brother's laps and my cousin's laps and I WOULD sit in the middle and the others but em, I think, some of them WOULD have to sit down on the bottom of the car, yeah, that's what we SHOULD do, that's what we had to do, what Mommy said we SHOULD do at my party last time, even Katy's little sister" (JW5).

In the course of this stanza, the child switches from I to it to we until finally Mommy, a nominal, has the last word. Initially the child is assuming total responsibility for her plans and only repairing *I think* to *it WOULD be better* to provide independent rationale for why she should have the best position in the car. Then she resorts to an appeal to authority and to citing a precedent in that this was what her mother had recommended before.

However even her initial active position is mitigated somewhat in that she uses I with CAN'T to indicate that it is not her own choice. Then she shifts, repairing *I think* to the more neutral it with WOULD as a hypothetical situation and finally makes a last pronouncement on the matter by shifting to a nominal, Mommy, with the form SHOULD as the final arbiter whose previous recommendations fit here with what this child wants to happen.

Another child makes the switch from we to neutral it in order to make an appeal for independent support for what she reckons is unfair:

"We had good fun in Juniors 'cos there's a cooker in juniors but we don't have it, we only have a box of toys and they don't, they have a library as well but they don't have a box of toys because then it WOULD be really fair, WOULDN'T it not, if they had a box of toys as well as a cooker and a library but we have a library as well and it's great fun" (CMcG5).

---

[44] See Harré and Mühlhaüsler (1990, p. 148) for a very comprehensive study of the personal pronouns.

According to Stubbs (1996, p. 227) when the polarity of the modal used in a tag is different, that is, reversed, to the polarity of the main clause it is because it is expressing the speaker's own beliefs (as opposed to a situation where the tag modal has the same polarity as the main clause which refers to a proposition whose source is the addressee). She is using it with WOULD as an appeal for confirmation, an independent source of authority, to support her own opinion.

The use of generic you is also often highly egocentric. "The deeper we go into impersonal you the more personal it seems" (Bolinger, 1979, p. 205). Sometimes the generalizations one makes are of such a low order that they are really a reiteration of personal experiences or of personal habitual behavior.[45] In this example, by not saying "*I could have been going to get something*" or "*I was going to get something*" the child is trying to turn this incident into a general premise.

> "My teacher is not my favourite 'cos she is, sometimes she does get very cross when like you be bold and you're out of line. Once I got lines 'cos I was out of my seat at breaktime, that's a silly rule, you're not allowed out of your seat at breaktime, you COULD be going to get something" (EF5).

When used at very subjective moments like this, the impersonal pronoun you is actually very personal, like using WOULD as we saw in relation to marking personal emotions or desires when you also want to create distance. Impersonal pronouns, rather than simply being objective, help speakers to conceal subjectivity. They function to reduce the responsibility and individuality of the speaker. She continues the saga and her use of the possessive pronoun my with WOULD here is also interesting: "My favourite WOULD be Miss French and Miss Barber, the head, because they don't really get very cross with people, they're more the nice ones" (EF5). Why not "*my favourite is*" or "*I like*"? This construction provides more distance in some ways and therefore registers only as an implicit complaint but also makes the statement a highly personal one, as in by naming hypothetical favorites she is indicating displeasure with own her teacher in contrast.

Later she wants to justify having a boy for a friend (in contrast with the typical scenario where boys play with boys and girls with girls) so again she uses the impersonal or nonreferential it that confers some external authority on the matter in support of her argument. In other words, she tries to present her opinion as a general norm.

> "I'm going to Speech and drama class today and Simon's coming back after to my house, he's my friend except he's a boy, he's a bit rough,
> [pause]
> it isn't nice to just like girls or just like boys, it WOULDN'T be fair" (EF5).

---

[45] See Wales (1996) for a very interesting discussion of the personal pronouns in present day English.

Another area in which the children frequently want to put some distance between themselves and their utterances is when they are talking about their wishes or desires. It is interesting that in many of the cases where the children have tried to create distance via genericity, that is, by switching pronouns midstream, from first-person I to generic you, they also often use WOULD or its contracted form 'D in the utterance.

> "I'D like to be a dentist, not like my dad, I'D like a dentist or a doctor 'cos you'D get loads of money, no, I don't want to be a dentist cos you'D have to pick little pieces out of people's teeth, sounds horrible" (MS8).

First his own desire or wishes, then he switches to generic you to give reasons for his choice.[46]

Using a similar distancing procedure:

> "I'D like to make children enjoy doing stuff, like, I'D like to do something with children where, in, like, you'D help the children, like, lots of children are into watching theatres and things and that's what I'D like to do" (AC8).

The speaker suddenly becomes a bit self-conscious that it might sound silly or too personal so she shifts to generic you in order to introduce or sound an impersonal note. This interpretation of slight hesitancy or modesty is supported by her use of the discourse marker like.

Sometimes, particularly when talking about personal traits or characteristics, the children seem to feel that to be too personal is to be egotistical, so here, out of modesty, the speaker is using the device of "some people" to say what he thinks without seeming to boast. This device could be said to actually highlight the subjectivity or agency involved despite the surface function of modesty.

> "Some people WOULD think I'm nice, like, and that I'm grand, other people WOULD probably think that I'm a bit arrogant" (SM12).

Also, for example,

> "Well, I'm in this drama class and the teacher, well did you ever hear of the independent workshop? Well it WOULD be the head em drama class of the country" (JOR8).

He tries to present this aside as an objective opinion but his use of WOULD rather than for example, it is, renders it more than likely his own subjective opinion.

---

[46] Müller (1996) and Rizzuto (1993) have very good discussions of pronouns and subjectivity, especially Rizzuto on how pronouns refer to "the exquisite particularity" of our affective experiences and how without them, the "entire range of human resonance would remain in obscure undiffrentiation" (p. 541).

Frequently impersonal constructions are used to play down the speaker's anxieties. Here it is used to set up fact rather than opinion so he's right to be scared. Note the switch from I to you.

"At one stage, in '95, late '95, I was actually a bit scared of my snake because when you went to pick it up, it used to hiss sometimes and if you've ever been hissed at by a snake, it's a really high pitched hiss and it CAN be really nerve-racking, but now I'm well over it" (AK12).

The next speaker is presenting his experience as a typical scenario, as what is bound to happen to anyone under similar circumstances, so he lapses into the generic form, "*like, you'D miss them*",

"I'm going to Gonzaga next year, but like, 8 years with these people, you get used to it, like, you'D miss them, but it doesn't mean I'm just going to go away from them, I know where they all live, I have their phone numbers so we CAN hang around normally" (PF12),

and then he hastily sets about repairing the impression left and attempts a more active agentive presentation of himself, although the intended impression of taking control is considerably diminished by his use of such a circumlocutious doubly negativized construction: "But I'm not saying I WON'T get new friends" (PF12).

Similarly, this child's switch to it[47] sounds like trying to convince herself, "*it'll be fine*" rather than "*I'll be fine*."

"I'm worried about next year and I don't want to go at all, I want to stay in this school, like, I'm in 6th class now and I'm at the top and then I have to go right down to the bottom again and work up,
but I think it'LL be fine" (HG12).

Another similar function of an impersonal construction here is to take some distance from the implied complaint, one could get tired but not her.

"I have something on nearly every day except for Fridays, that's my only free day after school, em em em,
I like doing it all except sometimes you CAN get a bit tired and you kinda feel you don't want to go, but I don't know, you kinda get used to it, then em em em" (SL12).

---

[47] Berman and Slobin (1994, p. 173) on the use of expletive (or dummy) "'it' with modal and affective predicates for evaluative commentary only by older children, younger ones use 'it' as a pronominal either deictically or as a neuter-gender pronoun, also as an impersonal or nonreferential pronoun in copula constructions (*it was night-time, it wasn't as quiet here*)".

Pronoun Positioning: Agent or Victim?

The second point is that explicit positioning of the self as agent or victim is achieved via the use of the pronominal system. The pronouns allow a privileging of subject or agent positions that can be traced in the course of a child's narratives. The situation is not so neat of course, that a child is either agent or subject. Subject positions need not be automatically privileged, but we can often identify the dominant subject-agent position apparently preferred by the speaker and that provides the flavour or tone of the autobiography.[48]   Seemingly unimportant grammatical distinctions often conceal functionally quite distinct positions, for example, as Bamberg (1994) pointed out positioning oneself as the subject of mere reporting is quite different to positioning oneself as a character in a drama.

Overall the child is the experiencer (45%) of their modal utterances more often than the agent (36%). Except in the case of the 5-year-old group who cast themselves as agent when they use the first person pronoun over half the time (55%) compared to less than one third of the time for the other two groups. Interestingly the 5-year-old group do not talk about themselves as a patient at all, that is, as an entity acted on or affected.

The 12-year-olds make very little use of the recipient category preferring instead to talk about themselves in terms primarily of mental experiences, for example, emotions, feelings and thoughts. Another parallel trend pertains to the use of third-person generic forms that primarily refer to specific activities in the discourse of the 5- and 8-year-old groups, whereas the 12-year-olds once more seem to concentrate on mental experience verbs.

This child's narratives are highly agentive, lots of I, and I as agent. She frequently refers to herself as asking questions and requesting permission but in an assertive way, often using the personal active past.

> "I got very interested in it so I asked my dad COULD I go" (karate)
> "I asked COULD I bring in that so I brought my flower dress in" (for a school play)
> "I'm going to read it all out to myself and then see what I CAN do on my project" (SM8).

Compare that with the tone of the following narratives in which the lack of agency is equally obvious. Most I's are used with negative modal auxiliaries or occur in reported speech in which he is the subject of, and/or at the receiving end of, a negative modal.

> "But the others said 'no, you CAN'T use it' 'cos it's not yours"
> "Mum said the computer is just for the others and I CAN'T really play with the others" (StJS8).

---

[48] See for instance Gee (1991, p. 31) on grammatical subjects as "psychological launching off" points: "the psychological subject structure of a narrative tells us something about the narrator's stance and how she changes it across the narrative. It makes interpretative demands and constrains how these demands are to be met".

or his options are limited and depend on others:

> "Lego was the only thing I COULD get"
> "I CAN have one more song which James didn't really want" (StJS8),

or he is subject to the will of others:

> "Andrew WOULDN'T hold on, I was the one who had to".
> "I have one friend that I kinda miss, he lives far away from me so I CAN'T
> really visit him" (StJS8).

Another transcript provides some very good examples of the speaker positioned as subject rather than as agent. Note his use of me rather than I.

> "Except for one sleepover I've always been in the house, except for once it
> was in my small sister's friend's house 'cos my mum and dad were going out
> and I WOULDN'T have them here, there was no-one to mind me, there
> WOULD be noone to mind me so I had to go over there. Oh, you know, I
> never have a nice time in the world, never, I never get one, even at Christmas
> I didn't get a right toy, at Easter I didn't get my, at the sleepover, and when
> they were there, you see, at nighttime they were eating Easter eggs and I
> didn't have any but then at the end I did and they gave me bits at the
> sleepover, when they were eating them, only little bits though, they COULD
> have given me big bites, I love Easter eggs" (CM5).

In this passage, he never represents himself as actor or agent, it is either me as done to, or hard done by, or I as passive victim of circumstance or blaming others for being inconsiderate. This is a consistent tone throughout his narratives:

> "When I was in my Mum's belly you know, I didn't get anything there"
> "At Christmas they didn't get everything right, I didn't have a good time
> there, at that either, I never have a good time"
> "My Dad always gets cross and real mad, sometimes at me too, we went to a
> match once, I don't know who won or anything, I didn't have a flag" (CM5).

As part of this positioning function there can be an explicit positioning via identification with, for example, parents by using we to distinguish oneself from younger siblings and also identification and comparison between the self now and a younger earlier self. This child is alternately positioning herself with younger siblings:

> "I have a baby brother and you know what he CAN say? He's a bit like me,
> he has blonde hair and blue eyes but my Mum and Dad don't"
> then "my baby brother loves my Daddy, my favourite is Mummy" (LC5),

and then trying to distance herself, to align herself complicitously with the adults:

"When I was 5 my Mummy and Daddy gave me a clown puppet and I still have it but Max MIGHT tangle up the strings so we put it up high so he CAN'T reach it" (LC5).

Some confusion enters here however: "But I CAN'T either" (LC5).

Also this child is aligning himself with his parents to make it look like he had a say but in fact makes a rather contradictory statement: "We decided we MIGHT come back tomorrow so we did" (NR5, about holidays).

The next example shows the child being very equivocal, she starts by asserting her seniority than by switching to the generic you form, she fails to carry it through. She ends up reversing her stance and presenting herself as victim.

"I'm the oldest which is good sometimes and bad sometimes, it's good when you CAN get your own way and you CAN tell them what to do and bad when the others go,
you know, my brother Sarah and Stuart, they always pick on me" (KM12).

There are interesting examples of identification and comparison with younger self (e.g., AK8 and AW12 although in very different ways). In this next case the switch from I to you is supposed to represent what he is talking about as a general problem, something everyone experiences not just him. Generic you here makes this an everyman type scenario, what Gerhardt and Savasir (1986, p. 525) called the "I-just-like-anyone".

"How COULD you ever have been that age, you never realise that you WOULD like that and that next year you'LL be looking back" (AW12).
"I forget everything 'cos when you're a baby you don't, you forget ever-, you don't know anything when you're older, that's a problem, 'cos you have to tell somebody" (DG5).[49]

And then compare this reflective interpretative attitude to the confused stance taken when recounting a received story. Here the child is obviously telling a family folklore story rather than something he remembers himself, hence the pronominal confusion (we to you, also the repair of WOULD to COULD), that is, a story told to him about him.

"You see, my-, there was this barrier trying to keep me from getting down the stairs and I kept on climbing over it and my mum put it up higher and I kept on crawling under it, and we WOULD hear all the bumps com-, eh, when I was going down the stairs you COULD hear me falling, falling over, I COULD have died, and em" (AK8).

---

[49] An interesting unsolicited attempt to account for what he understands by autobiography and memory.

The situation broken down by age is very similar with the main difference being that the incidence of first-person future tense increases with age (from 40% for the 5-year-olds to almost 52% at age 12). Present tense is very consistent and the 12-year-olds have the least past-tense first-person modal utterances (19% compared to the 5-year-olds' 32%). The only other anomaly is that the youngest children tend to make generic type statements in the present tense (usually therefore related to notions of ability) compared to a much more even distribution across all tenses for generic utterances by the other two age groups.

The main trend is for first person, I or we, modal utterances to refer to some future state, that is, talk specifically about the self, about themselves, is set mainly in the future. On the other hand when talking about third parties, the children tend to be referring to specific events set in the past. Again we see how important the future is in children's talk about themselves.

Although even the 5-year-olds sometimes compare their present and younger selves, the younger children are not always at ease in their use of the pronominal system in this way and certainly are not as skilled in its manipulation as the older children. In this passage, for instance, there is constant tension between using the generic you and we:

> "We hafta, the juniors don't like being boy/girl, boy/girl 'cept you hafta, in
> junior infants you have to, we have to
> 'cos they don't like to sit beside girls but you have to do it in Miss McG's
> class
> we sit beside anybody in Miss Ruttle's, you don't have to go boy girl
> and now all the juniors are copying, the boys, what we did last year, the boys
> were on the blackboard side, the girls were on the other side and then it
> WOULD be boy other girl on the end or behind you at the four tables"
> (NE5).

There are also cases of the speaker trying to set up some sort of identification with the researcher, what I have called the "interpersonal you." In this case the child is using it in order to evoke empathy for his position and in an attempt to elicit some reassurance that he is right to be indignant. His switch to you is an appeal for empathy by decentring the narrator in the space of intersubjective understanding:

> "Did you hear me on the radio? It was the Friday before Mother's day, you
> WOULD have heard all about it, did you hear that?
> I definitely said the most embarrassing thing, even, you know Simon Young?
> From the radio? he said, he made a rude remark.
> WOULD you like after being on the radio and suddenly em a man says"
> (JOR8).
> "My favourite site is something called The Reading Room, you CAN tell that,
> I just go on to his Netsearch" (JOR8).

There is also the you of prescription, of habitual scenarios (often with unmarked present tense):

"You CAN write in letters and you COULD say" (DPB8).
"It's got a stone in the middle, you CAN just eat it normally" (JOH8).
"I had fish fingers and you CAN get sausages, you CAN get burgers, and you CAN get chicken bits" (NE5).

And finally, one case of ellipsis that finally takes the subject out of the equation altogether: "CAN'T remember names" (SOH12).

Summary

This analysis has highlighted the importance of tense for our sense of personal identity and continuity of self and how in the main it is the simple present and the future conditional together which constitute these narrators' autobiographical subjectivity: the present tense as used to express the essential constitution of the children's lives and their plans for the future as another very important source of self-identity. In particular the 12-year-olds are very future oriented in their modal utterances. An exploration of the verbs chosen to represent events, each set entailing its own distinctive premises from a particular point of view and degree of agency, cast the 5- and 8-year-old children in the role of determined actors and the 12-year-olds as more reflective beings. There was also the interesting scenario, from an autobiographical point of view, that the child was frequently absent as actor or even experiencer from their modal statements. A lot of the time the 5-year-olds in particular were actually talking about other people, other agents beside themselves. The 8- and 12-year-old children spent more time talking directly about themselves, in the context of trying to explain and motivate actions and thoughts. The point of view constructed or plotted by the pronouns in these narratives was typically that of a first-person narrator (although as we have seen not necessarily as active agent) but laced heavily with generic statements of such a low order that they can probably be interpreted subjectively also without impunity. The particular linguistic forms chosen for analysis in this context revealed the ways in which different grammatical options and choices functioned for these children to allow them to situate narrative events (and I argue also themselves) temporally, socially, and even morally. Now it remains to broaden the scope of this discussion to a discursive level and to attempt a reading of the discursive effects of the children's autobiographical narratives.

III

Constructing a
Narrative Identity

Grammar is not necessary and sufficient for meaning. Situations, context, history and a form of life all play a part. Genova (1995, p. 120)

The child's work on a word is not finished when its meaning is learned. Vygotsky (1987, p. 322)

To correlate discourse choices directly with social categories is to abstract away from the real reason language choices are made: In service of the expression of and creation of self. Johnstone (1996, p. 89)

The grammatical analysis was to establish the construction of autobiographical discourse, the material resource of the modal auxiliaries in the narratives. Now for the function of this construction, in which discourse function refers to the intention of the speaker with regard to the addressee.[1] The self is both the object and the subject of autobiographical discourse and the functions associated with talk about the self are the expression, the assessment and the evaluation of that self. Modal structures are similarly always an evaluation of one sort or another.[2] Therefore, in the context of autobiography, a modal utterance can be mined for how speakers are evaluating what they are talking about, namely, themselves.

All the children told stories.[3] As soon as we are asked about ourselves, to tell our autobiography, we start to tell stories. We tell what happened, what we said, what we did. But our identities are not only influenced by past events and situations and their consequences but also by how we interpret and talk about them now, retroactively, and by how we feel and think about the future. In the same way that the narrator organizes the elements of her or his story in a certain

---

[1] The term discourse function is used in the sense of interpersonal or affective function as discussed by Guo (1994, p. 212) and Lyons (1977, pp. 50-51), that is, how the speaker intends to influence the mental state or behaviour of the addressee.
[2] Modal structures are "combinations of modal relationships between the enunciator and the actants appearing in the utterance." They always imply an evaluation if modalities are seen as intersubjective relationships rather than logical categories (Sülkunen & Torrönen, 1997, p. 54).
[3] Emotional closeness of narrative to children's worlds, especially in traditional form (e.g., fairy tales): "narrative as a type of discourse in which children can easily insert or articulate their own point of view" (Pontecorvo, 1994, p. 144). Early mastery of the "grammar of stories".

way, in autobiographical narratives we are organizing and arranging the elements of our identity in certain ways. Rather than what the story means, we ask what does the story do?

We are not born with an identity, we have to identify to get one. And the stories we tell in turn tell something of our identifications. "It is not a question of knowing whether I speak of myself in a way that conforms to what I am, but rather of knowing whether I am the same as that of which I speak" (Lacan, 1977, p. 165) and Zeldin (1995, p. 46) "when people tell the story of their life, the way they begin reveals at once how free they consider themselves to be and how much of the world they feel at home in."

I have shown what can be accomplished by the deployment of various syntactic structures and combinations, and now I need to explore how all these elements fit together or are brought together in situated speech to achieve the speaker's purpose, to create a particular discourse context.[4] This entails going back and forth between detailed linguistic analysis of language forms and functions and the context and positionings of the speaker (and the spoken about) established by the use of these forms in particular ways.[5]

This is where a discussion of the discourse functions comes in. A particular modal auxiliary used in a particular utterance is not necessarily straightforward. There is no one-to-one correspondence whereby you can start from a linguistic form and definitively establish its function with regard to the construction of discourse around it. The difficulty is in "analyzing particular forms as a function of their context *as well as* the context as a function of these forms: Each produces the other" (Bamberg, 1987, p. 112). It has to be approached from both sides: On the one hand, you have to try and work with the distributional frequencies of forms to get at the overall structure and tendencies of the children's narratives; on the other hand you are looking for any unexpected forms that stand out and in so doing contribute something else to the construction of meaning. As Lakoff and Johnson (1980) pointed out, more of form is more of content.

Putting everything together, the idea is to ascertain what situation or context is actually being set up by the modal utterance and what surrounds it. The analytic framework proposed here means moving or fanning outward from the modal auxiliaries. Despite making use of a modal categorization scheme that specifically takes the speaker and the discourse context into account, a scheme like that will always be inadequate without a detailed description of the grammatical environment and an attempt to describe the discourse function, the product of the utterances in their situated particularity. Although linguistic

---

[4] Gerhardt and Stinson (1994, p. 153): "talk not only occurs in a context but is organized with respect to certain features of that context. The discourse itself will be organised on the basis of particular demand characteristics inherent to this mode of encounter. Different types of talk have been shown to be organized in particular ways depending on the type of task being carried out."

[5] See Berman and Slobin (1994, p. 535) for a discussion of grammatical constructions and narrative development: "the challenge of narrative syntax lies in the flexible use of a range of construction types. The separate linguistic devices needed for building well-structured narratives are available long before these more advanced discourse challenges are fully met."

analysis can describe the structure of the children's modal utterances, the task is to link those constructions to the ways in which the children are using these forms in their stories, the form functions. These linguistic forms are understood to function as part of the social practice of language.

With the ability to tell stories, to make use of the language of narrative (including crucially, temporal, causal, conditional, and intentional forms) comes the ability to narrativize experience. Activities and events experienced as a participant can now be made into stories that include motivations, goals and relations that were previously only partially understood. In this way, children's goals and meanings begin to take on more of the meanings of the wider community as well as the child's own understanding of events and experiences. This sort of narrative development heralds some other very important advances.[6] For instance, now there is the possibility of other previously unknown worlds. Stories can be understood as about a different time and a different place, where the child himself or herself has never been. Second, this level of linguistic achievement means language can be used to reanalyze and reinterpret previous experiences and representations of those experiences on another level. Third, the collaborative constructions in narrative provide the basis for understanding the perspectives, motivations, goals, and emotions of others in a way that is not possible on the mimetic level alone when different roles in activities are understood but not yet the internal states of the other actors (Nelson, 1996, p. 351).

Summary of Age-Related Patterns for Discourse Functions of the Modal Auxiliaries

Bearing in mind that it is the child's own system that must be accounted for, a set of eight discourse categories are described that seem to capture what it is the children are doing with the modals they use in the context of autobiographical discourse (see the Appendix for a full list of the 62 discourse functions making up the eight categories coded in the transcripts). As "interpretations arise *in confrontation* [italics added] with the material at hand,"[7] the object of the exercise was to allow categories to emerge from reading (and rereading) the transcripts. In other words, the question posed for each utterance containing the target form (a modal auxiliary) concerned its role with respect to the surrounding discourse. What is the child trying to do or say based on the linguistic forms recruited? There is not just one discourse goal, rather a series of moment-by-moment locally organized goals and decisions. "'Life-stories' are best understood as expressions of multivoiced individuals" (Bamberg, 1991a, p. 161).

---

[6] See Nelson (1996, pp. 4-6) for an experiential theoretical approach to narrative development that has the child "an acting and interacting person [whose] primary cognitive task is to make sense of his or her situated place in the world in order to take a skilful part in its activities."

[7] Gee (1985, p. 199). My italics, a striking term to use in this context and reminiscent of those theories mentioned earlier which view grammar and grammatical constructions as a solution to a problem, namely, the construction and maintenance of discourse.

In discussing the particular discourse functions at work in these accounts, we should note what Bowers (1988) says on the functionality of discourse. His main critique was directed at what he called "an overly constricted linking of discourse to function". He suggested that "rather than relate discourse functions 'down' to the cognitions of individuals we might attempt to forge links with grander social theory" (p. 187). So in the course of addressing what the child might be saying or doing at the particular point or juncture in the text, I am also relating the discourse functions up to wider issues in psychology, to what is known of the self and its development, for instance, to the literature on narrative development, to theory on the development of the child's morality system, and so on. The discourse categories generated in this study often relate to what Gerhardt and Stinson (1994, p. 156) have called a speaker's "modes of entry," which include the speaker's attitudes, self-reflective evaluations, or emotional reactions toward the events recounted, which they suggested are usually marginalized in accounts of narrative. These are also some of the roles I want to focus on as these are brought about primarily by the modal auxiliaries in this context. For instance, there is a distinct lack of emotional terms and references that I argue is because the modal auxiliaries are doing that work in the narratives.

The two most frequent discourse categories for all the children are **reporting** and **agency**, including **theory of mind** uses by the 12-year-old group.

- The **Problem-Solving** category shows a slight but steady decrease from 5 to 12, and within this category the 5-year-olds do not use the possibility or options function.

- **Reporting** uses are fairly evenly distributed across age groups, and are highest for the 8-year-olds, especially in relation to elaborating on background material.

- **Prescribing** uses dramatically decrease in the 12-year-old narratives, while being fairly well represented for the 5- and 8-year-olds, with the 8-year-olds using this category the most.

- **Interpersonal Narrative** functions are fairly consistent but there is a small steady increase with age. The 5-year-olds most typically make use of the boasting function within this category.

- **Agency** is important for all the children but decreases with age, with 5-year-olds tending to express forms of intention and the older groups marking agency through expression of desires and preferences.

- **Emotional** uses hardly feature at all in the 5-year-old narratives, they are beginning to be used by 8-year-olds and are fairly well established by age 12, particularly with regard to expressing hope and doubt. It is noteworthy that there is a temporal pattern to the age differences in relation to marking emotions via the modal auxiliaries.

- **Theory of mind** uses shows a similar pattern of increase with age. This category is used twice as much by 8- as by 5-year-olds, and three times as frequently by 12-year-olds. The older group focus especially on character assessments, both of themselves and of others and on **theory of mind** statements in relation to self and to others.

- Reference to **Unreal States** as a category features very largely in the 5-year-olds' narratives, particularly fantasy and imaginative uses. This category is used less but equally by the 8 and 12-year-olds, in which the 12-year-olds in particular use it to make predictions and to hypothesise and the 8-year-olds to make forecasts.

- The **Theory of mind** and **Emotion** categories together, for the 12-year-olds, account for over 27% of their total modal utterances. The ability to use these categories is very important for self development and for narrative development (8-year-olds =14%, 5-year-olds = 7%).

It is not as clear cut as all this of course, distinct discourse functions cannot easily be ascribed to utterances, modal, or otherwise. In trying to assign categories it becomes obvious very quickly that there are large areas of overlap in relation to the concepts and situations engendered by the use of the modal auxiliaries. For example, a major distinction in the **reporting** category is between reporting on actions and reporting on happenings that raises issues of responsibility, volition and intention, issues which are also at the forefront of the discourse category of **agency**. These discourse functions overlap with those in the categories of **emotionals** and **theory of mind** statements to the extent that they are used to index and construct motivations and rationales in relation to third person characters as well as those of the speaker. In the course of this type of discursive episode, the speakers make use of various narrative devices of an **interpersonal** nature, a category that often overlaps with the **prescriptive** function of the modalized utterances in these transcripts. And in the course of prescribing behaviour and constructing moral worlds, the speakers often engage in an on-the-spot form of **problem-solving** discourse, which in turn often requires the enlisting of fantasy and *irrealis* scenarios. The difficulties in trying to definitively describe the discourse function of any particular utterance containing a modal auxiliary are apparent but nevertheless there are some important and interesting distinctions that can be made.

6

Accounting for Oneself: The Discourse of Agency

REPORTING

This discourse category comprises those cases in which the modal auxiliaries seem to be performing a descriptive function without, for the main part, any explicit expression of personal affect toward what is being described, overt assessment or evaluation of the event or situation, and in the absence of explicitly reflective elements. Of course the fact that an event or situation is being described or reported on at all means it cannot be neutrally charged in this context.[1] However this category is trying to account for those cases in which the speaker appears to adopt the role of a reporter laying out the facts in order to make a later commentary.

It has been established that when modal forms are involved, it is not a straightforward mapping of words to world but reporting in order to recast, showing different levels of involvement, taking different measures of distance in relation to what one is reporting (e.g., perfective or imperfective statements) and taking up of different positions in relation to your narratives. In reporting, you are always in essence constructing the event or scenario for the listener.[2] In the very process of singling out and ordering events, you are at the same time conveying how they are related or relevant to the present discourse experience, where they fit into your autobiography.[3]

Overall, this category accounts for 23% of all modal utterances, which is possibly much less straightforward reporting than would be expected of this discourse type. Even within a monological autobiographical context, the descriptive function is less important than the indexical instrumental function, the speaker is still trying to do or to effect something, not just to tell something.

Action or Event

One point of interest here is the children's reporting of happenings or events

---

[1] Harré and Mühlhäulser (1990, p. 131): "Responsibility is assigned to human beings both for their actions in the world and for their reports as to how the world appears from their point of view."
[2] Portelli (1981, p. 175): "The remembering and the telling are themselves *events*, not only descriptions of events" and "an event lived is finished, bound within experience. But an event remembered is boundless, because it is the key to all that happened before and after it".
[3] Bamberg and Reilly (1996, p. 337): "The self as the narrator, as well as the events (including processes and states) that are reported in the narrative, *emerge* in the interaction; they are jointly co-constructed. Content and performance both are contextualization factors in the process of how narrators intend to be understood in interaction and how they ultimately constitute their self-understanding."

(overall 57%) versus their reporting of (non)actions (43%). The shift in perspective required brings up issues of intention, volition and responsibility. In first-person narratives, events, and actions are the result of particular linguistic choices, they must be constructed in different ways. We have already seen this operate at the level of grammatical subjects and semantic roles, and it is also evident here in relation to whether the children primarily describe things or events and assert facts or report on specific instances of failure to do something or on constraints and conditions affecting themselves as actors or their characters.

Curiously the 8-year-olds provide the most background material in their narrative accounts, that is, they elaborate more frequently, which overall means they are reporting events more often (68%). This fits well with ideas[4] on the development of the self, which has children in the middle years tending to use more environmental and background terms and generally providing more clues than younger children who tend to just assume background. The 5-and 12-year-olds are more evenly divided on the two modes of reporting, that is, they reported intentions and existing conditions on actors about as often as they provided more straightforward descriptions of settings and situations. The older children however tend to be much more selective in their reporting of environmental or elaborative details, not just as background but used in interaction with other information.

AGENCY

Discussion of the self and what the past self is inevitably leads to debates on agency, that is, the status of the I who authors statements and of the subject.[5] This section focuses on where agency is constructed linguistically and discursively[6] in the children's autobiographies. This category of agentive uses of the modal auxiliaries differs from straightforward reporting or describing functions in that there is judged to be a measure of interpretation, explanation or reflection involved in relation to the role of the agent, whether the agent is the speaker or some other character in their narrative.

To Be Active Is to Be Moral

This category constitutes a cluster concept[7] (overall 18% of all utterances containing a modal auxiliary) as there are a host of different ways of signalling and adjusting agency at all levels of language and discourse. There is the relatively basic distinction between what we do and what happens to us, between

---

[4] For example, Wilkinson, Barnsley and Hanna (1980) on the development of the self in autobiographical writing.
[5] See Tonkin (1992) for a very good discussion.
[6] "The 'realism' of Self is probably built into folk psychology as a spin-off of the notion of agency. It is surely built into English language usage, though in a strikingly idiosyncratic way" Bruner (1990, p. 159, no. 2).
[7] In the sense that some of the functions accounted for here are less typically agentive than others (e.g., Wittgenstein's, 1953, analysis of games or Rosch's, 1978, analysis that showed that categorization judgements often contain a cline of typicality ranging from typical to atypical exemplars of the category).

actions and happenings. And then there is the fact that active subjects in the process become moral persons also (Duranti, 1994; Tonkin, 1992) that introduces levels of responsibility and commitment. This basic premise, that an active subject is by the same token a moral subject, means that a large part of autobiographical narrative is taken up with accounting for our actions, supplying reasons and excuses, and persuading someone of our version.[8] Indeed, we can either offer our point of view or impose it via the modals.

The reason for including expression of desire and expression of preference as indicators of agency is that there are actually very few instances in which the children make any form of explicit comment or evaluation about themselves and much less stories and talking directly about themselves than you would perhaps expect in autobiographical discourse. Those utterances expressing wishes or stating preferences were the ones in the narratives most likely to be in the first person. The children, by using these type of sentences, are assigning feelings and ideas to themselves or alternatively claiming them for themselves and, as such, they constitute a real measure of agency. They represent an explicit marking of "what I am like," "what I like to do," and "what I would like to be." It is a way of separating oneself out from others, of standing apart. Also as Serniak (1992) pointed out, the priorities and preferences selected by the narrator are not just expressions of the self but actually constitute the autobiographical self and serve to demarcate it by circumscribing the manner in which a life is lived. Talking about what you intend to do of course is also an obvious marker of agency. In general, the 5-year-olds report on quite straightforward, concrete, realizable intentions, for example,

> "I'm gonna ask for a magic wand on Christmas and a Dr Dreadful and you CAN make dreadful things" (NR5).
> "So we decided we MIGHT come back tomorrow so we did" (NR5).[9]

while the 8- and 12-year-old children more frequently mark future oriented desires and abstract preferences:

> "I'LL keep it for rollerblades 'cos that's what I've always wanted" (CK8).
> "I'D love to go there again" (JOR8).
> "I'D like to be an actress or a dancer or a singer" (AC8).
> "I'D like to work in a shop, a clothes shop" (SM8).
> "I hope I get into Vet 'cos I'D really like it" (AK12).
> "I'D prefer to be like my Mum than my Dad" (KM12).
> "I think I'D like to stay in primary school" (DH12).
> "And, like, I know this WOULDN'T happen but I'D love to be an actor" (PF12).

---

[8] Edwards (1997, p. 223) on "acceptable" descriptions and consequential alternatives: a speaker who can establish their own version as the criterial version is in a very powerful position that leaves anyone who challenges it open to being accused of nit-picking.
[9] Note the contradiction of a juxtaposition of DECIDE and MIGHT.

Also included in this category is the function of offering to disclose or reveal information that could conceivably have been included in the category of interpersonal-narrating functions. However the contexts in which these offers were made were explicitly agentive in that the children were making clear that it was up to them what they told, and also, they knew that it was of interest and that they could withhold it or choose to divulge the information. It was used mainly rhetorically to explicitly mark just such a position, hinging on the established, if not overtly conscious, connection between knowledge and agency.[10] If disclosing or withholding information is one way of assuming agency or control, then this child is firmly in the driver's seat:

> "There's two things I'D like to find out about, one's a secret, I'LL tell you the other" (DPB8).
> And later: "I'LL tell you a bit about a programme I watched" (DPB8).

And some of the older children:

> "I don't actually know what hospital but I CAN find out for you" (AK12).
> "I remember lots of awful days but I don't really like talking about them though,
> if I remember something that's not too awful I'LL tell you" (SOH12).

Presentation of Self

There are (at least) two construals of self. The child can present himself or herself as a causal agent, an active, changing, effective entity in space-time. This child's transcript overall was highly agentive, lots of I in relation to her own abilities, and she even repairs in the second example so that she is once more the instigator of the action.

> "I got very interested in it and I asked my Dad COULD I go" (SM8)
> "Last year we done a play in the summer in the hall and I was a little flower girl so I had to, I asked COULD I bring in that so I brought my flower dress in" (SM8).

Or the child can present himself or herself as an experiencer or a recipient of actions, where the self is seen as an objective static entity. The speaker portrays himself or herself as the brunt of forces and effects, as a social construct.[11] At a very young age children adopt a simple solution. They tend to use I to index themselves as effective agent (often with progressive aspect) and use me or my

---

[10] See Serniak (1992) for a fascinating discussion of autobiographical discourse as a degenerate case of empirical knowledge.
[11] Frawley (1997, p. 205) on Nelson's (1989) subject, Emily.

(with the simple present tense) to index the person as constructed form.[12] But they learn eventually to fuse these into the single form I[13] and that it is up to the speaker and hearer now to calculate the particulars of the situation.

The flip side of agency, how we react to the agency of others, what Bruner (1995) called "reactive agency" or victimcy, is also included in this category. For instance, there is a sense of agency here but somehow it is negatively defined:

> "I'D like to be a dentist, not like my Dad, my Dad's an auctioneer,
> I'D like a dentist or doctor 'cos you'D get loads of money,
> No, I don't want to be a dentist 'cos you'D have to pick little pieces out of
> people's teeth, sounds horrible" (MS8).

> "I CAN have one more song which James didn't really want but he has loads
> of blank tapes but he really wanted them , but he gave me one blank tape
> but my Mum has recorded this song that I hate and she,
> they were taking all the spaces so I COULDN'T really put anything onto it"
> (StJS8).

Or this next child whose narratives tend to suggest a much more pervasive lack of agency and passivity. Note also some of the only uses of the passive tense in the entire corpora.

> "Except for one sleepover I've always been in the house,
> except for once it was in my small sister's friend's house 'cos my Mum and
> Dad were going out and I WOULDN'T have them here,
> there was no-one to mind me,
> there WOULD be no-one to mind me so I had to go over there
> oh, you know, I never have a nice time in the world,
> never, I never get one" (CM5).

Challenging[14] as a form of agentive behavior in reaction to the agency of others, or to assert one's own agency in a particular situation, is often achieved using the modal auxiliaries, whether challenging someone's assertions:

> "My minder thinks there's a big shop in town what have all all doughnuts
> but I don't really think that CAN be true" (CMcG5).

their behavior:

> "And I'm there "Mark, CAN you please be quiet, I'm trying to say my
> prayers
> and I said "Mark, if you don't be quiet, I WI-ILL kill you" (CK8).

---

[12] Budwig (1986, 1990),Gerhardt (1989): It has been suggested that the modal system of middle and late childhood incorporates earlier functions and uses of the self-reference system.
[13] In English
[14] See also Guo (1994) on the mandarin modal *neng* (roughly CAN) and interpersonal challenge.

"My Mum is afraid of the water cos she fell in the water but I don't think she
SHOULD have,
she SHOULDN'T have done, em, like,
she didn't actually came, she SHOULD have still come,
usually when we go, em, my Mum is usually careful but then she just fell in"
(StJS8).

or their thinking:

"They even had a snake which I thought was quite funny,
you COULDN'T see it, the whole cage was covered in ferns and it says eh
"people WILL be prosecuted if they tap on the glass" because they were so
rare,
personally I thought why bother putting it on show when you CAN'T see it,
that was the only snake I didn't see but, you see, having snakes I COULD
kinda spot them but most people COULDN'T see anything at all" (AK12).

Accounting . . .

One of the really important aspects involved with notions of agency revolves
around giving reasons, being able to account for oneself, being held accountable
for failure. That is, notions of morality and responsibility.[15] We should look at
"the pieces of language which make up giving reasons for one's actions"
(Canfield, 1981, p. 13). Autobiographical accounts often involve expression of
reasons and excuses and modalized statements tend to be co-opted to carry out
this "reason-giving" function.

"I'm the oldest which is good sometimes and bad sometimes,
it's good when you CAN get your own way and you CAN tell them what to
do" (KM12).
"At parties I used to wait till everyone else was finished just so I COULD eat
everything,
instead of like, people seeing me eating so much,
as I ate quite a lot and I'D be embarrassed,
I was quite shy but I'm not really anymore, I've come out of that" (TA12).

To introduce a narrative character (or oneself) as an agent is to set up a moral type
who can therefore be praised or blamed for their actions. It is to set up a moral

---

[15] Hill and Irvine (1993, p. 1): "To say an individual, a social actor, is 'responsible' is a relatively new
way of speaking. Deriving from an older version of 'responsiveness,' a quality of participation in
dialogue, the newer sense of responsibility indexes the development of an idea of the continuity of a
self with a relatively consistent scheme of interpretation of what it is reacting to [and] continuity in
the community of agents to which response is being made". This "quality of participation in
dialogue" is a sense of the term that could be central for us. See also Shotter (1993a, b)
responsiveness = responsibility + addressivity.

world.[16]   This point must be particularly salient in the case of autobiographical discourse (it forms a large part of the category of prescriptive discourse functions in these narratives also). But remember in these narrative accounts the child as the subject of the verb in modal utterances is only the agent 20% of the time. Overall the discourse constructed by these children is not all that densely populated by themselves as active agents.

However one of the main functions of autobiographical speech in particular is still to be able to account for both your own actions and the actions of anyone else mentioned and frequently this amounts to ordering or structuring your account in such a way as to be able to change, mitigate or modify potential assessments. To be accountable arises from the fact that agents can be held responsible or answerable for their actions and even for their reports. Accounts involve talk designed to recast the pejorative significance of one's action or one's responsibility for it and thereby transform other's negative evaluations (Buttny, 1993).

This child starts out in a vaguely accusatory manner as he recounts the story of his dog dying but in the course of the episode he becomes anxious to defend his mother's actions (or failure to act in this case).

> "One time when I came back from playschool Thatcher was dead,
> Thatcher is the dog,
> and em, I said 'where's Thatcher' and she said oh I brought it to the vet'
> and then one of them said 'she died'
> my Mom never kept a photograph of her, she never kept one of her,
> because em, like, she, em, she usually just kind of comes and runs away and
> you just look and she runs away when the camera faced her and my Mom
> never thought of that
> so she COULDN'T have done it" (St.JS8).

This transformative function is the most distinctive feature of accounts as a discursive practice. And the modal auxiliaries are the transformers, they transform an event from being a *fait accompli* to being somehow psychologically in progress (Todorov, 1976). Here this child tries shifting the responsibility for choosing which friends to bring along.

> "But I think in May I'm going to Disneyland
> but I MIGHT go hostelling for my birthday and ponyriding 'cos it's not too
> far from the hostel
> but I CAN'T really bring all my friends 'cos we don't have a really big car
> but I MIGHT bring 3 of mine, my best friends" (JW5).

As individual actors we usually think we know more about the conditions, circumstances, and constraints on our actions than others do. These conditions

---

[16] See Duranti (1994) on the building of moral worlds in political discourse as well as in everyday speech.

and circumstances are usually conveyed in accounts as reasons, excuses, and explanations in the hope that they can transform the significance of the event. The event can be seen differently by reconfiguring the event's underlying conditions or previously unknown or unappreciated circumstances. This transformative power of speech shows that events remain open to (re)interpretation because the significance of a particular event depends on a web of interrelated events, actions, social actors, motives and so on, a change in one of these parts may effect a change in the whole (Buttny, 1993, p. 5). Events and our stances toward them are not stored somewhere waiting to be spoken about but are constructed in the act of talking about them. And in this way the speaker establishes a moral world through the acts of accounting and transforming.

What the child chooses to try to account for, or to give reasons for, also points to what they think needs them, that is, it is something they consider to be out of the ordinary or remarkable in some way and therefore to require some form of warrant (Potter, 1996). Not all actions require motives. Motives are generally offered as a reason for behavior when there is a departure from conventional expectations.[17]

. . . and Being Held Accountable

Another interesting aspect to agency is that being held accountable for failure reflects certain assumptions, in particular that a certain stage of development has been reached. For instance, anyone judged not to have acquired a certain level of competence or ability (the beginner, children, the developmentally disabled) cannot therefore be seriously blamed for their actions or errors. A lack of skill or ability has reflexive implications regarding the individual's status or category of personhood, as a not yet competent member or adult (Buttny, 1993, p. 3). It is usually around the age of 8 that children are beginning to be held accountable, to be trusted with tasks and responsibilities. It could be this new responsibility that is being reflected in their autobiographical accounts, maybe in the 20% of their modal utterances that involve accounting for personal motives and desires.

This can also work in another way. Wolf (1990, p. 208) points out that the significance of these changes in children's language may actually lie in the opposite direction. To speak as subject and object, author and critic, or character and narrator, may or may not result in a more differentiated sense of self. The significance of these new discourse forms may be that children now appear substantially different to others. They sound old enough to be involved in discussions about what is right and wrong, about their motivations and intentions. They may now reasonably be called on to explain themselves. The linguistic acquisitions may not so much create a diversified self as signal to others that a child is old enough to become a part of those situations that will develop the

---

[17] Insofar as accounts offer "a valuable site for uncovering a culture's taken-for-granted assumptions and folk logic of right action" (Buttny, 1993, p. 2).

"several minds" of the self. The way in which the child presents himself or herself (e.g., as volitional agent, as passive victim, or as actor) will affect, in turn, how others see and react to the child. This can herald the child being treated as a responsible agent, being held newly accountable.

Of course in order to successfully account for your actions or to transform the listener's evaluation requires that your accounts be accepted. You need to persuade the listener of your account (as we saw, the modal auxiliaries are excellent devices to recruit if you want to engage in some subtle persuasion). You need to structure your account around accepted social and moral orders. Is this the main difference between the children's autobiographies? Are the 12-year-olds better at giving accounts? Are they better at outlining circumstances, motives, and conditions into a coherent whole? If this is any indication, then they have used reference to emotions and theory of mind statements to much better avail than the younger children to set up situations, to give account of their motivations and to rationalise and explain their actions.

EMOTIONS

This category includes all reference to emotional states and any utterance that serves to convey an emotional reaction or feeling state to what is being described, through explicit or oblique reference, whether experienced by the speaker or by other characters in their narratives. Overall, this discourse category represents only 5% of all the modal utterances. It is in fact the least used category of all, but it is also one of the more interesting ones in terms of the many issues raised by even this small number of cases.

As mentioned, there are actually very few overt references to emotions, emotional states or feelings of any kind.[18] The rarity of emotionals co-occurring with the modal auxiliaries in these accounts is a function of the fact that it is the modal auxiliary itself that is providing the evaluative element in the utterance. If one of the main functions of emotion marking in narrative is to provide an evaluation, the speaker's, then we can see that for the speaker to refer to an emotional in combination with using one or other of the modal auxiliaries would almost constitute an overmarking (and therefore also especially deserving of attention). Looking at the transcripts overall there is very little explicit stating of traits, characteristics, dispositions, or of anything even approaching typecasting of themselves on the children's part. Some possible exceptions are references to being good at something, or not as the case may be: "I like Art but I'm not very good at it, I'D like to be good at ART" (SOH12).

Accident or Design

Overall there are very few trait type references, very few statements of the type "I am (a)" or "I felt". Maybe this is because children do not readily appreciate

---

[18] Wilkinson, Barnsley, and Hanna (1980, p. 40): "The ability to express affect in words is not easily come by, in spoken language emotion is carried by paralinguistics and there is little reason to express it otherwise".

that characteristic as a coherence structure is preferable to opportunity in terms of the telling of one's autobiography and establishing of agency. An explanation rooted in the self and self's agency is preferable to one rooted outside because an externally based account invites attribution to either accident or determinism (Linde, 1993, p. 131).

In argument against Linde's (1993) assertion that there is no point in asking a child to tell their life story: It is precisely the average 5-year-old's lack of skill in putting together a coherent story, their lack of concern with plotting a series of events that establish a trajectory of either stability or intended change in their narrative, which leads us to think that they do not have a "self" established on the concept of autobiography but they do. Or rather this is their self-in-the-making, fragmented, oscillating between one way of being and another, primarily because they are not yet cognisant of the pressure, as culturally situated beings, that one ought to be able to account for oneself, along a continuum, along a certain path with certain identifiable points or junctures to explain and situate coherently any deviations or developments.

The young child's self is made up of a mixture of the here-and-now and things that have happened, not only to themselves but to anything or anyone deemed an extension of themselves (we see how important the concept of possession is developmentally and in terms of constitution of the self for the young child). In other words, they are not driven by the need to make sense, to come up with or to present a unified self/story for the listener when they are asked to speak autobiographically. If these 5-year-olds have difficulty narrating, to our adult ears at least, a coherent satisfying autobiography, it is not because they are having difficulty expressing their real self, the real them, but rather because they are in the process of developing the ability to identify themselves under particular conditions: "It is part of the process of learning how to have identity-further specifying and changing it" (Cronen & Pearce, 1991, p. 59). The younger children have not yet organized their autobiography through telling and retelling.[19]

For example, the 12-year-olds tended to get much more anxious in relation to the request for their autobiography and became immediately concerned with what they thought was expected of them, with figuring out what was wanted. They repeatedly ask where they should start, apologize for not remembering something, and in general seem to be much more aware that they are expected to be able to link everything up and to give it its own place in the scheme or order of their life, their autobiography, their self. They are much more obviously striving for coherency and attempting to structure their account. They want to establish patterns. As children get older, they buy into social and cultural norms and views of self and identity.

We could see the 5-year-old children not as deficient or as lacking something but as yet a more fluid self. They do not seem to presume a core and stable

---

[19] See also Nelson's (1992, 1993) research on the autobiographical memory system and reinstatement through language and narrative.

identity which they match everything against, that they check their accounts against to see if they are authentic or "in keeping" with previous accounts but instead have a more open sense of multiple selves in social encounters. Missing also is the idea that as you tell your life story you are "pigeon-holing" yourself, establishing a reputation, presenting (a version of) yourself. The public is not yet incorporated and fixed as the private only to be (de)flected outwards again in edited form (Harré, 1995). Also 5-year-old children tend to have much less of an extended sense of their own history so they will see less need for coherence between one narrative and another. Having only a superficial sense of the past (only around 8 does a sense of the narrative whole emerge) it could be argued that there is therefore less necessity for them to behave in ways that are considered to be internally consistent or coherent with their past behavior. I would even argue that there is no realization that it should be so. Narratives, and autobiographical narratives in particular, are supposed to center around the notions of change-stability. Society values both strongly but change is actually more salient and more important for children.

There is only one explicit reference to an emotion experienced by one of the 12-year-olds. (And even this is qualified by the use of *actually* and *a bit*).

> "Mary is moving to Churchtown, which I WOULD actually be a bit jealous of because they're opening a new petshop, but I'm hoping to see the new shop,
> I'm petshop mad, it's kind of like people going shopping" (AK12).

Even this single example raises an interesting point in relation to the use of the modal auxiliaries (in this case WOULD) with emotionals. This combination generally serves to imply that the emotion referred to is an habitual or a recurrent one.[20] Woofitt (1992)[21] called this use of WOULD its "fact constructional role," indicating that the speaker is not extrapolating from a single case but has made repeated observations. This is not a once-off situation or event but something that happens generally. So the issue of normality is closely connected to the issue of regularity. A description is produced that characterizes something as normal or regular.

Also, of course, it can be a means of distancing oneself[22] from less attractive emotions via the modals. The modals are being used to convey notions of speaker (non)involvement. On the one hand, most of the instances of (oblique) references to emotions are in the first person, that is, the children are talking about their own emotional states. They make practically no reference to the emotions or feelings of others. On the other hand, in the case of the 12-year-olds, many of their emotional references are generic type statements. As we have seen

---

[20] See Capps and Ochs (1995) on an agoraphobic woman's similar use of this device.
[21] See Potter (1996, p.195). This is also dealt with in Widdicombe and Wooffitt's (1995) study of youth identity.
[22] Or its corollary, showing commitment.

in the course of the modal analysis, emotions and feelings made reference to in this way, these lower order generalizations, can more properly be assigned to the speaker himself or herself than to the third-person "everyman" figure they are superficially speaking about.

> "I'm going to Gonzaga next year, but like,
> eight years with these people, you get used to it,
> like, you'D miss them,
> but it doesn't mean I'm just going to go away from them, I know where they
> all live, I have their phone numbers so we CAN just hang around normally,
> but I'm not saying I WON'T get new friends, em" (PF12).

WOULD, combined with the switch from first-person subject to the generic subject you when talking about his feelings, is a way of taking psychological distance. This boy is concerned to show disinterestedness at precisely the point where he is not, where it could be a particular issue.

Looking further at this passage, another thing to notice in this connection is that the modal auxiliaries tend to cluster, to co-occur. This is interesting in the sense that a single passage will often contain many of the modal auxiliaries found in any given child's transcript.[23] This tells us what the children are uncertain about, what is very subjective/emotive for them, what is unresolved or which accounts they are still working through.[24] We have seen that the modal auxiliaries very often have discourse marking functions, and it is said that discourse markers[25] in speech typically cluster at moments of uncertainty, of affect, and especially at the points of greatest self-disclosure. So although we do not see these children explicitly outlining their feelings and emotions, it is often the combination of a modal used as discourse marker within a story or account that gives up the emotional content.

Rather than making overt reference to what they feel or felt, or directly commenting on the sort of person they are, the children tell stories.[26] It is the narratives and anecdotes that are their autobiographies and that can be mined for this information. Only by looking at the utterance in context, and by trying to interpret what the utterance is meant to convey, can you assign to it its emotional

---

[23] McGregor (1997, p. 388, on the Australian Aboriginal language, Gooniyandi, and speech addressed to mother-in-laws) noticed a similar pattern. He said that it was the greater than normal frequency of modal markers, rather than any particular use of them, which served as an index of the interpersonal relationship, specifically the indirect nature of the relationship, iconically represented by the nondirectness of the interpersonal meanings. This was to show that patterns of usage of grammatical markers can index social meanings that have nothing to do with their own inherent meanings as grammatical signs.

[24] Taylor (1989) suggested that the language we use in articulating the import of emotions discloses what is important to us in our lives (what we feel upset, angry about and so on).

[25] See Schiffrin (1987) on discourse markers.

[26] Sülkunen and Torrönen (1997, p. 58): "A development in modal theory is the semiotics of emotions or passions. Modal structures are often combinations of different modalities in a narrative trajectory of a subject." In a seminal article on anger Greimas (1983) proposed that certain passions or emotions such as anger or jealousy may be articulated somewhat like modal chains in a story.

element or undertone. So rather than saying they are worried or anxious (in these next examples about the transition to secondary school which featured a lot in the older children's accounts), a typical construction in these transcripts is:

> "Having a different teacher for each subject seems different, I don't know what it'LL be like" (AW12).
> "You have to stand up and say "Good Morning" and I don't know if I'LL remember that all the time" (DH12).

Also the kinds of emotions the children ascribe to themselves can be sourced for levels of agency or victimcy, that is, how the emotion states and feelings mentioned orient the listener toward a particular positioning of the speaker. In this study, there are no very agentive type emotions constructed in discourse. The speaker is a victim, or at least is more often reacting than acting. There are very few displays of being annoyed or angry or being delighted or happy. More reactive and negative type emotional states are referred to, for instance, frustration, hope, or regret. States and agentless happenings typically result in sadness, and its variants with no animate agent to blame, whereas situations that evoke danger are more likely the results of wilful, intentional actions brought about by animate others (Bamberg & Reilly, 1996).[27]

These examples are mainly states or agentless emotions. Polar opposites like anger and sadness differ particularly in terms of actor involvement (transitive vs. intransitive acts) and type of action (intentional vs. accidental and justified vs. unjust). The kinds of emotions expressed by these children involve levels of victimcy, or at least passivity rather than agency, and tend to be directed inward rather than outward. The speaker is reacting emotionally to a situation but the impression is one of powerlessness or a lack of control in the face of whatever is provoking or producing an emotional reaction in the first place.

> "I baby-sit sometimes and there's a little boy and he's being bullied at school at the moment, it happened to me once
> I don't know, they just didn't like me for some reason
> but, like, now they're nice to me and everything
> but they just picked on me all the time,
> and if I said anything or they'D laugh at me doing something,
> I don't know, what happened, and I used to cry and everything,
> it was pretty awful,
> the teacher never did anything about it and I told her and she just laughed,
> well, she didn't laugh at me or anything but she said 'Tommy, now don't do it again', like, that WOULDN'T stop him or anything
> em, but he left the school and everything's going OK,
> practically " (HG12).

---

[27] See also Edwards (1997, chap. 7).

Emotions and Narrative

Reference to emotionals in modalized utterances have a particular role to play in terms of the overall development of narrative ability and increased sophistication in narrative skills. First, what is the narrator doing when making reference to emotions? How does it work? Basically references to emotions are "point-making devices." Bamberg (1994, p. 54) in fact says references to both emotions and to mental states are point-making devices within narratives. We see that reference to mental states as a category is much better represented in this study. This part of the discussion relies on the large body of research by Bamberg and colleagues on narrative development, on perspective taking in narrative, and particularly on the role of emotionals in narrative development. By marking emotions the speaker frames events and episodes in their narratives. "In this function they are pervasive qualifications of the events they span and inform" (Young, 1972, p. 23). The speaker almost steps outside of the plot to evaluate the event. Evaluation and reflexivity, the constitution of a moral world is the main objective of autobiographical discourse. Johnstone (1996, p. 52) said her subject, when asked to engage in a similar monologic narrative type task as I have set up here, had to find ways to compensate for lack of audience participation, for example, she frequently left the narrative line of her story to provide explicit evaluation of her own. It might well be the case that 5-year-olds in particular are used to collaboration in story-telling and yet in its absence, they do not have the requisite skills to fill in the gaps themselves. By marking emotions the speaker constructs and provides for the listener motivations for the episodes and events she or he is in the process of recounting.

According to Davis and Harré (1990), emotion words do the job of orienting toward a particular positioning (usually of those who are characterized by these terms) within social encounters. References to emotions can serve two listener-orientations. First, in the sense that they refer to internal states, they momentarily bring the flow of events to a halt. In so doing, these references mark the narrator's stepping out of the event line of the plot and present an evaluative stance or perspective with regard to the event under consideration. Secondly, these references often occur at episode boundaries, that is, at the beginning or end of event sequences. We have seen how the modal auxiliaries often occur at just such junctures also. In this way references to emotions serve to transfix two episodes and contribute to the flow of the narrative as a whole.[28] They signal to the listener how the different narrative units are connected and in so doing, reveal an overarching perspective from which the narrative whole is being constructed. They form the perspective-taking activity of the narrator.

Bamberg (1991) uses the idea of a horizontal and vertical axis[29] to explain

---

[28] See Bamberg (1991) for how emotional states serve as transfixes between two separate frames.

[29] Bamberg (1991, p.277) on binding (referential activity) and unfolding (discourse activity): "Local level linguistic units (sentences and clauses) are not only held together by boundaries to the right and left; rather linguistic units are also organised in the form of an intrinsic, hierarchical order constituted by the relevance of the particular propositions to the overall theme, discourse activity."

narrative development[30] (which is also relevant in terms of the theory of positioning). Horizontal ordering refers to the characters and events in the story, what is taking place within the narrative. Vertical ordering is where the narrator addresses characters' motivations, emotions, intentions, and so on and provides a running commentary or evaluation on the narrative's characters and events at the same time. References to an emotional state in a narrative are not referential in the same way as references to what happened. When someone talks about events and happenings they design their speech so the listener can make inferences about mental life and cognition. The converse is also true. We make assumptions about the world and the way it is or should be, about what happened and why it happened, from the way the speaker designs and presents us with the emotions and motivations of the actors and characters populating their narratives. Thus "event construal and the construal of character's 'inner psychologies' are closely orchestrated with regard to one another. Accounting for one to a large extent indexes the other." [31]

This is interesting when we consider the children are talking about themselves (or at least are talking in response to being asked to talk about themselves). There are three main phases of narrative ability (Bamberg and Reilly, 1996) that correspond roughly with the age groups in this study. In the early period, age 3 to 6, children start from the assumption that a story is a whole at the level of story-telling activity. They know what story telling is about, and they try to keep their audience engaged, but as is the case with these 5-year-olds, the narrative units are not held together well, either at the horizontal cohesive level or at a vertical hierarchical organizational level. On the whole, the 5-year-old children tend to use paralinguistic affective expression to bolster their still unsophisticated linguistic narrative abilities. In other words, direct expression of affect instead of reference to emotions marks the activity of story telling for this age group. None of these 5-year-olds' modal utterances make reference to emotions or to motivations. Instead their narratives (sometimes little more than a string of single propositions) are supplemented with miming activities, facial expressions or for instance using raised or hushed tones to convey emotional aspects of the story.[32]

Although it is reported that children as young as 5 are capable of using emotion terms as evaluative stances from a narrator's perspective, these children did not. What is lacking here seems to be an element of "recipient design" (Fox, 1994, p. 31) or a full set of underlying organizing principles. The 5-year-olds' stories have a chaotic, unmotivated aspect, a feeling of being organized locally.

---

[30] This development from using only horizontal relations to using a hierarchical set of both vertical and horizontal relations is also seen, for example, in the development of categorization and classification skills in children.

[31] See also Edwards and Potter (1992, pp. 42ff).

[32] Wilkinson, Barnsley, and Hanna (1980, p. 70) on the development of the self in children's autobiographical writing: expresses emotions, becomes aware of these emotions; evaluates them, recognizes their springs and complexities; becomes more able to tolerate conflicting emotions, becomes aware of motives behind apparent motives. Self becomes aware of self-image and possible image in eyes of others.

One story or event, or even a word sometimes, touches off another, seemingly unrelated. This is not to say that these elements are necessarily unrelated, only that they are not very coherently organized. The younger child cannot be credited with a highly developed sense of recipient design or of listener orientation requirements. This single example in the 5-year-old corpora was coded as an emotional reference more in reaction to the heightened and very excited rendition of the incident than for its straightforward marking of emotion. Note how we are left hanging as to the import of the fact that the dog belongs to her friend although the fact that it is stressed suggests it is a relevant factor in her delight and to the story overall.[33]   She has not yet learned what it is reasonable to expect her listener to infer. She is at the same time telling both too little and too much, suggesting that she is monitoring her output more for herself as the narrator than for the listener. She is not constructing and updating what Berman and Slobin (1994, p. 609) called "a representation of the listener."

> "I remember this dog, this puppy dog,
> guess what dog, a poodle, a baby poodle and yesterday when I saw this cute
> baby poodle,
> it was gorgeous and I went over to it and I lifted it up and it licked me,
> I COULDN'T believe it,
> my friend's dog" (HOB5).

The 5-year-olds' nonuse of emotion terms suggests that he or she does not yet understand that you must motivate the actions and events in your narratives for your listener,[34] via emotional references in this case. "Narrating means giving instructions to the recipient as to how to construct motives and actions through slipping into the protagonist's intelligence and this activity is not to be confused with the theme (or topic) of the narrative" (Bamberg and Reilly, 1996, p. 338).

     In the middle period, from around 6 to 9, children begin to tie together emotions, motivations and story events. They start to use linguistic references to emotions (and to internal states in general) to signal their own evaluations of particular story events.   Specifically, references to third-person character's feelings reflect their new ability to tie story happenings to story character's internal states from a narrator's point of view. But at this age, the listener is not given an overall perspective on the story as a whole, but a particular single focus on the local connection between a particular story event and its internal

---

[33] Tonkin (1992, p. 7): "most people don't recognize, consciously, that there are language-bound expectations about the placing of central and peripheral topics; they may then hear other placings as incompetent or stupid". Much the same situation holds when we listen to young children's accounts and narratives. Berman (1988, p. 489) said 5-year-olds know the rules of how to tell a story but typically do not know enough to avoid detail and to focus on the overall theme or to plan overarching discourse organization.

[34] Development in this respect must parallel developments in visual perspective taking, in conceptual perspective taking and in the acquisition of a theory of mind. See also Krauss and Glucksberg (1969) on children and referential communication, that is, communication in situations that require the speaker to describe an object to a listener or to evaluate the effectiveness of a message and Brown (1995) on speakers, listeners and communication.

(evaluative) outcome in one of the story characters (Bamberg, 1996). The narrator is operating primarily on the horizontal axis. The child is focused on the particular, on the parts, on the local links[35] that tie character's evaluations and motivations to the story events precipitating or following them. The construction of a narrative whole and the listener are still not taken fully into account.

It is interesting in this connection to note that these 8-year-olds mark emotions with regard to primarily past events. They are speaking retroactively when they speak about their emotions, whereas the 12-years-olds are more concerned to imagine and anticipate the emotional impact of future events, for example:

Regret:

> "If I had got the part of de Valera's son, I WOULD have been [mimes happy]" (JOR8).
> "He lives far away from me so I CAN'T really visit him" (StJS8).

Frustration:

> "And em, I COULD have been in a film but I have an English accent you see, it was so annoying because it was an Irish film" (JOH8).
> "We COULDN'T even watch the TV when we got home 'cos we had none" (IB8).

Excitement:

> "I CAN'T wait until a few weeks 'cos we're going over to England" (SL12).

Doubt:

> "When I grow up I want to be an actress but I don't know if I'LL be able to" (SL12).

This fits with the temporal patterns already outlined, where the oldest children were the most future oriented, talking about the future, whereas the 5-and 8-year-olds were telling stories about the past but it is not that neat. The sense is that the 8-year-olds are actually making a pronouncement as to their feelings or emotions about the events or happenings that they have recounted but from the point of view of how they feel now rather than telling me how they felt then, rather than putting their audience via their words into the picture then. So they tell the story and then as an addendum make reference to an emotional state. They are telling how they feel now about what happened in the past but not how they felt then as it happened, at the time. The 12-year-olds on the other hand are busy telling me how they feel now about something that may or may not happen in the future.

---

[35] Should these local and global links be seen as themselves given that they are talking autobiographically?

For all children, and presumably for all narrators, what we feel about something now is what is important, not how we did feel or will feel in the future, even if it was possible to make absolute distinctions of that order.

In the final stages of narrative development, from age 9 or 10 on and certainly by age 12, all the different levels of structuring are integrated. The children now make linguistic references to emotions and to other internal states that are evaluative from a much more global perspective. The overarching perspective from which they as narrator view events, settings, and character motivations as connected is much more obvious. And, because they are much less focused than the middle group on particulars, they are now concerned to present for the listener a character's mental and emotional states as being the outcome of story events and equally to show how events and actions in the story are the result of their character's (their own) motivations and emotions.

Overall, the 12-year-olds here have a much greater awareness of, and facility for, recipient design that are evident in the discussion of their use of the modals in interpersonal narrative roles. For instance when, as sometimes happened, the children became anxious about their performance, where to start or whether they were on the right track, it is because they were only too well aware of the conventions and the nature and design of these narrative occasions. There was also a steady increase with age in reference to mental states, what I call **Theory of Mind** statements. Together these two categories account for the discourse function of 27% of all modal utterances for the 12-year-olds. The ability to mark emotions and make reference to mental states are both very important developments, in terms of narrative development and also for self-development. Only at this age do the children consistently make strategic and relevant references to emotions in their narratives. They give insight not only into the motives of the characters but they are also used to signal the point of the story, why it was worth telling at all.

THEORY OF MIND STATEMENTS[36]

This category includes all modal utterances that include references to mental states, whether the speaker's own, held now or at any given time in the past, or any beliefs or mental states attributed to other characters in their discourse, whether about the speaker, about themselves as third parties or about some other character. Also included was any overt character assessment made by the speaker, again either about themselves or an other, when it directly related to

---

[36]This term is used in the same way as in recent psychological research on the child's development of a "theory of mind" as a personal account of one's own and other's mental states (e.g., Perner, 1991; Wellman, 1990). A very comprehensive review of research and theory that also advances the body of knowledge in this area of developmental psychology is provided by Mitchell (1996). He spent a lot of time treating developments in language and communication as he asserted that a uniquely human application of an understanding of mind falls within the province of verbal communication (p. 11).

some trait other than physical ability or appearance, that is, when it referred to mental traits or abilities.

There is a natural connection, and even an element of overlap, between this category and the discourse category that includes reference to emotions because in both cases you are talking about establishing motivations and reasons for people's actions and for the fact that they hold a set of beliefs. These modal utterances serve to display beliefs and to make opinions explicitly available. We need to know that people's actions are governed not just externally but by virtue of their beliefs. To engage in autobiographical discourse requires that speakers focus on what they once believed and what they now hold to be the case. We would expect speculation as to the beliefs a third party in the narrative must have held to direct their actions. We would also expect a certain amount of speculation as to what others think of the speaker or how actions and events in the past must have directed or influenced someone's thinking about us. (i.e., we would expect a certain amount of Goffman's, 1967, impression management, see accounts theory in the **agency** category).

Overall, this category accounts for 13% of all modal utterances, but when broken down by age, the situation is quite different. As with the category of emotional discourse functions, these so-called **theory of mind** functions are much more important for the older children. The 12-year-olds make use of these meanings more than three times as much as the youngest group. The 5-year-olds tend to comment in a fairly situation-specific fashion on other people's beliefs, whereas the 8-year-old group focuses more on their own beliefs and opinions but also in relation to quite specific events. The oldest children make the most explicit and the most general statements about mental states and beliefs, both in relation to themselves and others. They also frequently make statements amounting to a character assessment, again primarily about other people but they also refer to themselves in these terms.

In this discourse context, the modal auxiliaries were often used by the children in utterances whose function was ultimately to make statements about themselves, although under the guise of simply reiterating what others have said. These reported views are often complimentary to the child and by assigning them to others, the speaker is able to shift the source of, and hence responsibility for, the utterance elsewhere.[37]

Often the children actually used reported speech, a popular maneuver using the modal auxiliaries to distribute responsibility for the effect of an utterance. They also used double-voiced utterances to make their own statements authoritative, that is, to add the moral weight of other voices to their own. For example, this child uses both verbatim reported speech and paraphrasing to make her point. Note also the clustering of the modal auxiliaries that we have seen before.

"I CAN be real annoying sometimes I'D say,

---

[37] Responsibility framing devices on reported speech in regards to self.

my friend says "I CAN'T believe you are <u>so</u> mean to your brother and I
CAN'T believe he is <u>so</u> nice to you, 'cos you are so mean to him",
this is what my friends WOULD say to me
but he's being mean to me as well but they'D say he's quite nice to me
but I'D say I CAN be nice as well,
I've a lot of good friends" (RL12).

The next examples come from the transcript of a 12-year-old who frequently used
this type of construction to talk about himself:

"Some people WOULD think I'm nice, like, and that I'm grand,
other people WOULD probably think that I'm a bit arrogant" (SM12).
"Some people in the cricket club say I'LL be more successful than him but I
don't think so" (SM12 in relation to his older brother).

The same child in another extended passage combines reported speech, the
conversational historic present (which we have seen is a device used to make an
event or episode especially vivid), and explicit references to his mother's beliefs
and mental states to recount an obviously highly charged episode.

"Sometimes you get, like, an-, like any child with their parents you get,
we have rows, you know, and my Mum's getting a bit stubborn,
it feels actually as you get older your parents get more stubborn, you know,
more,
anyway my Mum's always going,
a few days ago my Mum said 'did you take any fig rolls, how many fig rolls
did you take?' 'n I said '2' and then she go-, she came over to me in a storm
and she said I had 3
and she screamed at me and said 'you're a liar, you're a liar',
she trotted up the stairs 'I'LL never believe you again' and I'm, like, 'God!'
and she goes 'you're a liar' and like, she, she just says that but she doesn't,
she <u>does</u> believe me, I <u>know</u> she does, and em" (SM12).

The modal auxiliaries were also used within this category to express a speaker's
opinions and beliefs on her or his own state of mind at some time in the past.
Note also the use of habitual WOULD here that has already been discussed in
terms of setting up an element of habituality.

"With the interview for the film, it was all I COULD think about, like, I
convinced myself I was gonna get it" (PF12).
"No, I used to think I'D like to work as an artist or something" (SM8).
"As I ate quite a lot and I'D be embarrassed" (TA12).
"There's me, I'm just finished reading a book 'cos I thought I MIGHT be
interested in books" (TA12).
"I didn't tell my minder 'cos I thought I'D just worry her" (RL12).
"I thought I'D be there for ages" (SC8).
"I COULD take his soother, but I WOULDN'T" (EF5).[38]

"I MIGHT have done that but I don't think the priest WOULD be so stupid"
(KB8).

And also in relation to other characters' states of mind:

"That's my sister, she CAN get in a very bad mood" (TA12).
"Dad's a bit strict, when he, when he CAN make his mind up" (SOH12).
"We call him fat and he just CAN'T come to terms with it but he is fat"
(SM12).
"He didn't tell because he knows he'LL get in trouble himself because he
normally does when he tells like that" (CMcG5).
"He'D really slag you, I've never known somebody like that" (AK12).
"I used to run off and my Mum's best friend, K, WOULDN'T know where I
was" (SM12).
"But when it comes to interviews I get real shy so they think I WOULD be
shy in front of the camera" (PF12).
"My Mum never thought of that so she COULDN'T have done it" (St.JS8).

If we compare the younger children's theory of mind statements in all the
different forms with an extended passage from one 12-year-old, we can see a
clear development in terms of actively reflecting on and evaluating one's former
self in relation to previously held beliefs, opinions, and ideas that had an effect
on our lives. The younger children tend to focus on specific incidents and events
in relation to past beliefs. For example,

"Oh yeah, when I was a baby I wrote on some carpet, I didn't know, I
thought it was some paper thing and I was thinking I'LL draw an X on it so I
did' (DG5).
"It MUST be, it MUST be you just don't know what paper is" (HOB5).
"He said Harry WILL keep on going into his room and taking things" (StJS8,
explaining why one brother wanted a lock for his bedroom).

"My brother taught me multiplication, he, and we, he taught me squares and I
nearly learnt square roots,
I, em, I figured out something to get a sweet from him
he gave me loads of questions
what's the square root of 64
and then I just thought it MIGHT be 9

---

[38] Interesting because an explicit use of the modal auxiliaries to indicate physical and circumstantial
capability outweighed by lack of volition or moral reasoning. "While it is nature that gives me the
capacity to initiate action, a sense of power in the world, it is only language and a social order which
can give me a sense of responsibility for what I do. Nature provides the 'can' but culture and
language provide the 'may' and 'must'" Harré (1993a, p. 5). Also see Wierzbicka (1996, p. 105) on
the difference between moral (based on the concept of good and bad) and social (based on the concept
of CAN) rules.

but I said I'D do 8 first and 8 was the right one and I got the sweet" (DPB8).

"we didn't think that he WOULD stay alive" (JOH8, about a lamb that had to be hand fed).

The older children tend to depict more general type scenarios based on and built around ideas and beliefs they had when younger. This particular child's speech was in fact very heavily modalized overall lending it an air of mature reflection and retrospective restructuring.

"But I like 6th class a lot because, like, in junior infants, Miss Ruttle used to give us little jobs, like, to give out books or something, but that was only to give us a false sense of responsibility whereas now we actually do have some importance,
I know next year we'LL have much more but this year, you just seem to be much more important than you were in 5th class,
and each year when you go up another class you actually look back and wonder how COULD you ever have been that age and been interested in the things, mutant turtles and all that,
you never realise that you WOULD like that and that next year you'LL be looking back and realising how COULD you support a team so much and just gradually you change so much
or that how were you ever that small, like, we look at 5th class and imagine how they're so small, and we were only that size a few months ago" (AW12).

Similarly, another 12-year-old recounts how his false beliefs at the time led to an unforgettable experience for him.

"I remember when I was young, my mum had her womb removed when I was about 7,
of course I thought she was real sick and that she was going to die
so I was in the hospital all the time and I was sitting there thinking 'oh my god, she's going to die, when is it?'
and then it turns out that she came home the next week after it
and I was going 'why aren't you in the grave?' and then my Mum, my Mum explained it to me and I was like, 'oh God, how stupid I've been'
and I, I was, I haven't forgotten th-, that situation for the rest of my,
I WON'T forget it for the rest of my life,
as you CAN imagine, it was very, em" (SM12).

Modal auxiliaries in their epistemic sense do not provide information about the world as such, what they do is provide information about the information of the speaker. Another use of these types of statements was for relational or identificatory purposes, either in relation to themselves (further examples of the tendency to introduce characteristic traits and feelings via general comments or stories rather than making explicit statements):

"I CAN never remember names" (SOH12).
"I CAN'T say I like learning but I like being in the class" (HG12).
"I'm always worried that I've forgotten something that I'LL need" (SL12).
"I was always afraid that I'D forget my lunch or something like that" (SL12).

Or in order to typecast other people:

"And he CAN'T, like, you WON'T ever do him, Dad, he's always in the right, he's perfect" (HG12).
"And he says 'Helen, you're only thinking about snobbiness, it's a good education and you'LL do well'"(HG12).

The importance of this function cannot really be overestimated in this context: "words alone do not create the world but they certainly contribute to make inner selves known and opinions available and hence vulnerable to the scrutiny of others" (Duranti, 1994, p. 42)

7

Evaluating Oneself:
The Discourse of Morality

INTERPERSONAL NARRATING FUNCTIONS

This category consists of those metacommentary type uses of modalized utterances, whether direct performative uses or more negatively nuanced affairs. Even in a monologic narrative there's a listener and meaning is interactively constituted. For the modal auxiliaries the interpersonal function precedes the informational one (Guo, 1994). The functions of boasting, showing off, and responding to perceived or anticipated challenges were included in this category as they were considered to be directed specifically at the listener, that is, to be occasioned by the discourse context and to be both outside, yet remaining part of, the events taking place within the narrative.[1] This category of discourse functions represents about 9% of the overall modal utterances. There is a small, steady increase in these types of utterances with age, but all the children make fairly good use of this function of the modal auxiliaries. The 5-year-old speakers do the most boasting, which fits well with their preoccupation with possessions. The 8-year-olds also engage in boasting and showing off but are beginning to use some types of discourse markers fairly well. Once more, we could interpret this movement in the direction of a more adult model, a more conventional model that is.

Modal Auxiliaries as Discourse Markers

The 8- and 12-year-olds use the most discourse markers (for example, "CAN'T remember" used apologetically or dismissively) showing they are more aware of narrative conventions, of recipient design than the younger children. Also they seem to have more of an idea of what should be included in an autobiography, the type of information and stories generally offered as autobiographical discourse.

---

[1] Fox (1994, pp. 30-31): "the study of grammar in use, in conversation, is the study of grammar in social interaction in socially organised contexts. Utterances are produced in real time for particular local interactional reasons. In a common misinterpretation, interaction is heard as referring to only the most obviously social phenomena, such as turn-taking and maybe adjacency pairs. But interactional motivations can be much less obviously social than these phenomena. All utterances created are recipient designed, that is, specifically constructed for a particular listener (or group of listeners) on a particular occasion of listening".

The older groups also make most use of rhetorical devices, a quite sophisticated discourse skill, related to the idea of recipient design.[2]

> "Did you hear me on the radio? It was the Friday before Mother's Day,
> you WOULD have heard all about it,
> I definitely said the most embarrassing thing" (JOR8).
> "I've already been in two movies so what else CAN I do?" (JOR8).
> "Well, where CAN I begin?" (SM12).
> "And where CAN I go back now?" (SM12).
> "What CAN I say about my Dad?" (SM12).

The older children's narratives appear more other directed, by which I mean more manifestly designed and organized with the listener in mind. For example, the same child keeps saying why he has related something whereas most of the 5-year-olds do not see the need for this sort of signposting. The 8- and 12-year-olds are well aware that if you can successfully explain or motivate why you are telling a particular story, why it could be important or relevant, then it has more chance of being accepted, of not being challenged and indeed the more general point that it will seem more coherent. They seem to realize that a particular incident is not in itself necessarily worth recounting unless you can get across to your listener not just what happened, the details, but why you are remembering it now, why you are telling the story.

> "And then we were in hysterics and I, I'LL never forget that really" (SM12).

> "And I, I was, I haven't forgotten th-, that situation for the rest of my,
> I WON'T forget it for the rest of my life as you CAN imagine,
> it was very. and em" (SM12).

Similarly only the older children, the 12-year-olds in particular, tend to express concern that they are doing it right, that they are telling, that is, remembering, the "right" things.

> "I'm not so sure where to start 'cos I CAN only remember from when my
> sister was born" (IOD12).
> "I was born on the 10th of the 10th 1983,
> I don't actually know what hospital but I CAN find out for you" (AK12).
> "How WILL I start off?" (DH12).
> "Do you want me to tell you like, my most recent or my most distant
> memories?
> my brother, I CAN'T really remember when he was younger cos I wasn't
> born yet
> but I'LL tell you some important things in his life" (SM12).
> "I CAN'T really think" (AC8).

---

[2] Theory of listener, representation of listener, recipient design, flip side = grammatical structures as interpretive demands, therefore discourse functions/activity demanded on both sides (Fox, 1994).

They also often use so-called frozen or idiomatic discourse makers[3] to dramatize events, highlight, and pick out for the listener the important bits.

> "I'm going to Alexandra's next year, I CAN'T wait" (SOH12).
> "I've had them in for 5 weeks today so I CAN take them out next week,
> I CAN'T wait,
> but I only have 2 pairs of earrings so I'LL have to borrow all my Mum's"
> (SOH12).

Some instances look like the sort of discourse markers that are used to bring about self-reflection.[4]

> "And also my favourite which I MUST remember was when I was,
> when I went to America, last summer,
> it was the West Indies, St Lucia and the prime minister's son, em, went there
> on his honeymoon just a week after we went" (JOR).

> "I CAN remember when I was in 3rd class and well, em,
> there was this boy and he was messing a lot and Mr T. came over to him and
> got,
> and dragged him up off the ground" (KM12).

> "But I remember my first day at school
> when I was walking along and my mum, she brought me in,
> and I was holding on to her
> as if I WOULD never see my parents again
> but I CAN remember my teeth actually shaking" (AW12).

And finally discourse markers used as responsibility for performance, another consequence of the older children's more developed (re)presentation of their listener, their increasing awareness of recipient design measures. Here the 8-and 12-year-olds are assuming responsibility for their discourse performance,[5] whether apologizing for a poor show, which is a way of signaling that the narrator knows the proper format, knows what is called for but for whatever reason can not do it now. The main thing conveyed in the next example is that the child

---

[3] According to Hoye (1997), such frozen or conventional phrases would therefore not qualify as discourse markers but as I outlined in the modal analysis, I consider these phrases in this context to be doing the work of discourse markers.

[4] Gerhardt and Stinson (1994, pp. 458-459): "these markers help bring about the analytic stance of self-reflection and self-investigation, [they] cluster at moments of greater self-disclosure moments of uncertainty".

[5] Bauman in Hill and Irvine (1993, p. 182) on responsibility for performance, *I can't remember*. "I understand performance as a communicative frame, the essence of which resides in the assumption of responsibility to an audience for a display of communicative competence (the knowledge and ability to speak in socially appropriate and interpretable ways [Hymes, 1971, p. 58]) highlighting the way in which verbal communication is carried out, above and beyond its referential content. The act of speaking is itself framed as display, objectified, lifted out to a degree from its contextual surroundings, and opened up to scrutiny by an audience".

knows she should include breaking her arm in her autobiography but she does not actually remember the incident and so tries to make good the gap by recounting another illness scenario.

> "I CAN'T remember when I broke my arm
> but once when I was in 3rd class last year, yeah, that was last year, em, I broke,
> I mean I was very sick" (SM8).

Or used to dismiss things they can not recall anyway as unimportant or irrelevant and to change the subject.

> "Only a few kids, only babies and myself and my brother James and another girl who was about 9 -CAN'T remember her name-
> I CAN never remember names" (SOH12).

> "In karate this, just last Sunday, I won a trophy for second place in team fights,
> I started when I was something like 6 or 5,
> I CAN'T remember,
> and I'm on my green belt now" (SM8).

> "And then of course we moved,
> but I CAN'T really remember that far back" (SM12).

And finally, to break off proceedings: "And that's all I CAN remember" (AC8, uttered at the end of a particular story).

PRESCRIBING

This category refers to the children's prescribing and assembling of possible and parallel worlds to indicate how things might have been, and particularly in the case of the younger ones, how things should have been different. This involves evaluating the way the world is in general and also an evaluation of specific events and happenings in their own spheres of experience. Even when the first impression is straightforward describing or reporting, the modal utterance can still be read for the speaker's take on the event or whatever is being so described.

The Discourse of Morality

An account must have a point. Often the point is to establish the morality of something or someone in relation to norms. This amounts to the view that utterances in discourse are organized in order to construct a moral world in which characters and events are continuously evaluated "over and against an emergent, jointly achieved, though not necessarily agreed upon, ethical perspective" (Duranti, 1994, p. 166).

"He's my friend except he's a boy
he's a bit rough
it isn't nice to just like girls or just like boys, it WOULDN'T be fair" (EF5).

This category also incorporates those utterances that prescribe against, that is, when the children proscribe certain behaviors or scenarios. Whereas descriptive discourse (or reporting) is used to indicate that something is the case, the role of prescriptive discourse is to guide conduct, both the speaker's and the hearer's. This form of discourse is used by the speaker to make something the case, to induce others to believe or to act in particular ways. The English modal auxiliaries play a pivotal role in the organization of this particular type of discourse, namely, the discourse of persuasive argument that is essentially prescriptive in nature (Gerhardt, 1990, p. 7). This is also the case in these autobiographical narratives, as a lot of them are taken up with account giving, reason giving, justification for actions, and so on.

Prescriptive discourse often de-emphasises subjectivity by describing normative procedures via impersonal constructions. The source of authority of the prescription is seen to change somewhat with age in that the importance of parents as a source of authority decreases in favor of friends and self. The 5-year-old children tend to confound age and status with epistemic authority. To the extent that moral development is thought to proceed from external obligation to personal responsibility,[6] the 8- and 12-year-old children tend to use more principled modals rather than interactive ones, which is also part of the diachronic movement in modal meanings outlined earlier. And as Gerhardt (1990, p. 47) pointed out, the child's developing awareness that social conventions actually exist brings in its wake a sense of the child himself or herself having rights (i.e., the right to engage in those activities that are sanctioned by convention as well as the right to expect others to comply). This also involves the child's sense of having duties (i.e., the duty to acknowledge the force of the convention over one's own and others' activities).

The younger children, the 5-year-olds (and also sometimes the older ones) often judge themselves, others, and events in terms of punishments or rewards:

"He never lets me on the beanbag so I just go on it but he didn't tell 'cos he knows he'LL get in trouble himself because he normally does when he tells like that" (CMcG5).

---

[6] See especially Leman and Duveen (1996) on developmental differences in children's understanding of epistemic authority; Serniak (1992) on epistemic bravado; Raviv, Bar-Tal, Raviv, and Houminer (1990, p. 159): "the conception of epistemic authority places a unique focus on subjective beliefs concerning the source." There are also many theories in the psychological literature of which Kohlberg's (1976) theory would be well-known. He postulated three main stages of moral development: Premoral: punishment and obedience orientation, naive instrumental hedonism; Morality of conventional role conformity: the 'good boy' morality of maintaining good relations, approval of others, authority-maintaining morality; and the morality of self-accepted moral principles; and Morality of contract, of individual rights and of democratically accepted law, morality of individual principles of conscience.

Or according to the status quo where for example, parents, teachers, and policemen are good or in the right simply by dint of status:

> "I MIGHT have done that but I don't think the priest WOULD be so stupid" (KB8).

Judgments are also made in terms of conventional norms and rules:

> "She loves her school now
> but you CAN only stay there for 2 years" (CK8).
> "It isn't nice to just like boys or just like girls,
> it WOULDN'T be fair" (EF5).

Another development around 8 is where the children are now seen to judge self and others in terms of intention or motive regardless of power or status (if she did not mean to do it, she should not be punished or held accountable).

> "My mum never keeped a photo of her, she never keeped one of her
> my mum never thought of that so she COULDN'T have done it" (StJS8).

The 12-year-olds tend to reason more often in terms of abstract concepts such as a basic respect for the individual rather than in terms of conventional norms of right or wrong conduct.

> "Our teacher now is strict but he's nice, he teaches you well,
> if you don't understand something he goes over it again
> but he CAN be, he shouts a lot sometimes
> but he's a nice teacher" (HG12).

This is the morality of individual conscience. Rules are seen as arbitrary and changeable:

> "They have to be 2 pages but you CAN have 3 if you want" (JOH8).
> "You had to answer it in your own words,
> you COULDN'T copy, you COULDN'T answer it from the sheet, like"
> (RL12).

and people and events are judged now in terms of a personally developed value system:

> "He'D really slag you, I've never known someone like that" (AK12).
> "I don't think it's fair that we get homework as well as school, 'cos like,
> I WOULDN'T mind spending an extra hour at school and getting no
> homework" (AK12).

Looking for Support

This category accounts for a little more than 10% of the modal auxiliaries used. In particular, the 5- and 12-year-olds are appealing for support for their argument or to have their version accepted or validated. In fact, this is a fairly consistent theme in many of the categories, probably because of the crucial role of the modal auxiliaries in persuading, in challenging, in giving and in constructing accounts. The 8-year-olds in this category do the most recommending, stating of rules and blaming, which fits with the pattern we already saw whereby this is the age group that is most concerned with rules, obtaining permission, what people around them should and should not do, and so on. This age group's narratives, as is the case with most narratives of personal experience, are frequently told as "moral or behavioral *exempla*, suggesting how the addressee should behave in a similar circumstance in his or her life" (see Linde, 1993, p. 112ff).

> "My mother, she always likes me, but she said to me 'Linda's not here today,'
> my minder's gone home, but she SHOULDN'T go home that way
> but I've got my mother and father to look after me and my sister" (VMcG5).

Positioning via Reported Speech

The discourse function of appealing for support for your account or version as you present it and try to have it accepted is very informative here. What is spoken and who may speak are issues of power. A basic principle might be that the higher the rank of the speaker the more individualistic she or he is allowed to be: "[a high chief] can 'own' as it were the meaning of his own words and expect others to comply with his own interpretation" (Duranti, 1994, on Samoan society). This is manifestly not the case with children. Duranti's point in relation to, for example, a high chief is that words often do not emanate from individuals in the Western sense but from the locus of a positional identity,[7] such as a particular noble title. A similar point but in the reverse direction can be made for children's discourse, as in, their relatively low position occasions frequent recourse to authority. It is often the case that what a child says is not allowed to stand on its own, unchallenged, and this I think explains in part why they use more persuading techniques, more challenging and anticipatory manoeuvres, and especially the device of reported speech.

Reported speech, a discourse device pointed out many times in the examples already, is very interesting in this context. It seems on the face of it like the simple insertion into a narrative of an unbiased rendition of what someone else said, but we have to ask why at that point? Why has that particular remark been chosen? Why not paraphrase what was said? The device of reported speech is

---

[7] Cohen (1994, p. 1) on the anthropologist F. Gearing's study of the Fox Indians of Iowa who apparently regard their behaviors as inhering in the structural niches in which they are placed, so that any Fox who happened to be similarly located would behave in the same way. Interesting parallels with positioning theory.

frequently used in these narratives as a means of validating the child's own position. It is suggested (e.g., Hill & Irvine, 1993) that in cases where the speaker's personal identity or social position is insufficient as a guarantee of a statement's truth or authenticity, for example, in a young or a low-ranking speaker, double-voiced utterances, or reported speech is used to make utterances authoritative. They function to add the moral weight of other voices to the speaker's own. The speaker uses reported speech as a way of claiming, in effect, that an utterance has already been coconstructed.

This can work in two ways, either to back up the speaker's position and to validate their version or account or, alternatively, it can be employed in order to distance the speaker from an utterance (but still making the point or passing on the information). Speakers in this way are trying to evade responsibility by invoking some other source for an utterance rather than rather than trying to enhance their own utterances' force. "Reported speech and other responsibility framing devices because of 'leakage' distribute responsibility, thinning out and socializing its central focus rather than absolutely relocating it at a distance from the animator" (Bauman, 1993).

Here the speaker is trying to marshal support (not only via reported speech, although it is used here also to show how reprehensible the DJ's comments were):

"My Mom, did you hear me on the radio? it was the Friday before Mother's Day, you WOULD have heard all about it, did you hear that?
I definitely said the most embarrassing thing, even you know Simon Young? From the radio? he said, he made a rude remark about my Mom at the very end, he said I was the, no, he actually said it about me, 'well, there's the science fiction kid,'
I did not like that at all and if I ever meet him I'm going to beat the living daylights out of him
WOULD you like after being on the radio and suddenly em, a man says 'oh yeah, there's the sci fi kid'?
I said that my Mom smokes a lot and she didn't really like TV
but sometimes she watches Sci Fi movies with my Dad at night" (JOR8).

PROBLEM-SOLVING

This category refers to those modal utterances that are not just recounting some event or idea but are actually used by the child in the process of working through unresolved stories and accounts.[8] Discourse itself, in this theoretical framework, is both problem and solution. The problem-solving genre is directed to the solution of epistemic puzzles and makes use of markers of argumentation, possibility and modality.[9] Overall this category of discourse functions accounts for 10% of the modal utterances that shows that autobiographical speech and

---

8 See Bruner (1987) on the engine of narrative, trouble, as an imbalance or disequilibrium among the elements of the narrative.
[9] See, for instance, Feldman (1989) on monologue as problem solving.

discourse is not just about the past per se. It does not always, or even mostly, involve straightforward narrating or retelling of bounded perfective events. The problem-solving scenarios in these narratives take many different forms and cover a wide range of experiences but some of the familiar patterns are evident in this category. For instance, the temporal pattern we have seen whereby many of the 5-year-old children's unresolved accounts center around working out the logic of some past event, how it must have happened. The older children, the 8- and 12-year-olds, are, as usual, more future oriented in their problematic accounts.

> "I got, I got em, I was going to ask for, I got em, I got the sticker case that I
> asked for
> but I said em 'if you CAN'T get me Skiing Barbie get me Glitter Cindy' and
> I got her instead and I got a big bike with a dolly seat and a basket but no
> bell,
> I MIGHT get one from the guy in the shop who is, who gonna, who was, em,
> who had that bike, but I think he still has it 'cos Santa gave me the one
> my Mommy showed Santa what bike I WOULD like and then he gets it,
> I think he went back, he MIGHT have gone back after and leaved it when
> everybody was asleep, he left nearly all the presents out when we were asleep
> and Mommy went up to bed and Daddy went up to bed before him and we
> heard a knock,
> we heard a door,
> and it MIGHT be 'cos the bike was too heavy to get in the chimney" (JW5).

Note how the language of problem solving involves especially the language of logical inference (*but, so because, not*)[10] and qualifications of knowledge states via for example, epistemic adverbs (*maybe, probably, certainly*). One of the main tendencies is for the older children, especially the 12-year-olds, to use the more tentative options, which reflects their tendency to be more reflective in general.

The children engage also in a lot of on-line rationalization as they get caught up in working out a plan of action:

> "I'D like to be an actress or a singer or a dancer
> I'D like to,
> make children enjoy doing stuff
> like, I'D like to do something with children where, in-, like, you'D help the
> children ,
> like, lots of children are into watching theatres and things
> and that's what I'D like to do,
> hopefully I WILL,

---

[10] As opposed to the use of temporal connectives (Feldman, 1989, p. 98).

I mean, I'LL, I'm gonna force my Mom to get me into the Billy Barry
MAYBE in the summer" (AC8).

Similarly, there are a lot of justificatory episodes:

"I never really liked Irish, I just hate languages, I don't speak any,
my Mum is trying to make me speak French but, like, I don't want to speak
it,
no, it just sort of gets in the way of Irish and I'm trying to get into Irish, I'm,
I'm not very good at Irish at all cos I don't like it,
I mean if I liked it, I'D try but I don't really try,
I kind of feel it's pointless as well, I don't think I'LL use it,
I mean it COULD be handy for quite a lot of things but I don't really think
I'D use Irish for a job" (TA12).

The oldest group of children often told narratives that involved exploring their
options:

"I'm going to Gonzaga next year, but like,
eight years with these people, you get used to it,
like, you'D miss them,
but it doesn't mean I'm just going to go away from them, I know where they
all live, I have their phone numbers so we CAN just hang around normally,
but I'm not saying I WON'T get new friends, em" (PF12).

And working out the implications of sequences of events and situations,
something that was not found very often in the 8-year-old's narratives and hardly
featured at all in the first-person narratives of the 5-year-old children:

"I think she missed us a bit but I didn't miss her at all, the advantages
weighed out the downside for me, I had much more, not responsibility, I
don't know, that I had all the time, more space, Someday she says she'LL
bring me but I think it WILL be a while yet
there's a big gap between us but I don't mind that,
it's sometimes good 'cos she knows what secondary school and college are
like and I'LL have that headstart, sort of, to know what it'LL be like"
(AW12, about sister).

This leads into a category of discourse functions that is in fact very closely
related, although the natural affinity between problem solving and *irrealis*
functions is often not recognized.

UNREAL STATES

This category reiterates the importance of the future and the possible as important
elements of autobiography. It encompasses references to unreal states, the
forecasting of events, predicting courses of action, all these functions allow the

speaker to make her or his opinions available and to comment on nonexistent states in ways that will point up the speaker's own very subjective stance in relation to these things.

The modal auxiliaries are the most important way we have of "living beyond the fact", the here-and-now. Children also need to view their lives as projecting beyond the moment, as being internally related to a larger structure: "our permanent need to live by the pattern rather than the fact." (Gee, 1985, p. 216, citing Kermode, 1966). In fact this point may be even more salient in relation to children. Are children allowed inhabit the present? Children are always, for example, asked to think of themselves in relation to the future, what they want to be when they grow up, what will happen when they get older, bigger, and so on. The organization of the present in terms of the future is a fundamental cultural source of developmental change and a powerful environmental source of developmental continuity (Cole & Cole, 1993).[11] And this also supports the assertion that change may be more important in children's autobiographical narratives than stability.

Overall this discourse category accounts for 11% of the modal auxiliaries used by the children. In the case of the 5-year-old narrators, this is mainly in the form of fantasizing and imagining. This trend supports Feldman's (1989, p. 118) idea of a common origin in story forms for two activities that are not usually seen as related in development: problem solving and fantasy.

"Imagine if the water came swishing in here, all of the water,
then, and if all of the puddles came in here we'D be swimming around the place
and d'ya know what Cormac said? 'It'D be cool, I COULD skateboard'"
(EF5).

"I was, when I was only, I said to my mother 'where is my gold dishes?'
before I was born and I found it, I found a gold [ ] with wings on and every single plates,
I was very rich but I had lots of money, I'm a rich man you know,
but then I hid them where no-one CAN find them" (VMcG5).

"I'D like to be a sly fox 'cos I like to eat chickens" (VMcG5).

The 8-year-olds spend more narrative time forecasting events and outcomes:

"My Mum is going away tomorrow, I don't know where she's going,
I think she is just going for two days, you see the games WILL cheer me up"
(StJS8).

---

[11] Cole (1996, p. 186 on White, 1942, p. 120): "Temporally the culturally constituted mind is 'a continuum extending to infinity in both directions.' In this manner the medium of culture allows us to project the past into the future, thereby creating a stable interpretative frame which is then read back into the present as one of the important elements of psychological continuity".

"I'LL be making my communion on the 11th of May" (KB8).
"And then we're also going to Legoland and MAYBE to the world of
adventures,
this WILL be the second time we've been in England" (JOR8).
"I like swimming and we'LL be going there in a few weeks in school,
I learned when I was away in Spain" (SC8).

And the oldest children use the modal auxiliaries for predicting, hypothesizing
and speculating, often in relation to their own emotional reactions. Again in this
discursive context, the adolescents tend to be very future oriented and actually
also quite pragmatic.

"And em, like, I like going up on stage, I think it's fun but sometimes I get
really shy,
in the Feis I get awfully shy, it gets really embarrassing, there's all these
people staring at you and, but not in the play cos I'LL know all the people
there and I know all my friends" (DH12).
"If we win that, we go to England but I don't think there is an awful lot of
chance
but you have to hope anyway,
it WILL be great to go to England because I have never, I have been to
England but never by myself, I've never really been away by myself for more
than a week
so it WOULD seem very strange to be in a different country" (AW12).
"I'LL miss all my friends 'n stuff but most of them are going to Muckross
except,
but Margaret, I don't really get on well with her any more, she's so lazy,
I WOULDN'T mind if she didn't go to Muckross, but eight others from our
class are going so I'LL be fine but I'D say it'LL be real different" (RL12).

"I'm worried about next year and I don't want to go at all
like, I'm in 6th class now and I'm at the top and then I have to go right down
to the bottom again and work up, but I think it'LL be fine" (HG12).

"When I grow up I want to be an actress but I don't know if I'LL be able to
'cos if I'm an actress I WON'T really get to see my family that much, but so,
I don't know, I just love acting" (SL12).

Summary

The modal auxiliaries were used primarily in their reporting and agentive
functions by all age groups, not surprising given the nature of the task but not, as
we have seen, straightforward either. Reporting in this context is rarely a direct
mapping of words to world but revealed different levels of involvement and
different measures of distance in relation to what the children were reporting.
One of the basic tenets of this study, that an active subject is a moral subject, is

reflected in the use of the modal auxiliaries in the context of agency, in the distinction between actions and events, between what we do and what happens to us.

There were some interesting age-related patterns in relation to the other discourse functions associated with the use of the modal auxiliaries. Many of the 5-year-olds' modals were in the context of problem solving and unreal states, which we saw are very closely related conceptually and that highlight the overall importance of the future and the possible in autobiography. Issues of moral development were mirrored nicely in the use of the modal auxiliaries as development proceeded from external obligation to a heightened sense of personal responsibility. The middle group, aged 8, was primarily concerned with prescribing thought and behavior, usually of other people. In fact, the 8-year-olds overall had the highest incidence of pre- and proscriptive discourse uses of the modal auxiliaries. They also had least use for modalized *irrealis* statements, underscoring once more their tendency to stick to the facts or at least to restrict themselves to trying to establish them. The older children's transcripts were much more evaluative and reflexive and accounted for the majority of the modal auxiliaries as used in theory of mind statements and the relatively few references to emotions and emotional states documented. This in effect meant the 12-year-olds were better at accounting and providing motives for themselves and at organizing circumstances and conditions into some sort of meaningful, narrative whole. Significantly, all the children, the two older age groups in particular, had grasped the rhetorical potential of the modal auxiliaries. What do these discourse patterns, temporally organized as they are, tell us about the child's construction of a narrative identity? After all: "Stories never live alone: they are the branches of a family that we have to trace back, and forward." (Calasso, 1994, p. 10).

8

Conclusion

The self is essentially a being of reflexivity, coming to itself in its own narrational acts. Wolf (1990, p. 189)

It is not child's play to make meanings that relate self to other subjectivities, to be the fulcrum of control, to be bound by commitment to norms and yet remain autonomous, and to be self in a world of causes beyond one's control. Bruner (1996, p. 27)

And yet most children can do it. Apparently autobiography is much easier than it should be because of some push even in the earliest normal development towards the elaboration of a reflective self (Bruner, 1995, p. 170) which means that even at age 5, children can engage with some form of autobiographical discourse. Although these 5-year-olds can make a stab at it, they are not very accomplished in this activity. If, as Henry James is quoted as saying, "adventures happen only to people who know how to tell them" (Bruner, 1995, p. 163), then, in the case of autobiographies, it seems that only people who can tell them, have them. Johnstone's (1996, p. 186) assertion that "this, I think, is what articulateness really is: successful self-expression" helps explain why this should be the case. She said "people who are not articulate are people who fail to assert themselves or in everyday terms, to make themselves felt". And Tonkin (1992, p. 133): "the development of oral genre is an important component of self-awareness as the articulate representation of oneself. An inarticulate interviewee may be so through having had so little authority over the life described that actions and events can only be rendered blurrily and inconsequentially." This must be the case with young children. Narrative development is really only beginning at this stage.[1] The 5-year-old child is as yet quite inarticulate, and perhaps most importantly for autobiographical discourse, she or he is quite unmotivated to parcel up events and emotions into one package as adults have learnt to do. We should not dismiss these early narratives because of their relative incompetence. A narrator's skills (or lack of in this case) in organizing and plotting are the means through which they direct interpretation, they are part of the meaning. They tell us something about the child's autobiographical self, but they also reveal something of the self-constructive implications of being

---

[1] For example, Montangero (1996, p. 7): "while 4 and 5 year old children are able to verbalize sequences of events, stories only take on an episodic structure for most children from the age of 8 onwards and the distinction between a narrative with canonical structure and an incomplete story or a simple script does not become operative until the age of 9 or 10 onwards."

skilled at these narrative practices. Maybe Lemke (1995, p. 96) was right, what we need is a latter-day Jean Piaget to write *The Child's Construction of the Sense of Self* that would tell the story of how we are taught to think of ourselves as Selves. Ultimately, the achievement of an autobiographical self is accomplished via the articulate expression of that self. What we acquire is not a true self or a true identity but the ability to communicate and perform a self: "to be someone is clearly a rhetorical achievement" (Shotter, 1993a, p. 16).

The value of the autobiographical voice is not a function of its informativeness or accuracy or even of its truthfulness but, as Johnstone said, it is about being articulate which is precisely what your average 5- or even 8-year-old narrator is not. But they are, nonetheless, trying to depict themselves in some particular relationship to their object and, of course, their interests and preferences have influenced their perceptions and accounts of that object.[2] "The self is the object as well as the subject of this mode of discourse and what is recounted amounts to an expression, assessment and evaluation of that self." (Gerhardt & Stinson, 1994, p. 161).

Initially the infant is limited to being either experiencer or actor and has multiple selves only insofar as she or he enters or experiences different events.[3] Around 3 or 4 years, children begin to show an authorial self independent enough of any given situation to select voices and versions of experience. They now can speak as object or subject, observer or participant. They can operate as author, can adopt various stances, and can move between different possible worlds. At this point they also have a much richer syntax that enables them further to do this[4] and they use different voices to signal different perspectives. They use language, and frequently the modal auxiliaries, to compare their older and younger selves. It is in the context of "a sharply differentiating sense of self that children acquire a set of linguistic markers which may either partake of or amplify their shifting notion of self" (Wolf, 1990, p. 190). And as I noted earlier, the modal system for the children in this study replaces the very early system of self-referential contrasts and provides the child with a more sophisticated and flexible way of differentially referring to, reflecting on and indexing self.

These 5-year-old children's narratives comprise fairly simple sentences, consisting in the main of action verbs with very little, if any, modification. Their sentences tend to be chronologically organized with elementary cohesion devices.[5] This means ideas are not so much related within their narratives as simply juxtaposed. Overall there is very little coherent or global structure evident at this stage. In the case of the 8-year-olds, the syntax is more exact and the overall organization of their narratives is much more coherent, partly as a result of this age group's new mastery of a range of cohesive devices. A

---

[2] Serniak (1992, esp. pp. 50-51) has a good discussion on the authority of autobiographical discourse as confused by the identity of subject and object in the autobiographical conception of knowledge.
[3] See Wolf (1990) for this discussion of the experience of self as multifaceted.
[4] See Wilkinson, Barnsley, and Hanna (1980) on children's autobiographical writing.
[5] They still have a "structure-dependent knowledge of narrative" (Berman, 1988, p. 492).

relationship between parts and whole is established and can be seen in the appropriate subordination of material within the narratives. The children are not so singlemindedly devoted to a simple linear framework but will often interrupt the straight sequential path of their narrative and indulge in retrospection or anticipation. There is a developing awareness of the listener, and the listener's status vis-à-vis the narrative, and in addition they are better able to select among, and make use of, appropriate registers.

There is what you could call a "U-shape" evident in the data from 5 to 8 years, back to 12, where the 8-year-olds' narratives are the most straightforward or "boring", as it were.[6] In the process of becoming better knowers and users of their native language, children become increasingly constrained by its particularities.[7] The middle age group tends to tell quite standardized, fairly stereotypical stories as though they know what is expected of them in telling a story. Just as the 12-year-olds sometimes got quite anxious in relation to the request for autobiographical narratives, the 8-year-olds were quite happy and comfortable with the situation as they seemed to have quite conventionalized notions of what a story "should" include, most notably, very definite beginnings, middles, and ends. The 12-year-olds do not use such explicit markings of sequentiality, they are able to alternate between perspectives and to select particular discourse options depending on the narrative situation. There is much clearer evidence of a developing personal style in the narratives of the 12-year-old children. [8]

Harter's (1983) description of the development of the self or I as story teller outlines much the same process of development as this study. The child aged 3 to 5 years first uses verbs that describe the actions of others before using verbs that describe observed persons altering the status of an object in the environment, what Harter called the self as an action-guiding storyteller. We saw how the 5-year-olds in this study frequently paired their modal auxiliaries with activity-specific verbs whereas the 12-year-olds showed a clear preference for co-occurring mental-experience verbs. The 7- or 8-year-old storyteller can compose only a limited range of stories for enactment by self-as-actor. They describe themselves in terms of action competencies and are concerned with how their competencies compare to others. The young adolescent in this scheme can manipulate and monitor her or his storytelling activity and is able to tackle contradictions and inconsistencies. And in late adolescence (a cohort not included in this study) according to Harter there is the emergence of an ancillary story teller, the unconscious self.

---

[6] See Engels (1995) for the types of stories children of different ages and genders tell.

[7] See also Berman (1993, pp. :253-257).

[8] Hermans (1995) said the self is a polyphonic novel in which each $\underline{I}$ position has its own valuation system. "The $\underline{I}$ moves in imagination from one authorial position to another as if it were a single body moving over a variegated landscape offering many different scenic views. Certain positions or viewpoints become important over time and these are the positions from which the $\underline{I}$ develops a distinctive voice." Hermans and Kempens (1993 on the dialogical self) also feel the temporal dimension of the self narrative in psychology is emphasized at the expense of spatial aspects.

The pattern or patterns in these narratives could be captured by saying that development of the narrative or autobiographical self is a change in the questions that are being asked and answered. To the extent that 12-year-olds are beginning to ask themselves questions, to the extent that they realize they are accounting for themselves, there is an epistemic or evaluative feel to their autobiographical narratives. In exactly the same way, development proceeds for the 5-year-old from the fact that they neither ask nor answer questions of this sort in the main. Very few 5-year-olds are concerned with "the work of finding the through-lines in the moment-to-moment flux of living and thinking" (Britton and Pellegrini, 1990, p. 206). In the case of young children, their experience, and hence the listener's narrative experience, is largely unrealized, unexamined, unshaped. Events and actions are related and recounted but there is little or no contextualization. There is very little attempt on the child's part to make the listener aware of the significance of what she or he is told. The 8-year-old child's accounts are somewhat more conventionally coherent. The narratives are given more shape in the telling, primarily via elaborative and background material (the 8-year-olds as a group in fact provided the most embellishment and description of this sort for their narratives: over 64% of their discourse functions in the category of reporting). But there is still a sense in which there is little examination or reflection on the part of the narrator. The 12-year-old narrator though shows much greater self-awareness and is able to take a reflective and reflexive stance in relation to her or his own story. The older child tends to use a wider variety of devices to expand the experience for the reader (e.g., this group used the conversational historical present, direct and indirect reported speech, and rhetorical speech). The recounted experience is more fully realized and explored. Older children try to shape and determine events for the listener in line with their acute awareness of their image in the eyes of others and their awareness of the possibility of manipulating that image.

In short, if the narrative is not yet a whole for the younger children, can we say that in much the same way the self, at least the autobiographical self, is not a unified whole for them either? An interesting aspect arose as a result of using photographs with the children and that corresponds with what Montangero (1996, p. 75) reported in his investigation of the development of children's diachronic thinking. He found that when presented with a series of photographs or drawings depicting the stages in the life of an individual, 8- to 9-year-old children tend to describe a number of pictures rather than characterising the set using a noun or a verb. I asked the children to bring family photographs with them to the interview session to give them something to focus on and to talk about initially. Many of the children then started off by talking about their photographs. What was noteworthy was the different ways in which the younger and older children approached this. In Montangero's terms, the 5- and even 8-year-olds were clearly dealing with snapshots and evoked the past and future less frequently when they described a picture. The 12-year-olds though would depict the stages of a process. They showed a more interactionist or constructivist viewpoint than the younger children. So one 5-year-old who had brought several photographs with her went through them all intoning:

> "This is me in my pram"
> "This is my granny"
> "This is me in the swimming pool" (JW5).

One 12-year-old narrator on the other hand said:

> "That was my eating phase, I liked food a lot as you CAN see"
> "There's me, I'm just finished reading a book 'cos you see, I thought I MIGHT
> be interested in books"
> "That's my sister, she CAN get in a very bad mood" (TA12).

Another striking aspect associated with the use of photographs is the crucial element of possession in the child's initial formulation of self. Bruner (1996, pp. 35-38) cites two aspects of selfhood that he considered to be universal: agency and evaluation. Agency is more than the experience of oneself as an independent agent carrying out activities. It also takes into account autobiographical memory that records and organizes all our agentive encounters with the world. It is "a record that is related to the past but that is also extrapolated into the future, self with history and with possibility". Evaluation refers to the moral aspect of selfhood that is arguably the most important aspect (and was certainly the case in these narratives). In portraying the self, the narrator is creating a moral world, and in the process, creating a position for which she or he can be (and is prepared to be) held responsible. The self "increasingly takes on the flavour of these valuations", a flavor largely contributed by the modal auxiliaries.

To the agentive and epistemic selves, here is a third on foot of these children's autobiographies: the self of possession or of ownership. The children's modal utterances were further analyzed as to how they functioned to construct the self as either *narrator* (the observing self, 46% overall), as *character* (the acting or experiencing self, 29% overall) or as *owner* (the having or extended self, 26% overall). This is not to suggest that these aspects of self develop in age-related stages, rather that all these selves can be seen in the speech of all three groups. But in this analysis they are very differently important or present in the autobiographical discourse of the different age groups. The individual is essentially "a basket of selves which come to the surface at different social moments as appropriate" (Turner, 1994, p. 11). The 5-year-olds' modal utterances were fairly evenly distributed across all three categories but they made slightly more modal statements from a position of self-as-owner (35%) than they did as either narrator (32%) or as actor (33%). They also wore this self-as-owner "hat" more often than either of the 8-year-olds (27%) or the 12-year-olds (20%). Both the 8- and the 12-year-olds made more modal statements from the perspective of narrator/author (43% and 56% respectively), and in keeping with trends so far, the oldest children made most use overall of this reflexive objective stance.

This leads to the other essential aspect in this analysis of these autobiographical identities-in-the-making, the temporal system and most especially the importance of the future in this study of the modal auxiliaries in autobiography.   It is illustrative to look at how the children arrange their modalized discourse.   Do they start before their own life?   Do they look backward from the present?   Or start at the beginning and build up (maybe in the present or historic present)?   We saw across all the children's narratives that the modal utterances showed a slight bias towards the future tense (39%), with the 12-year-old autobiographies being the most heavily oriented toward the future (46% of their modal utterances).   But when we look at the situation now, in terms of the type of self I am arguing each modal utterance sets up or constructs, a very interesting pattern emerges (see Table 8.1).

TABLE 8.1
The Tense in Which Each Type of Modal Utterance Appears
for Each Category of Self by Age of Speaker in Years (%)

	Narrator			Actor			Owner		
	5	8	12	5	8	12	5	8	12
Present	27	27	27	33	27	23	44	40	43
Past	27	22	17	39	47	41	42	37	25
Future	46	52	56	28	27	36	15	23	32

For all age groups, the extended self or self-as-owner is mainly present tense, whereas the observing self or self-as-narrator is predominantly future and the agentive self or self-as-actor is mainly in the past tense. The 5-year-old narrators are most preoccupied with possessions and associations and are least able to compare present-with future-and past-time frames.   The 8-year-olds, concentrating on action stories are the most conservative in some ways and tend to stick to the past tense as the proper story-telling mode. Finally, the 12-year-olds spend most of their accounts talking about the future. The future orientation in the discourse of the 12-year-olds has already been highlighted but take a further look at the concept of possession in the younger children. The essential element, the cohering force of the concept of possession, is also the future. If to be, or to have, a self means to be located in space and time, then even the 5-year-old children's autobiographical narratives, heavily shot through with notions of possession and ownership, are frequently firmly located in the future.

The patterns of use of the modal auxiliaries and their grammatical and discursive environs develop alongside the child's concept of self and autobiography and alongside narrative and language development in general. This is because whatever it is interests the child, or whatever the child is oriented toward in general terms, is manifested at any given point in their language. Take pronouns, which develop from a context of possession to action and then to description.   We can map this onto Bosch's (1962) schema of development from having or owning to influencing or doing and finally, being.[9] According to this, children first use pronouns to convey the concept of ownership or possession. Next they become capable of viewing the self and others in action contexts. The third and most advanced level of pronominal use is in the context of description. Now the child can represent subjects abstractly apart from the realm of action. On a broader scale, when children begin to be able to talk about themselves, they are primarily interested in talking about their things, their toys and also their family. One child explicitly states: "I only have stories about other people" (KB5). Later children focus more on activities and what they are capable of and later still, at adolescence, they are more given to reflection on their place and role within their families and peer groups but also in wider society.

Jaspers (1970, p. 607) summarized what it means to appropriate things, to make them one's own. He said that as property is acquired for future use, then the acquisition thereof must be closely linked to expectations for the future and thus to having a sense of history, of continuity. "To be a self requires that one have the power to dispose of things that are not self. It is the pathos residing in property that makes possible intercourse with objects that are in my power and my acting on these things; hence the coming into being of my personal world." This involves, crucially, entering into an existence bound up in time, establishing a sense of continuity of self. Bosch (1970, p. 78) said, for example, the autistic child who has not acquired the possessive pronoun, has not developed the possibility of acquiring and keeping property, of "developing its consciousness of self in future" and that by the same token he or she cannot distinguish self and nonself insofar as this delineation is structured via "having". The next context in which pronouns develop is that of action, the child sees himself or herself as an acting agent, acting on things, causing things to happen, and being acted on and can also therefore see others in action contexts. The autistic child is often restricted by seeing only in the present, missing entirely the essential element of action: the intention reaching into the future, the purposiveness, the "in-order-to" of action, and the co-operative acting in a common world.

We could see possession as a sort of early self-awareness that is later expanded to an abstract representation of self in description. The essential point for our purposes is that possession is linked to future use. The young child uses possession to formulate an initial sense of self (which is why family photos were used to elicit personal narratives). Their sense of self is anchored in possessiveness. They are disclosing themselves in their possessions and in relation to the people they associate with themselves. The young child's (and

---

[9] Bühler (1935) proposed a "trivalent semantic" relationship that he identified with the terms indication, signal and symbol and that are related to Bosch's three pronoun contexts. Speech is an indicator in that it expresses the individuality of the speaker. When speech is addressed to a partner in conversation it is a signal. And it is a symbol in respect to the object, the fact that the word denotes and to the existence of which it refers. Snell (1952, p. 62) traced these relationships back to elementary sense forms that he called "primary phenomena of meaning": language as indication he traced back to having; language as signal to acting; and language as symbol to being.

indeed also the adult's) sense of identity is bound up with objects but possession indicates not only boundaries, but also agency. Following Cassirer (1946, p. 90): "a concept maintains its sphere despite all its synthetic supplementation and extension; the new relations into which it may enter *do not cause its boundaries to become effaced but lead rather to their more distinct recognition* [italics added]." I argue that it is by means of these aspects of "self/not-self" and "mine/not-mine" that a distinct sense of self is constructed initially. This continuum of Possession-Action-Description ties in very well with the findings in this study. We have the essential element in possession being the acquisition of property for future use. The child's experience of action or agency similarly implies an element of intention for the future. And acts of description (especially in light of their future tense status) underline the temporal aspects of the child acting into future possibilities and the future consequences of stories. This is the crucial contribution of the modal auxiliaries. This future element also highlights the aspect of change that is so important to children: to establish continuity of self by advancing into the realm of the future (what they will be when they grow up); in order to maintain a sense of distinctness (how they compare with, and are different to, everyone else)[10] and of agency (what they will do and how they will act in the future); and to bring about a stance of reflexivity (evaluating the likelihood of various scenarios, evaluating and assessing the future consequences of their actions, projecting their expectations into the future). Change, rather than stability, and a sense of the future is bound to be more salient to a narrator who has little real sense of the past. We "act into" future possibilities as much as we "act out of" the past.

> How it was that he could remember poems by heart was a mystery to him, and he often reflected that perhaps he would have done better to learn his life by heart so that in these recurring nocturnal last moments he could at least have watched an orderly film instead of all those loose fragments without the cohesion you might have expected of a life just ended. (Nooteboom, 1996, p. 8)

The modal auxiliaries are a particularly sensitive class of words. They are exploited to create distance, to maintain formality, to be tentative rather than direct, and to construct a narrative as opposed to a commentary. In the absence of the modal auxiliaries it would be a much more circumlocutious affair to commit yourself to your statements, whether in terms of emotional involvement (or noninvolvement) or in the sense of taking or denying responsibility and committing yourself to, or evading if necessary, a course of action. This analysis

---

[10] Johnstone (1996, p. 128): "doing things differently from others is how we express selfhood and expressing selfhood is both an important function of talk and a prerequisite for successful talk".

of children's autobiographies-in-the-making shows that the child's life story, just like the adult's is formed in the telling.[11]

> What we refer to confidently as memory-meaning a moment, a scene, a fact that has been subjected to a fixative and therefore rescued from oblivion-is really a form of storytelling that goes on continually in the mind and often changes with the telling. Too many conflicting emotional interests are involved for life ever to be wholly acceptable and possibly it is the work of the storyteller to rearrange things so that they conform to this end. In any case, in talking about the past we lie with every breath we draw. (William Maxwell, *So Long, See You Tomorrow*, 1980/1997:27)

---

[11]"Very soon we discovered that we were listening to people in the act of *constructing* a longitudinal version of self" (Bruner, 1990, p. 120).

Appendix

CODING SCHEME: MODAL AUXILIARIES IN AUTOBIOGRAPHICAL DISCOURSE

Modal Auxiliary full/contracted form (eight main forms and variations)
CAN (can't)
COULD (couldn't, could've)
WILL (won't, 'll)
WOULD (wouldn't, 'd)
SHOULD (shouldn't)
MUST
MIGHT (mightn't)
MAY (maybe)
*SHALL/OUGHT not used at all

Modal Category
can
could
will
would
should
must
might
may

Transcript ID Number
1–12:   5-year-old transcripts
13–24:   8-year-old transcripts
25–36:   12-year-old transcripts

Age
5 years
8 years
12 years

Sex
female
male

Syntactic Information for Modal Auxiliaries

Type of Use
imitation
repetition
direct to researcher
false start
unintelligible
codable

Intonation
modal auxiliary stressed
modal auxiliary unstressed

Polarity (must not be on main verb)
positive
negative

Modification of Modal
double modal
adverbial intensifier
adverbial delimiter
none

Utterance Type in Which Modal Auxiliary Appears
statement
desire-command, wish, entreaty
question-request
exclamation

Type of Preposition in Which Modal Auxiliary Appears
action
description
motivation
elaboration
reaction

Position of Modal Auxiliary in Utterance
main clause, single modal
main clause, more than one modal
subordinate clause, single modal
subordinate clause, more than one modal

Clause in Which Modal Auxiliary Appears
main clause
sub clause
main clause, reported speech
sub clause, reported speech
tag

Mood Category of Utterance in Which Modal Auxiliary Appears
declarative/assertive
declarative/conclusion
performative/warn
exclamative
performativepromise
performative/predict
performative/bet
performative/challenge
interrogative/request
interrogative/rhetorical
interrogative/speculative/musing
interrogative/guess question
interrogative/expository
imperative force from speaker
imperative force from other
performative/prohibitive
performative/permissive
performative/recommendation

Grammatical Person and Number of Subject in Modal Utterance
(surface subject of sentence where modal is used, i.e., NP placed immediately before the VP. If two pre-verbal noun phrases, take more agentive as subject. Can be explicit or implicit.)
No sentence subject
1st person singular
1st person plural
1st person inclusive
2nd person singular
2nd person plural
3rd person singular (human)
3rd person plural (human)
3rd person (inanimate)
Generic (referring to anyone)
Sentential subject (s is a whole sentence)

Point of View of Modal Utterance
inside statement, from experiencer's point of view
outside statement, experiencer and listener positioned outside event

Pronoun Used with Modal Auxiliary
I
you singular
he
she
us/we
you plural
they
it animate/nonhuman

it/there/that non-animate (e.g., it would be better)
that
generic you
nominal
possessive pronoun

Type of Discourse in Which Modal Utterance Occurs
autobiographical narrative to researcher
fantasy/dream/film-story plot narration
reported speech-speaker's
reported speech-other
autobiographical metalinguistic/asides

Semantic Case Relation Between Surface Subject and the Verb
surface subject is actor/experiencer of main verb
surface subject is patient of main verb
surface subject does not belong to above 2 categories
a sentence is the subject of the verb phrase
no surface subject

Semantic Role of Narrator in Modal Utterance
narrator is agent
narrator is experiencer
narrator is patient
narrator is recipient
narrator is absent

Verb used with modal auxiliary

Main Verb of Modal Utterance
verb present
verb absent/elided

Verb Semantic Type
physical state
internal state
process
event

Verb Type
transitive (direct object) N-V-N
transitive (deleted object) N-V
intransitive (no direct object) N-V point of view of agent as the object affected
intransitive (no direct object) N-V point of view of agent with no affected object
intransitive (no direct object) N-V point of view of object and action affecting it
verb absent

Verb Encodes
dynamic event, action/movement/change
state, rather than event
absent

Hierarchical Classification of Verb Used With Modal Auxiliary
(Schlesinger, 1996)
activity-specific
activity-diffuse
momentary
transitional-intentional
transitional non-intentional
process
stance
mental-stimulus
mental-experiencer
relational verb
bodily sensation-intransitive

Agentive Features and Verb Hierarchy
(Schlesinger, 1996)
Group 1, subjects have all 3 agentive features (change, cause, control)
Group 2, subjects have only cause and control
Group 3, subjects have only change
Group 4, subjects have only control
Group 5, subjects have no agentive feature

Aspect
imperfective: from inside an ongoing event, event time + utterance time
perfective: from outside an event already completed or about to begin

Voice
active: event presented from the point of the agent
passive/full: event presented from the point of the object affected (the patient or theme) by the action initiated by the agent (primary emphasis on object, only secondary on agent)
passive/truncated: focus on object affected but ignore agent entirely
middle: focus on action as it affects the object (the patient) (rare in English but may occur with adverbial modification)

Tense of Modal Utterance
simple present
simple past
simple future
present perfect
past perfect
future perfect
present continuous
past continuous
future continuous

present, incorrect, should be past
past, incorrect, should be present
absent
future conditional
past conditional
present conditional
present historical

Semantic Information for Modals

Auxiliary Type (Bybee et al., 1994)

Agent-oriented: all modal meanings that predicate (internal/external) conditions on a wilful agent with regard to the completion of an action referred to by the main predicate.

Speaker-oriented: includes all directives (commands,, demands, requests, entreaties) as well as utterances in which the speaker grants the addressee permission, utterances that impose or propose some course of action or pattern of behavior and indicate that it should be carried out, does not report conditions on the agent but allows the speaker to impose such conditions on addressee, that is, speech acts through which a speaker attempts to move an addressee to action, to impose conditions of obligation.

Epistemic: clausal scope indicators of a speaker's commitment to the truth of a proposition, applies to assertions, unmarked case is total commitment, markers of epistemic modality indicate something less.

Source of Modal Force With Regard to Modal Auxiliary
Regardless of Surface Subject (Bybee et al., 1994)

- **Agent-oriented:**

root (im)possibility, it *is (im)possible* for the agent to carry out the action of the main verb, s/he is able and external conditions allow it.

(non)ability, existence of *internal enabling* conditions in the agent with respect to the predicate action – *physical.*

(non)ability, existence of *internal enabling* conditions in the agent with respect to the predicate action-*menta .*

necessity, existence of *physical* conditions *compelling* an agent to complete the predicate action.

obligation, existence of external *social* conditions *compelling* an agent to complete the predicate action-*strong* (absolutely incumbent on the agent).

obligation, existence of external *social* conditions *compelling* an agent to complete the predicate action-*weak* (it is recommended that).

permission, agent *is allowed* to complete the action of the main verb.

intention, agent *intends to* carry out the action of the main verb.

desire, existence of *internal volitional conditions* in the agent with respect to the predicate action, the agent of the verb desires or wants to complete the action of the main verb.

used in directives, used to elicit action, *subjective* where the speaker is involved in creating obligation, granting permission.

- **Speaker-oriented:**

imperative, used to issue a direct command to a second person.

prohibitive, a negative command

optative, wish/hope of speaker expressed in a main clause, the proposition represents the
    speaker's will.
hortative, speaker encouraging/inciting someone to action.
admonitive, speaker issuing warning.
permissive, speaker granting permission.
recommendation, speaker advising/urging.
* **Epistemic:**
possibility, speaker indicates that the situation described in the proposition is possibly true.
probability, speaker indicates that the situation described in the proposition is probably
    true, greater likelihood.
certainty, the speaker is emphasizing that the proposition is true.
inferred certainty, speaker infers from evidence that the proposition is true, strongly
    implies that the speaker has good reason for supposing it to be true.
epistemic uncertainty, the speaker is emphasizing that he or she does not know that the
    proposition is true.
counterfactual, the proposition describes an unreal or imagined situation that could have
    been true but was not.
speaker, question.
hypothetical, the situation is unreal or imagined but one that could be true.
hypothetical prediction.

Source Category
agent-oriented
speaker-oriented
epistemic

Macro Function of Modal Auxiliary
descriptive function
evaluative function
mixed
action

Discourse Information of Modals

Discourse Micro Functions of Each Modal Utterance in Autobiographical Speech
allowing/discounting possibility
exploring options
planning
reasoning
inferring
concluding
confirming
rationalising
asserting facts
describing events/things
elaborating on background
reporting on own action/ability/failure
reporting on other action/ability/failure

reporting conditions affecting self
appealing for support /external validation/ inviting agreement
recommending
stating rules
stage-managing
apologizing/discourse marker (I can't remember)
boasting (self/ability/possessions/others connected to self)
dismissing discourse marker (I can't remember)
dramatizing/discourse marker (I can remember, I can't wait)
responding to anticipated/imagined challenge
rhetorical device
showing off
accusing
blaming
criticizing (open/veiled)
protesting (unfair/restrictions)
whining
accounting for motives/desires
admission (failure/guilt)
assuming responsibility
challenging
defending self/other
excusing own failure/bad behavior
explaining own action
explaining own inaction
indicating initiative explicitly
offering to disclose/reveal information
expressing desire
expressing intention
expressing preference
expressing anxiety
expressing doubt
expressing excitement
expressing frustration
expressing hope
expressing jealousy
expressing regret
expressing incredulity
character assessment: other
character assessment: self, explicit
comparing self and other
fantasizing
forecasting events
hypothesizing
imagining
predicting events/reactions
speculating on likelihood
referring explicitly to Theory of mind of other, also in relation to self
referring explicitly to Theory of mind of self

Discourse Category of Modal Utterance

Problem-Solving (discourse functions 1-8)

Reporting (discourse functions 9-14)

Prescribing, including negative prescription (discourse functions 15-18; 26-30)

Interpersonal narrating functions (discourse functions 19-25)

Marking agency (discourse functions 31-43)

Marking emotions (discourse functions 44-51)

Making Theory of mind Statements (discourse functions 52 -54; 61-62)

Referring to Unreal States (discourse functions 55-60)

Self Described in Modal Utterance

Observing Self: self as narrator

Experiencing Self: self as character:

Possessive Self: self as owner

Full Utterance Containing Modal Auxiliary

Full list of utterances transcribed for each modal auxiliary for each child.

References

Aarts, B., & Meyer, C. F. (Eds.). (1995). *The verb in contemporary English: Theory and description*. Cambridge, England: Cambridge University Press.

Antinucci, F., & Parisi, D. (1971). On English modal verbs. *Papers from the Seventh Regional meeting of the Chicago Linguistics Society*. Chicago: Department of Linguistics, University of Chicago.

Austin, J. L. (1962). *How to do things with words*. London: Oxford University Press.

Baker, C. L. (1981). Learnability and the English auxiliary system. In C. L. Balker & J. J. McCarthy (Eds.), *The logical problem of language acquisition*. Cambridge, MA: MIT Press.

Bamberg, M. (1987). *The acquisition of narratives: Learning to use language*. Berlin: Mouter de Gruyter.

Bamberg, M. (1991a). Conceptualisation via narrative. *Journal of Narrative and Life History*, 1, 155-167.

Bamberg, M. (1991b). Narrative as perspective taking: The role of emotionals, negations and voice in the construction of the story realm. *Journal of Cognitive Psychotherapy*, 5(4), 275-290.

Bamberg, M. (1994). Actions, events, scenes, plots and the drama: Language and the constitution of part–whole relationships. *Language Sciences*, 16(1), 39-81.

Bamberg, M. (Ed.). (1997a). *Narrative development: Six approaches*. Mahwah, NJ: Lawrence Erlbaum Associates.

Bamberg, M. (1997b). Language, concepts and emotions: The role of language in the construction of emotions. *Language Sciences*, 19(4), 309-340.

Bamberg, M., Budwig, N., & Kaplan, B. (1991). A developmental approach to language acquisition: Two case studies. *First Language*, 11, 121-141.

Bamberg, M., & Dammad-Frye, R. (1991), On the ability to provide evaluative comments: Further explorations of children's narrative competencies. *Journal of Child Language*, 18, 689-709.

Bamberg, M., & Marchman, V. (1990). What holds a narrative together? The linguistic encoding of episode boundaries. *Papers in Pragmatics*, 4, 58-121.

Bamberg, M., & Marchman, V. (1991). Binding and unfolding: Towards the linguistic construction of narrative discourse. *Discourse Processes*, 14, 277-305.

Bamberg, M., & Reilly, J. (1996). Emotion, narrative and affect: How children discover the relationship between what to say and how to say it. In D. I. Slobin, J. Gerhardt, A. Kyratzis, & J. Guo (Eds.), *Social interaction, social context and language: Essays in honour of Susan Ervin Tripp*. Mahwah, NJ: Lawrence Erlbaum Associates.

Banville, J. (1993). *Ghosts*. London: Picador.

Barwise, J., & Perry, J. (1983). *Situations and attitudes*. Cambridge, MA: MIT Press.

Bates, E., Dale, P. S., & Thal, D. (1995). Individual differences and their implications for theories of language development. In P. Fletcher & B. MacWhinney (Eds.), *The handbook of child language*. Oxford: Blackwell.

Bauman, R. (1986). *Story, performance and event: Contextual studies of oral narrative*. Cambridge, England: Cambridge University Press.

Benson, C. (1993a). Psychology, culture and discourse: A new paradigm? *The Thornfield Journal*, 16, 3-7.

Benson, C. (1993b). *The absorbed self: Pragmatism, psychology and aesthetic experience*. Hempstead: Harvester Wheatsheaf.

Benveniste. E. (1971). *Problems in general linguistics*. (M.E. Meek, Trans.) Coral Gables, FL: University of Miami Press.

Berman, R. A. (1988). On the ability to relate events in narrative. *Discourse Processes*, 11, 469-497.

Berman, R. A., & Slobin, D. I. (Eds.). (1994). *Different ways of relating events in narrative: A cross-linguistic developmental study*. Mahwah, NJ: Lawrence Erlbaum Associates.

Biber, D., & Finegan, E. (Eds.). (1994). *Sociolinguistic perspectives on register*. Oxford/New York: Oxford University Press.

Binnick, R. I. (1991). *Time and the verb: A guide to tenses and aspect*. Oxford/New York: Oxford University Press.

Bliss, L. S. (1988). Modal usage by preschool children. *Journal of Applied Developmental Psychology*, 9, 253-261.

Bloom, L., & Harner, L. (1989). On the developmental contour of child language: A reply to Smith & Weist. *Journal of Child Language*, 16, 207-216.

Bolinger, D. (1979). *Meaning and form*. London: Longman.

Bosch, G. (1970). *Infantile autism: A clinical and phenomenological-anthropological investigation taking language as the guide*. (D. Jordan & I. Jordan, Trans.) Berlin: Springer-Verlag. Original work published 1962.

Bowers, J. (1988). Review essay: Discourse analysis and social psychology. *British Journal of Social Psychology*, 27, 185-92.

Bowie, M. (1993). *Psychoanalysis and the future of theory*. Oxford: Blackwell.

Brazil, D. (1995). *A grammar of speech*. Oxford: Oxford University Press.

Britton, B., & Pellegrini, A. (Eds.). (1990). *Narrative thought and narrative language*. Hillsdale, NJ: Lawrence Erlbaum Associates.

Brown, G. (1995). *Speakers, listeners and communication: Explorations in discourse analysis*. Cambridge, England: Cambridge University Press.

Brown, G., & Yule, G. (1983). *Discourse analysis*. Cambridge, England: Cambridge University Press.

Brown, R. (1973). *A first language: The early stages*. London: Allen & Unwin.

Brown, R., Cazden, C., & Bellugi, U. (1969). The child's grammar from I to III. In J. P. Hill (Ed.), *Minnesota symposium in child psychology*. Vol 2. Minneapolis, MN: University of Minnesota Press.

Brown, R., & Gilman, A. (1960). The pronouns of power and solidarity. In T. A. Sebeok (Ed.), *Style in language*. Cambridge, MA: MIT Press.

Bruner, J. S. (1983). The acquisition of pragmatic commitments. In R. Golinkoff (Ed.), *The transition from prelinguistic to linguistic communication.* Hillsdale, NJ: Lawrence Erlbaum Associates.

Bruner, J. S. (1986). *Actual minds, possible worlds.* Cambridge, MA: Harvard University Press.

Bruner, J. S. (1987). Life as narrative. *Social Research,* 54(1), 11-32.

Bruner, J. S. (1990). *Acts of meaning.* Cambridge, MA: Harvard University Press.

Bruner, J S. (1995). The autobiographical process. *Current Sociology,* 43(2/3), 161-177.

Bruner, J. S. (1996). *The culture of education.* Cambridge, MA: Harvard University Press.

Budwig, N. (1985). I, me, my and "name": Children's early systematizations of forms, meanings and functions in talk about the self. *Papers and Reports on Child Language Development* 24.

Budwig, N. (1986). *Agentivity and control in early child language.* Unpublished doctoral diss. University of California, Berkeley.

Budwig, N. (1989). The linguistic marking of agentivity and control in child language. *Journal of Child Language,* 16, 263-284.

Budwig, N. (1990). A functional approach to the acquisition of personal pronouns. In G. Conti-Ramsden & C. Snow (Eds.), *Children's language.* Vol. 7. Hillsdale, NJ: Lawrence Erlbaum Associates.

Budwig, N. (1995a). *A developmental-functionalist approach to child language.* Mahwah, NJ: Lawrence Erlbaum Associates.

Budwig, N. (1995b). Language and the construction of self: Developmental reflections. *http://www.massey.ac.nz/~ALock*

Budwig, N. (1996). What influences children's patterning of forms and functions in early child language? In D. Slobin, A. Kyratzis & J. Guo (Eds.), *Social interaction, social context and language: Essays in honour of Susan Ervin-Tripp.* Hillsdale, NJ: Lawrence Erlbaum Associates.

Bühler, K. (1935). *Sprachtheorie.* Jena: Gustav Fischer.

Buttny, R. (1993). *Social accountability in communication.* London: Sage.

Bybee, J. (1985). *Morphology: A study of the relation between meaning and form.* Philadelphia: Benjamins.

Bybee, J., & Fleischman, S. (Eds.). (1995). *Modality in grammar and discourse.* Amsterdam: Benjamins.

Bybee, J., & Pagliuca, W. (1985). Cross-linguistic comparison and the development of grammatical meaning. In J. Fisiak (Ed.), *Historical semantics, historical word formation.* Berlin: Mouton.

Bybee, J., Perkins, R., & Pagliuca, W. (1994). *The evolution of grammar: Tense, aspect and modalities in the languages of the world.* Chicago: University of Chicago Press.

Byrnes, J. P., & Duff, M. A. (1989). Young children's comprehension of modal expressions. *Cognitive Development,* 4(4), 369-387.

Calasso, R. (1994). *The marriage of Cadmus and Harmony.* (T. Parks, Trans.) London: Vintage.

Calvert, S. L. (1992). Pictorial prompts for Discursive Analysis: Developmental considerations and methodological innovations. *American Behavioural Scientist,* 36(1), 39-52.

Canfield, J. V. (1981). *Wittgenstein: Language and world.* Amherst, MA: University of Massachusetts Press.

Canfield, J. V. (1993). The living language: Wittgenstein and the empirical study of communication. *Language Sciences,* 15(3), 165-195.

Capps, L., & Ochs, E. (1995). *Constructing panic: The discourse of agoraphobia.* Cambridge, MA: Harvard University Press.

Carey, K. (1995). Subjectification and the development of the English perfect. In D. Stein & S. Wright (Eds.), *Subjectivity and subjectivization: Linguistic perspectives.* Cambridge, England: Cambridge University Press.

Cassirer, E. (1946/1953). *Language and myth.* (S. Langer, Trans.) New York: Dover Publications.

Chafe, W. (Ed.). (1980). *The pear stories: Cognitive, cultural and linguistic aspects of narrative production.* Norwood, NJ: Ablex.

Chafe, W. (1994). *Discourse, consciousness and time: The flow and displacement of conscious experience in speaking and writing.* Chicago: University of Chicago Press.

Chafe, W. (1996). Beyond beads on a string and branches in a tree. In A. E. Goldberg. (Ed.), *Conceptual structure, discourse and language.* Stanford, CA: CSLI Publications.

Choi, S., & Gopnik, A. (1993). *Nouns are not always learned before verbs in Korean: An early verb explosion.* Paper presented to the Child Language Seminar, University of Manchester.

Chomsky, C. (1969). *The acquisition of syntax in children from 5 to 10.* Cambridge, MA: MIT Press.

Clark, E. (1987). The principle of contrast: A constraint on acquisition. In B. MacWhinney (Ed.), *Mechanisms of language acquisition: Proceedings of the 20th annual Carnegie Symposium on Cognition.* Hillsdale, NJ: Lawrence Erlbaum Associates.

Clark, E. V. (1990). Speaker perspective in language acquisition. *Linguistics,* 28, 1201-1220.

Clark, H. H. (1994). Discourse in production. In M. A. Gernsbacher (Ed.), *Handbook of psycholinguistics.* San Diego/New York: Academic Press.

Clark, H. H. (1996). *Using language.* Cambridge, England: Cambridge University Press.

Coates, J. (1983). *The semantics of the modal auxiliaries.* London: Croom Helm.

Coates, J. (1988). The acquisition of the meanings of modality in children aged eight and twelve. *Journal of Child Language,* 15, 425-434.

Coates, J. (1995). The expression of root and epistemic possibility in English. In J. Bybee & S. Fleischman (Eds.), *Modality in grammar and discourse.* Amsterdam: Benjamins.

Cohen, A. P. (1994). *Self consciousness: An alternative anthropology of identity.* London: Routledge.

Cole, M. (1996). *Cultural psychology: A once and future discipline.* Cambridge, MA: Harvard University Press.

Collins, P. (1991). The modals of obligation and necessity in Australian English. In K. Aijmer & B. Altenberg (Eds.), *English corpus linguistics: Studies in honour of Jan Svartvik*. London/New York: Longman.

Comradie, C. J. (1987). Semantic change in modal auxiliaries as a result of speech act embedding. In M. Harris & P. Ramat (Eds.), *Historical development of auxiliaries*. Berlin/Amsterdam: Mouton de Gruyter.

Comrie, B. (1985). *Tense*. Cambridge, England: Cambridge University Press..

Corson, D. (1995). *Using English words*. Boston: Kluwer.

Cromer, R. F. (1968). *The development of temporal reference during the acquisition of language*. Harvard University: Unpublished doctoral dissertation.

Cromer, R. F. (1974). The development of language and cognition: The cognitive hypothesis. In B. Foss (Ed.), *New perspective in child development*. Harmondsworth: Penguin.

Cromer, R. F. (1991). *Language and thought in normal and handicapped children*. Oxford: Blackwell.

Cronen, V. E., & Pearce, W. B. (1991/1992). Grammars of identity and their implications for discursive practices in and out of academe: A comparison of Davies and Harrés' views to coordinated management of meaning theory. *Research on Language and Social Interaction*, 25, 37-66.

Crystal, D. (1997). *A dictionary of linguistic and phonetics*. 4th ed. Oxford: Blackwell.

Damasio, A. R. (1994). *Descartes' error: Emotion, reason and the human brain*. New York: Grosset/Putnam.

Damon, W., & Hart, D. (1988). *Self-understanding in childhood and adolescence*. Cambridge, England: Cambridge University Press.

Davies, B., & Harré, R. (1990). Positioning: The discursive production of selves. *Journal for the Theory of Social Behaviour*, 20(1), 43-63.

Davies, B., & Harré, R. (1991/1992). Contradiction in lived and told narratives. *Research in language and Social Interaction*, 25, 1-36.

Denzin, N. K. (1995). Symbolic interactionism In J. A. Smith, R. Harré & L. Van Langenhove (Eds.), *Rethinking psychology*. London: Sage.

Dore, J. (1979). Conversational and preschool language development. In P. Fletcher & M. Garman (Eds.), *Language acquisition*. Cambridge, England: Cambridge University Press.

Dore, J. (1989). Monologues as reenvoicement of dialogue. In K. Nelson (Ed.), *Narratives from the crib*. Cambridge, MA: Harvard University Press.

Duranti, A. (1994). *From grammar to politics: Linguistic anthropology in a Western Samoan village*. Berkeley: University of California Press.

Duranti, A. (1997). *Linguistic anthropology*. Cambridge, England: Cambridge University Press.

Duranti, A., & Goodwin, C. (Eds.). (1992). *Rethinking context: Language as an interactive phenomenon*. Cambridge, England: Cambridge University Press.

Eakin, J. P. (1974). *Fiction in autobiography: Studies in the art of self-inventing*. Princeton: Princeton University Press

Edwards, D. (1997). *Discourse and cognition*. London: Sage.

Edwards, D., & Potter, J. (1992). *Discursive psychology*. London: Sage.

Enç, M. (1996). Tense and modality. In S. Lappin (Ed.), *The handbook of contemporary semantic theory*. Oxford: Blackwell.

Engels, S. (1995). *The stories children tell: Making sense of the narratives of childhood*. London: Freeman.

Ervin-Tripp, S. (1977). From conversation to syntax. *Papers and Reports on Child Language Development*, 13, 1-21.

Ervin-Tripp, S. (1989). *Speech acts and syntactic development: Linked or independent?* Berkeley Cognitive Science report, No. 61. University of California, Berkeley, Institute of Cognitive Studies.

Feldman, C. (1989). Monologue as problem-solving narrative. In K. Nelson (Ed.), *Narratives from the crib*. Cambridge, MA: Harvard University Press.

Finegan, E. (1987). English. In B. Comrie (Ed.), *The major languages of Western Europe*. London: Routledge.

Finegan, E. (1995). Subjectivity and subjectivization. In D. Stein & S. Wright (Eds.), *Subjectivity and subjectivization: Linguistic perspectives*. Cambridge, England: Cambridge University Press.

Fingarette, H. (1996). *Death: Philosophical soundings*. Chicago/Illinois: Open Court.

Firth, J. R. (1957). *Papers in linguistics*. Oxford: Oxford University Press.

Fleischman, S. (1982). *The future in thought and language: Diachronic evidence from Romance*. Cambridge, England: Cambridge University Press.

Fleischman, S. (1991). Discourse as space/Discourse as time: Reflections on the metalanguage of spoken and written discourse. *Journal of Pragmatics*, 16, 291-306.

Fletcher, P. (1979). The development of the verb phase. In P. Fletcher & M. Garman (Eds.), *Language acquisition*. Cambridge, MA: Cambridge University Press.

Fletcher, P., & MacWhinney, B. (1995). (Eds.). *The handbook of child language*. Oxford: Blackwell.

Foucault, M. (1972). *The archaeology of knowledge*. (A. M. Sheridan Smith & A. Mark, Trans.) London: Tavistock.

Fox, B. A. (1987). *Discourse structure and anaphora: Written and conversational English*. Cambridge, England: Cambridge University Press.

Fox, B. A. (1994). Contextualization, indexicality and the distributed nature of grammar. *Language Sciences*, 16(1), 1-37.

Fox, B. A, Hayashi, M., & Jasperson, R. (1996). Resources and repair: A cross-linguistic study of syntax and repair. In E. Ochs, E. A. Schegloff & S. A. Thompson (Eds.), *Interaction and grammar*. Cambridge, England: Cambridge University Press.

Fox, B. A., & Hopper, P. J. (1994). (Eds.). *Voice: Form and function*. Amsterdam/Philadelphia: Benjamins.

Frawley, W. (1997). *Vygotsky and cognitive science: Language and the unification of the social and computational mind*. Cambridge, MA: Harvard University Press.

Gathercole, V. C. (1986). The acquisition of the present perfect: Explaining differences in the speech of American and Scottish children. *Journal of Child language*, 13, 537-560.

Garcia, E. C. (1990). A psycho-linguistic crossroads: Frequency of use. *Journal of Semantics*, 7, 301-317.

Gee, J. G. (1985). An interpretative approach to the study of modality: What child language can tell the linguist. *Studies in Language*, 9(2), 197-229.

Gee, J. G. (1986). *Beyond semantics: A discourse analysis of the verb inflectional system in distinct narrative-like and communicative formats in the speech of a two-year old.* Paper presented at the Symposium on the Acquisition of Temporal Structures in Discourse, Chicago Linguistic Society Meetings, Chicago. Chicago: University of Chicago Press.

Gee, J. G., & Savasir, I. (1985). On the use of *will* and *gonna*: Toward a description of activity-types for child language. *Discourse Processes*, 8, 143-175.

Gee, J. P. (1990). *Social linguistics and literacies: Ideology in discourses.* Hampshire: Falmer Press.

Gee, J. P. (1991). A linguistic approach to narrative. *Journal of Narrative and Life History*, 1(1), 15-39.

Geertz, C. (1973). *The interpretation of cultures.* New York: Basic Books.

Genova, J. (1995). *Wittgenstein: A way of seeing.* New York/London: Routledge.

Gentner, D. (1982). Why nouns are learned before verbs: linguistic relativity versus natural partitioning. In S. Kuczaj (Ed.), *Language development. Vol 2. Language, thought and culture.* Hillsdale, NJ: Lawrence Erlbaum Associates.

Gerhardt, J. G. (1988). From discourse to semantics: The development of verb morphology and forms of self-reference in the speech of a two-year old. *Journal of Child Language*, 15, 337-393.

Gerhardt, J. G. (1990). The relation of language to context in children's speech: The role of HAFTA statements in structuring three-year olds' discourse. *IPrA Papers in Pragmatics*, 4, 1-57.

Gerhardt, J. G. (1991). The meaning and use of the modals HAFTA, NEEDTA and WANNA in children's speech. *Journal of Pragmatics*, 16, 531-590.

Gerhardt, J. G., & Savasir, I. (1986). The use of the simple present in the speech of two- to three-year olds: Normality, not subjectivity. *Language in Society*, 15(8), 501-535.

Gerhardt, J. G., & Stinson, C. (1994). The nature of therapeutic discourse: Accounts of the self. *Journal of Narrative and Life History*, 4(3), 151-191.

Gibbs, R. W. (1994). *The poetics of mind: Figurative thought, language and understanding.* New York: Cambridge University Press.

Givón, T. (1979). *On understanding grammar.* London: Academic Press.

Givón, T. (1982). Evidentiality and epistemic space. *Studies in Language*, 6, 23-49.

Goethe, J. W. von. (1983). *Goethe: Poems and epigrams.* (M. Hamburger, Trans.) London: Anvil Press Poetry.

Goffman, E. (1967). *Interaction ritual: Essays on face to face behaviour.* New York: Anchor Books.

Goldsmith, J., & Woisetschaeger, E. (1982). The logic of the English progressive. *Linguistic Inquiry*, 13, 79-89.

Goossens, L. (1987). The auxiliarization of the English modals: A functional grammar view. In M. Harris & P. Ramat (Eds.), *Historical development of auxiliaries.* Berlin: Mouton de Gruyter.

Greenbaum, S. (1969). *Studies in English adverbial usage.* London: Longman.

Greimas, A. J. (1983). *On meaning: Selected writings in semiotic theory*. (P. J. Perron & F. H. Collins, Trans.) London: Pinter.

Grice, H. P. (1975). Logic and conversation. In P. Cole & J. L. Morgan (Eds.), *Syntax and semantics. Vol. 3: Speech acts*. New York: Academic Press.

Gumperz, J. J. (1982a). *Discourse strategies*. Cambridge, England: Cambridge University Press.

Gumperz, J. J. (1982b). *Language and social identity*. Cambridge, England: Cambridge University Press.

Guo, J. (1994). *A developmental study of the Mandarin modal auxiliaries*. Unpublished doctoral dissertation, University of California, Berkeley.

Guo, J. (1995). The interactional basis of the Mandarin modal *neng* "CAN". In J. Bybee & S. Fleischman (Eds.), *Modality in grammar and discourse*. Amsterdam: Benjamins.

Haiman, J. (1993). Life, the universe and human language (a brief synopsis). *Language Sciences*, 15(4), 293-323.

Halliday, M. A. K. (1973). *Explorations in the functions of language*. London: Arnold.

Halliday, M. A. K. (1994). *An introduction to functional grammar*. 2nd ed. London: Arnold.

Hammersley, M. (1995). *The politics of social research*. London: Sage.

Harré, R. (1983). Identity projects. In G. Breakwell (Ed.), *Threatened identities*. London: Wiley.

Harré, R. (1988/1989). A metaphysics for conversation: A Newtonian model of speech-acts in people-space. *Research on Language and Social Interaction*, 22, 1-22.

Harré, R. (1989). Language games and texts of identity. In J. Shotter & K. J. Gergen (Eds.), *Texts of identity*. London: Sage.

Harré, R. (1992). The second cognitive revolution. *American Behavioural Scientist*, 36(1), 5-7.

Harré, R. (1992). What is real in Psychology: A plea for persons. *Theory & Psychology*, 2(2), 153-158.

Harré, R. (1993). *Social being*. 2nd. ed. Oxford: Blackwell.

Harré, R. (1993). Universals yet again: A test of the "Wierzbicka hypothesis". *Language Sciences*, 15(3), 231-239.

Harré, R. (1995). The necessity of personhood as embodied being. *Theory & Psychology*, 5(3), 369-373.

Harré, R., & Gillett, G. (1994). *The discursive mind*. London: Sage.

Harré, R., & Mühlhaüsler, P. (1990). *Pronouns and people: The linguistic construction of social and personal identity*. Oxford: Blackwell.

Harré, R., & Stearns. P. (1995). (Eds.), *Discursive psychology in practice*. London: Sage.

Harré, R., & van Langenhove, L. (1991). Strategies of positioning. *Journal for the Theory of Social Behaviour*, 21(4), 393-408.

Harré, R., & van Langenhove, L. (1993). Positioning in scientific discourse. In R. Harré (Ed.), *Anglo-Ukrainian studies in the analysis of scientific discourse*. Lewiston/ Queenston/Lampeter: Edwin Mellen Press.

Harris, C. L. (1989). Connectionist explorations in Cognitive Linguistics.

Harter, S. (1983). Developmental perspectives on the self-system. In E. M. Hetherington (Ed.), *Handbook of child psychology: Vol 4. Socialization, personality and social development.* 4th ed. New York: Wiley.

Heeschen, C., Perdue, C., & Vonk, W. (1988). *Annual report.* Nijmegen: Max Planck Institute for Psycholinguistics.

Heidegger, M. (1973). *Being and time.* (J. Macquarrie & E. Robinson, Trans.) Oxford: Blackwell.

Heine, B. (1993). *Auxiliaries: Cognitive forces and grammaticalization.* New York/Oxford: Oxford University Press.

Heine, B., Claudi, U., & Hünnemeyer, F. (1991). From cognition to grammar: Evidence from African languages. In E. C. Traugott & B. Heine (Eds.), *Approaches to grammaticalizations. 2 Vols.* Amsterdam: John Benjamins.

Heritage, J. C. (1984). *Garfinkel and ethnomethodology.* Cambridge: Polity.

Hermans, H. J. M. (1995). The limitations of logic in defining the self. *Theory & Psychology*, 5(3), 375-382.

Hermans, H. J. M., & Kempen, H. J. G. (1993). *The dialogical self: Meaning as movement.* New York: Academic Press.

Hermeren, L. (1978). *On modality in English: A study of the semantics of the modals.* Gleerup: CWK.

Hermeren, L. (1980). Testing the semantics of English modals. *Papers in Linguistics*, 13(3), 501-513.

Hickmann, M. (Ed.). (1987). *Social and functional approaches to language and thought.* London: Academic Press.

Hill, J. H., & Irvine, J. T. (Eds.). (1993). *Responsibility and evidence in oral discourse.* Cambridge, England: Cambridge University Press.

Hirst, W., & Weil, J. (1982). Acquisition of epistemic and deontic meaning of modals. *Journal of Child Language*, 9, 659-666.

Hopper, P. J. (1987). Emergent grammar. *Berkeley Linguistics Society Proceedings*, 13, 139-157.

Hopper, P. J. (1991). On some principles of grammaticalization. In E. C. Traugott & B. Heine (Eds.), *Approaches to grammaticalization. Vol. 1. Focus on theoretical and methodological issues.* Amsterdam: John Benjamins.

Hopper, P. J., & Thompson, S. A. (1980). Transitivity in grammar and discourse. *Language,* 56, 251-299.

Hopper, P. J., & Traugott, E. C. (1993). *Grammaticalization.* Cambridge, England: Cambridge University Press.

Hornstein, N. (1977). Towards a theory of tense. *Linguistic Inquiry*, 8, 521-557.

Hornstein, N. (1990). *As time goes by.* Cambridge, MA: MIT Press.

Howard, B. (1953/1889) Shenandoah. In A. H. Quinn (Ed.), *Representative American plays.* New York: Appleton Century Croft.

Hoye, L. (1997). *Adverbs and modality in English.* London: Longman.

Jaspers, K. (1932/1970). *Philosophie.* 3 Vols. Berlin: Springer. (E. B. Ashton, Trans.) London: University of Chicago Press.

Jesperson, O. (1924). *The philosophy of grammar.* London: Allen & Unwin.

Johnstone, B. (1996). *The linguistic individual: Self-expression in language and linguistics.* Oxford/New York: Oxford University Press.

Johnstone, B., & Bean J. M. (1997). Self-expression and linguistic variation. *Language in Society*, 26, 221-46.

Joos, M. (1964). *The English verb: Form and meanings.* Madison/Milwaukee: University of Wisconsin Press.

Karmiloff-Smith, A. (1979). *A functional approach to child language: A study of determiners and reference.* Cambridge, England: Cambridge University Press.

Keizer, B. (1996). *Dancing with Mister D.* London: Doubleday.

Kemmer, S. (1995). Empathic and reflexive -*self*: expectations, viewpoint and subjectivity. In D. Stein & S. Wright (Eds.), *Subjectivity and subjectivization: Linguistic perspectives.* Cambridge, England: Cambridge University Press.

Kerby, A. P. (1991). *Narrative and the self.* Bloomington: Indiana University Press.

Klinge, A. (1993). The English modal auxiliaries: From lexical semantics to utterance interpretation. *Journal of Linguistics*, 29, 315-357.

Klinge, A. (1996). The impact of context on modal meaning in English and Danish. *Nordic Journal of Linguistics*, 19, 35-54.

Knowles, M., & Malmkjær, K. (1996). *Language and control in children's literature.* London/New York: Routledge.Kohlberg, L. (1976). Moral stages and moralisation: The cognitive developmental approach. In T. Lickona (Ed.), *Moral development and moral behaviour: Theory, research and social issues.* New York: Holt, Rinehart & Winston.

Krauss, R. H., & Glucksberg, S. (1969). The development of communication. *Child Development*, 40, 255-266.

Kress, G., & Hodge, R. (1979). *Language as ideology.* London: Routledge.

Kuczaj, S. A. (1976). Arguments against Hurford's "Modal auxiliaries copying rule". *Journal of Child Language*, 3, 423-27.

Kuczaj, S. A. (1977). The acquisition of regular and irregular past tense forms. *Journal of Verbal Learning and Verbal Behaviour*, 16, 589-600.

Kuczaj, S. A., & Marastos, M. (1983). Initial verbs of yes-no questions: A development kind of general grammatical category. *Developmental Psychology*, 19, 440-444.

Labov, W. (1972). *Language in the inner city: Studies in the Black English vernacular.* Philadelphia: University of Pennsylvania Press.

Labov, W. (1994). *Principles of linguistic change. Vol.1. Internal factors.* Oxford : Blackwell.

Lacan, J. (1977). *Çcrits: A selection.* (A. Sheridan, Trans.) New York: Norton.

Lakoff, G. (1970). *Irregularity in syntax.* London: Holt, Rhinehart & Winston.

Lakoff, G., & Johnson, M. (1980). *Metaphors we live by.* Chicago/London: University of Chicago Press.

Langacker, R. W. (1976). *Non-distinct arguments in Uto-Aztecan.* Berkeley/London: University of California Press.

Langacker, R. W. (1990). *Concept, image & symbol: The cognitive basis of grammar.* Berlin: Mouton de Gruyter.

Leman, P. J., & Duveen, G. (1996). Developmental differences in children's understanding of epistemic authority. *European Journal of Social Psychology*, 26, 683-702.

Lemke, J. L. (1995). *Textual politics: Discourse and social dynamics.* London: Taylor & Francis.

Levinson, S. C. (1983). *Pragmatics.* Cambridge, England: Cambridge University Press.

Linde, C. (1993). *Life stories.* Oxford/New York: Oxford University Press.

Lyons, J. (1977). *Semantics.* Vols. 1 & 2. London/New York: Cambridge University Press.

Lyons, J. (1981). *Language, meaning and context.* London: Fontana.

Lyons, J. (1982). Deixis and subjectivity: *Loquor, ergo sum?* In R. J. Jarvella & W. Klein (Eds.), *Speech, place and action: Studies in deixis and related topics.* New York: Wiley.

Lyons, J. (1995). *Linguistic semantics.* Cambridge, England: Cambridge University Press.

Lyons, J. (1996). *Semantics, subjectivity and localism: Essays in linguistic theory.* Vol. 1. Cambridge, England: Cambridge University Press.

Major, D. (1974). *The acquisition of modal auxiliaries in the language of children.* The Hague: Mouton.

Mallarmé, S. (1974). *Passion and vision: Poems and prose of Baudelaire, Mallarmé and Rimbaud.* (D. Paul, Trans.) New York: Vintage Books.

Maratsos, M. (1982). The child's construction of grammatical categories. In E. Wanner & L. R. Gleitman (Eds.), *Language acquisition: The state of the art.* Cambridge, England: Cambridge University Press.

Matthews, R. (1996). "Oblique" modals in English and German. *Language Sciences*, 18(1/2), 363-79.

Maxwell, W. (1980/1997). *So long, see you tomorrow.* New York: Harvill.

McCune-Nicolich, L. (1981). Toward symbolic functioning: structure of early pretend games and potential parallels with language. *Child Development*, 52, 785-97.

McGregor, W. B. (1997). *Semiotic grammar.* Oxford: Clarendon Press.

McGuire, W. J., & McGuire, C. V. (1992). In G. R. Semin & K. Fiedler (Eds.), *Language, interaction and social cognition.* London: Sage.

Mead, G. H. (1934). *Mind, self and society.* Chicago: University of Chicago Press.

Menaugh, M. (1995). The English modals and established models of probability and possibility: A sign-based analysis. *Studia Linguistica*, 49(2), 196-227.

Mengham, R. (1995). *Language.* London: Fontana.

Menyuk, P. (1969). *Sentences children use.* Cambridge, MA: MIT Press.

Michael, M. (1996). *Constructing identities: The social, the nonhuman and change.* London: Sage.

Miller, G.A. (1971). Empirical methods in the study of semantics. In D. D. Steinberg & L. A. Jakobovits (Eds.), *Semantics: An interdisciplinary reader in philosophy, linguistics and psychology.* Cambridge, England: Cambridge University Press.

Miller, P. J., Mintz, J., Hoogstra, L., Fung, H., & Potts, R. (1991). The narrated self: Young children's construction of self in relation to others in conversational stories of personal experience. *Merrill Palmer Quarterly*, 38, 45-68.

Mills, S. (1995). *Feminist stylistics.* London/New York: Routledge.

Milroy, J., & Milroy, L. (Eds.). (1993). *Real English: The grammar of English dialects in the British Isles.* London/New York: Longman.

Mitchell, P. (1996). *Acquiring a conception of mind: A review of psychological research and theory.* Sussex: Psychology Press.

Modell, A. H. (1993). *The private self.* Cambridge, MA: Harvard University Press.

Montangero, J. (1996). *Understanding changes in time: The development of diachronic thinking in 7- to 12-year old children.* (T. Pownall, Trans.) London: Taylor Francis.

Moore, C., Bryant, D., & Furrow, D. (1989). Mental terms and the development of certainty. *Child Development,* 60, 167-171.

Much, N. C. (1992). The analysis of discourse as methodology for a semiotic psychology. *American Behavioural Scientist,* 36(1), 52-72.

Müller, J. P. (1996). *Beyond the psychoanalytic dyad: Developmental semiotics in Freud, Peirce and Lacan.* New York/London: Routledge.

Myhill, J. (1995). Change and continuity in the functions of the American English modals. *Linguistics,* 33, 157-211.

Nelson, K. (Ed.). (1989). *Narratives from the crib.* Cambridge, MA: Harvard University Press.

Nelson, K. (1992). Emergence of autobiographical memory at age four. *Human Development,* 35, 172-177.

Nelson, K. (1993). Events, narratives, memory: What develops? In C. Nelson (Ed.), *Memory and affect in development.* The Minnesota Symposium on Child Psychology. Vol. 26. Hillsdale, NJ: Lawrence Erlbaum Associates.

Nelson, K. (1993). The psychological and social origins of autobiographical memory. *Psychological Science,* 4(1), 7-14.

Nelson, K. (1996). *Language in cognitive development: Emergence of the mediated mind.* Cambridge, England: Cambridge University Press.

Nooteboom, C. (1996). *Rituals.* (A. Dixon, Trans.) London: Harvill.

O'Grady, W. (1987). *Principles of grammar and learning.* Chicago: University of Chicago Press.

O'Grady, W. (1997). *Syntactic development.* Chicago/London: University of Chicago Press.

Ochs, E. (1993). Constructing social identity: A language socialization perspective. *Research on Language and Social Interaction,* 26(3), 287-306.

Ochs, E. (1994). Stories that step into the future. In D. Biber & E. Finegan (Eds.), *Sociolinguistic perspectives on register.* Oxford/New York: Oxford University Press.

Ochs, E., Schegloff, E. A., & Thompson, S.A. (Eds.). (1996). *Interaction and grammar.* Cambridge, England: Cambridge University Press.

Ochs, E., & Schieffelin, B. B. (Eds.). (1979). *Developmental pragmatics.* New York/London: Academic Press.

Ochs, E., & Schieffelin, B. B. (1989). Language has a heart. *Text,* 9, 7-25.

Ochs, E., & Schieffelin, B. B. (1995). The impact of language socialization on grammatical development. In P. Fletcher & B. MacWhinney (Eds.), *The handbook of child language.* Oxford: Blackwell.

Okamura, Y. (1996). The grammatical status of pure future "WILL" and the category of future form. *Studia Linguistica*, 50(1), 35-49.

Palmer, F. R. (1979). *Modality and the English modals*. 2nd ed. 1990. London: Longman.

Palmer, F. R. (1986). *Mood and modality*. Cambridge, England: Cambridge University Press.

Palmer, F. R. (Ed.). (1995). *Grammar and meaning*. Cambridge, England: Cambridge University Press.

Perkins, M. (1983). *Modal expressions in English*. London: Frances Pinter.

Perner, J. (1991). *Understanding the representational mind*. Cambridge, MA: MIT Press.

Pieraut-Le Bonniec, G. (1980). *The development of modal reasoning: Genesis of necessity and possibility notions*. New York: Academic Press.

Pinker, S. (1984). *Language learnability and language development*. Cambridge, MA: Harvard University Press.

Pinker, S. (1994). *The language instinct*. Penguin.

Plank, F. (1985). The modals story retold. *Studies in Language*, 8, 305-364.

Pontecorvo, C. (1994). Narration and discursive thought in infancy. In M. Ammaniti & D. Stern (Eds.), *Psychoanalysis and development: Representations and narratives*. New York: New York University Press.

Pope, R. (1995). *Textual intervention: Critical and creative strategies for literary studies*. London: Routledge.

Portelli, A. (1981). The time of my life: Functions of time in oral history. *International Journal of Oral History*, 2(3), 162-180.

Potter, J. (1996). *Representing reality: Discourse, rhetoric and social construction*. London: Sage.

Quirk, R. (1986). *Words at work: Lectures on textual structure*. London: Longman.

Quirk, R., Greenbaum, S., Leech, G., & Svartvik, J. (1972). *A grammar of contemporary English*. London: Longman.

Raviv, A., Bar-Tal, D., Raviv, A., & Houminer, D. (1990). Development in children's perceptions of epistemic authorities. *British Journal of Developmental Psychology*, 8, 157-169.

Reilly, R. (1995). Sandy ideas and coloured days: The computational implications of embodiment. *Artificial Intelligence Review*, 9, 305-322.

Rizzuto, A. M. (1993). First person pronouns and their psychic referents. *International Journal of Psycho-Analysis*, 74, 535-546.

Rosch, E. (1978). Principles of categorization. In E. Rosch & B. B. Lloyd (Eds.), *Cognition and categorization*. Mahwah, NJ: Lawrence Erlbaum Associates.

Sacks, H. (1992). *Lectures on conversation*. (G. Jefferson, Ed.) Vols. 1 & 2. Oxford: Blackwell.

Salkie, R. (1996). Modality in English and French. *Language Sciences*, 18(1/2), 381-92.

Sapir, E. (1956). *Culture, language and personality*. (D. G. Mandelbaum, Ed.) Berkeley/London: University of California Press.

Schegloff, E. A. (1982). Discourse as an interactional achievement. In D. Tannen (Ed.), *Analyzing discourse: Text and talk*. Washington, DC: Georgetown University Press.

Schiffrin, D. (1987). *Discourse markers.* Cambridge, England: Cambridge University Press.

Schiffrin, D. (1994). *Approaches to discourse.* Oxford: Blackwell.

Schiffrin, D. (1996). Narrative as self-portrait: Sociolinguistic constructions of identity. *Language in Society,* 25(2), 167-203.

Schlesinger, I. M. (1995). *Cognitive space and linguistic case: Semantic and syntactic categories in English.* Cambridge, England: Cambridge University Press.

Searle, J. R. (1969). *Speech acts: An essay in the philosophy of language.* Cambridge, England: Cambridge University Press.

Semin, G. R., & Fiedler, K. (Eds.). (1992). *Language, interaction and social cognition.* London: Sage.

Semin, R., & Fiedler, K. (1992). The inferential properties of interpersonal verbs. In G. R. Semin & K. Fiedler (Eds.), *Language, interaction and social cognition.* London: Sage.

Serniak, R. (1992). In L. T. Winegar & J. Valsiner (Eds.), *Children's development within social context. Vol 1. Metatheory and theory.* Hillsdale, NJ: Lawrence Erlbaum Associates.

Shanon, B. (1993). *The representational and the presentational: An essay on cognition and the study of mind.* London: Harvester Wheatsheaf.

Shatz, M. (1987). Bootstrapping operations in child language. In K. E. Nelson & A. Van Kleek (Eds.), *Children's language,* 6. Hillsdale, NJ: Lawrence Erlbaum Associates.

Shatz, M., Grimm, H., Wilcox, S., & Niemeier-Wind, K. (1989). *The uses of modal expressions in conversations between German and American mothers and their two-year olds.* Paper presented at the Biennial meeting of the Society for Research in Child Development, Kansas City, MO.

Shatz, M., Hoff-Ginsberg, E., & MacIver, D. (1989). Induction and the acquisition of English auxiliaries: the effects of differentially enriched input. *Journal of Child Language,* 16, 121-140.

Shatz, M., Billman, D., & Yaniv, I. (1986). *Early occurrences of English auxiliaries in children's speech.* Unpublished manuscript. University of Michigan, Ann Arbor.

Shatz, M., & Wilcox, S .A. (1991). Constraints on the acquisition of English modals. In S. A. Gelman & J. P. Byrnes (Eds.), *Perspectives on language and thought: Interrelations in development.* Cambridge, England: Cambridge University Press.

Sheldon, E. (1911/1953). The boss. In A. H. Quinn (Ed.), *Representative American plays.* New York: Appleton Century Crofts.

Shepherd, S. (1982). From deontic to epistemic: An analysis of modals in the history of English, creoles and language acquisition. In A. Ahlqvist (Ed.), *Papers from the fifth International conference on historical linguistics.* Amsterdam: John Benjamins.

Shotter, J. (1993a). *Conversational realities: Constructing life through language.* London: Sage.

Shotter, J. (1993b). *Cultural politics of everyday life.* Buckingham: Open University Press.

Sinclair, J. (1991). *Corpus concordance collocation.* Oxford: Oxford University Press.

Slobin, D. I. (1973). Cognitive prerequisites for the development of grammar. In C. A. Ferguson & D. I. Slobin (Eds.), *Studies of child language development*. New York: Holt, Rinehart & Winston.

Slobin, D. I. (Ed.). (1985). *The cross-linguistic study of language acquisition*. Vols. 1 and 2. Hillsdale, NJ: Lawrence Erlbaum Associates

Slobin, D. I. (1991). Learning to think for speaking: Native language cognition and rhetorical style. *Pragmatics*, 1(1), 7-25.

Slobin, D. I. (1994a). Passives and alternatives in children's narratives in English, Spanish, German and Turkish. In B. Fox & P. J. Hopper (Eds.), *Voice: Form and function*. Amsterdam: Benjamins.

Slobin, D.I. (1994b). Talking perfectly: Discourse origins of the present perfect. In W. Pagliuca (Ed.), *Perspectives on grammaticalization*. Amsterdam: Benjamins.

Slobin, D. I. (1996). From "thought and language" to "thinking for speaking". In J. J. Gumperz & S. C. Levinson (Eds.), *Rethinking linguistic relativity*. Cambridge, England: Cambridge University Press.

Slobin, D. I., Gerhardt, J., Kyratzis, A., & Guo, J. (Eds.). (1996). *Social interaction, social context and language: Essays in honour of Susan Ervin-Tripp*. Mahwah, NJ: Lawrence Erlbaum Associates.

Smith, J. A. (1994). Reconstructing selves: An analysis of discrepancies between women's contemporaneous and retrospective accounts of the transition to motherhood. *British Journal of Psychology*, 85, 371-392.

Snell, B. (1952). *Der aufbau der sprache*. Hamburg: Claassen.

Snow, C. (1990). Building memories: The ontogeny of autobiography . In D. Cicchetti & M. Beegly (Eds.), *The self in transition: Infancy to childhood*. Chicago: University of Chicago Press.

Stein, D. & Wright, S. (Eds.). (1995). *Subjectivity and subjectivization: Linguistic perspectives*. Cambridge, England: Cambridge University Press.

Steiner, G. (1975). *After Babel*. Oxford: Oxford University Press.

Steingart, I., & Freedman, N. (1972). A language construction approach for the examination of self/object representation in varying clinical states. *Psychoanalysis and Contemporary Science*, 1, 132-178.

Stephany, U. (1986). Modality. In P. Fletcher & M. Garman (Eds.), *Language acquisition: Studies in first language development*. 2nd ed. Cambridge, England: Cambridge University Press.

Stephens, J. (1996). Linguistics and Stylistics. In P. Hunt (Ed.), *International companion encyclopedia of children's literature*. London/New York: Routledge.

Stromswold, K. J. (1994). The cognitive and neural bases of language acquisition. In M. S. Gazzaniga (Ed.), *The cognitive neurosciences*. Cambridge, MA: MIT Press.

Stubbs, M. (1985). A matter of prolonged field work: Notes towards a modal grammar of English. *Applied Linguistics*, 17, 1-25.

Stubbs, M. (1996). *Text and corpus analysis: Computer-assisted studies of language and culture*. Oxford: Blackwell.

Sülkunen, P., & Torrönen, J. (1997). The production of values: The concept of modality in textual discourse analysis. *Semiotica*, 113(1/2), 43-69.

Sweetser, E. (1990). *From etymology to pragmatics: Metaphorical and cultural aspects of semantic structure.* Cambridge, England: Cambridge University Press.

Talmy, L. (1988). Force dynamics in language and cognition. *Cognitive Science*, 12, 49-100.

Taylor, C. (1989). *Sources of the self: The making of the modern identity.* Cambridge, England: Cambridge University Press.

Todorov, T. (1976). The origin of genres. *New Literary History*, 8(1), 159-170.

Tomasello, M. (1992a). The social bases of language acquisition. *Social Development*, 1(1), 67-87.

Tomasello, M. (1992b). *First verbs: A case study of early grammatical development.* Cambridge, England: Cambridge University Press.

Tonkin, E. (1992). *Narrating our pasts: The social construction of oral history.* Cambridge, England: Cambridge University Press.

Traugott, E. C. (1982). From propositional to textual and expressive meanings: Some semantic-pragmatic aspects of grammaticalization. In W. P. Lehmann & Y. Malkiel (Eds.), *Perspectives on historical linguistics.* Amsterdam: John Benjamins.

Traugott, E. C. (1989). On the use of epistemic meanings in English: An example of subjectification in semantic change. *Language*, 65, 31-55.

Traugott, E. C. (1995). Subjectification in grammaticalization. In D. Stein & S. Wright (Eds.), *Subjectivity and subjectivization: Linguistic perspectives.* Cambridge, England: Cambridge University Press.

Trudgill, P., & Hannah, J. (1994). *International English: A guide to varieties of standard English.* 3rd ed. London: Edward Arnold.

Tudge, J., Shanahan, M.J., & Valsiner, J. (Eds.). (1997). *Comparisons in human development: Understanding time and context.* Cambridge, England: Cambridge University Press.

Tugendhat, E. (1986). *Self-consciousness and self-determination.* (P. Stern, Trans.) Cambridge, MA: MIT Press.

Turner, M. (1994). Design for a theory of meaning. In W. F. Overton & D. S. Palermo (Eds.), *The nature and ontogenesis of meaning.* Hillsdale, NJ: Lawrence Erlbaum Associates.

van der Merwe, W. L. & Voestermans, P. P. (1995). Wittgenstein's legacy and the challenge to psychology. *Theory & Psychology*, 5(1), 27-48.

Volosinov, V. N. (1976). *Freudianism: A Marxist critique.* (I. R. Titunik & N. H. Bruss, Trans. & Ed.) New York/London: Academic Press.

von Wright, G. H. (1951). *An essay in modal logic.* Amsterdam: North Holland.

Vygotsky, L. S. (1987). *The collected works of L. S. Vygotsky.* New York: Plenum.

Waksler, F. C. (1996). *The little trials of childhood and children's strategies for dealing with them.* London: Falmer Press.

Wales, K. (1989). *A dictionary of stylistics.* London: Longman.

Wales, K. (1996). *Personal pronouns in present-day English.* Cambridge, England: Cambridge University Press.

Warner, A. R. (1993). *English auxiliaries: Structure and history.* Cambridge, England: Cambridge University Press.

Wellman, H. M. (1990). *The child's theory of mind.* Cambridge, MA: MIT Press.

Wells, G. (1979). Learning and using the auxiliary verb in English. In V. Lee (Ed.), *Cognitive development: Language and thinking from birth to adolescence.* London: Croom Helm.

Wells, G. (1985). *Language development in the pre-school years.* Cambridge, England: Cambridge University Press.

Werner, H., & Kaplan, B. (1963). *Symbol formation.* New York: Wiley.

Whorf, B. L. (1956/1973). *Language, thought, and reality: Selected writings of Benjamin Lee Whorf.* (J. B. Carroll, Ed.) Cambridge, MA: MIT Press.

Widdicombe, S., & Wooffitt, R. (1995). *The language of youth subcultures: Social identity in action.* London: Harvester Wheatsheaf.

Wierzbicka, A. (1992). Lexical universals and universals of grammar. In M. Kefer & J. Van der Auwera (Eds.), *Meaning and grammar: Cross-linguistic perspectives.* Berlin/New York: Mouton de Gruyter.

Wierzbicka, A. (1996). *Semantics: Primes and universals.* Oxford: Oxford University Press.

Wilcox, S. A., & Woolley, J. D. (1989). *Children's evaluation of statements of belief as sources of information.* Paper presented at the Biennial meeting of the Society for Research in Child Development, Kansas City, MO.

Wilkinson, A., Barnsley, G., & Hanna, P. (Eds.). (1980). *Assessing language development.* Oxford: Oxford University Press.

Wittgenstein, L. (1953). *Philosophical investigations.* Oxford: Blackwell.

Wittgenstein, L. (1969). *On certainty.* Oxford: Blackwell.

Wolf, D. P. (1990). Being in several minds: Voices and versions of the self in early childhood. In D. E. Cicchetti & M. Beeghly (Eds.), *The self in transition.* Chicago: University of Chicago Press.

Wolf, D., & Hicks, D. (1989). The voice within narratives: The development of intertextuality in young children's narratives. *Discourse Processes, 12*(3), 329-351.

Wolfson, N. (1978). A feature of performed narrative: The conversational historic present. *Language in Society, 7,* 215-237.

Yavas, F. (1982). Future reference in Turkish. *Linguistics, 20,* 411-429.

Young, T. R. (1972). *New sources of self.* New York: Pergamon.

Zeldin, T. (1995). *An intimate history of humanity.* London: Minerva.

Index

PE 1315 .M6 Q54 2000 c.1
Quigley, Jean.
The grammar of autobiography

DATE DUE

GAYLORD   PRINTED IN U.S.A.